# SIMPLY THE BEST

*The Art of Seasonal Cooking*

# Tamasin Day-Lewis

# SIMPLY THE BEST
## *The Art of Seasonal Cooking*

Photography by David Loftus

A Seven Dials Paperback

'Good cooking is about having the confidence to subtract rather than add ingredients, about bringing out the essence of the thing itself, and both are elements as indispensable to the alchemy of good food as the most essential ingredient, passion.'

Tamasin Day-Lewis

# Contents

# INTRODUCTION

THE BIGGEST DECISIONS in our lives have a habit of deciding themselves, of just happening, more often than not when we are neither seeking nor expecting to be faced with them. Into the unknown we jump, instinct, caution, experience, fear, acting as a kind of natural rudder to propel us, if we are lucky, in the right direction.

And so it was when I was approached to write the *Daily Telegraph*'s Weekend Cook column. Out of the proverbial azure the offer came; it was neither something I had thought of as a natural progression from what I was doing, nor did I have the time to think long and hard about it. I said 'yes' immediately, the doubt, as with all things, came later. I had spent the previous 15 years making documentaries, first at the BBC then as an independent with my own small film company. Because of an innate fear of revisiting the same terrain, I had ploughed a varied and somewhat unquantifiable furrow, making social documentaries, music and arts films, religious, medical and educational films, what could loosely be termed entertainment films, and in talks production. I had burrowed into the worlds and subjects of the films, often to the point at which I thought about changing career, so inspiring was the research and the subject itself. When a series about gifted young musicians – the sequel to a series about a music school I had just made for Channel 4 – was turned down, and a year's work was lost as a result, I stepped up my irregular writing to full time.

A year later, I was summoned by Belinda Richardson and her boss Rachel Simhon, editor of the Weekend section of the *Telegraph*, and, over a very good lunch, invited to tell them how I would write the column if it were mine. Of one thing I was in no doubt. That we have a renaissance of dedicated and brilliant small producers, artisan craftsmen if you will, who are doing their best to transform our eating habits and bring back those essential ingredients, taste and quality, that largely went walkabout when the big conglomerates and factory farming lost us our way. My television life had involved a huge amount of interviewing; it is a pleasure which remains undiminished, and this seemed to me to be a fertile seam that the column should pursue, along with some political stories, essays, straight interviews with chefs and food writers, and personal pieces.

But I guess that what I felt most strongly about at the time, although I didn't quite dare voice it, was that I wanted people to read the column for the writing's sake, rather than because it was a food column. A vain hope perhaps, but not one inspired by vanity. This was somehow tied up with my sense that I needed to justify to myself and the reader that food was a subject that should be taken seriously, was serious enough to write about. Well of course it is. Food is as profound as any subject, and there is no aspect of human life that it doesn't touch. It exists at the very heart of our lives, and it is not, at heart, merely frivolous. We recapture memories and places through food, and it is a powerful and emotive thing to do. Nurturing, comforting, delighting, food is always the good thing, even in the most adverse and intransigent of human situations. We use all our senses for food, in fact they are never more unified than when we eat.

Setting out on this odyssey of writing a weekly food column, forced me to consider the defining principles of my own food philosophy, and sharpened my instincts for what it was the reader wanted to read. In fact, I still put myself in the position of reader, remembering that the touch-paper was kindled for me when, as a student, I began reading Jane Grigson's pieces in the *Observer*. After her unprecedented 22 years there, I have avidly followed her successor Nigel Slater, and, more recently, the talented Simon Hopkinson in the *Independent*, who has made the transition from chef to writer with seamless brilliance. If I were to count the torn and tawny edged cuttings in my ancient scrapbook of recipes, they are the leaders. So why does one tear a recipe out and consign it to one's deep litter system, or to an ageing heap of cuttings that one keeps, untranscribed but oft used for over 20 years? Because the good cook, the good cookery writer, makes one believe that, even if you have 18 recipes for *ragu*, pistachio soufflé or even a basic béchamel, suddenly you are in undiscovered country; this method, that detail or inspirational ingredient, coupled with the writer's passion, impels you to take note, and leaves you in a froth of excitement waiting to try it, tinker with it, allow it a place in your repertoire. Originality is not always the key. A classic or post-modern rendering of a recipe can be more tempting than something new. What the good food writer has done is to fill you with desire, make you feel you've never cooked the dish in question as well as you are about to cook it. And instilled in you the confidence to feel you can do it, for that too is at the heart of all good food writing.

My premise, since writing my weekly column, has been that people want to be made to feel hungry. They want food they can cook. And they want ingredients they can find. There are many subclauses to this, but I feel these are the three great imperatives; it would be perilous to ignore them, though presenting people with food they can cook is the most difficult clause to interpret with any obvious degree of accuracy. Does one assume that everyone who reads the column is at least a good basic cook? I fear not. It has become apparent, through interviewing some of the best of our small food producers, that their assumption that there is a lost generation of 25 to 35 year olds who don't know how to scramble or baste is accurate. These waifs and strays have subsisted on fast food, had no cookery lessons at school, are the offspring of working mothers who DON'T DO BAKING, and they have precious little domestic culture beyond taking the jacket off the convenience dinner before it gets the heat-and-eat treatment. There is no connection, that vital artery, between producer, rearer, grower and these kitchen-starved consumers; no touch, feel, peel involved; food has lost its animacy, its rawness, its sexiness to a generation of deskilled diners more concerned with speed and consumption than the pleasure of the process from growing to picking to recipe to mouth.

It goes beyond that. Supermarkets play God with the seasons, seducing us powerless-to-resist customers with the fruits and vegetables that the winter months deny us. I am not always able to resist temptation, but doing the season is a constant, one of the chief pleasures of my cooking life. The turning year is about waiting, anticipating, discovering; about picking the first crimson and primrose crab apples, downy quinces and wet walnuts from my trees, eating the tiny embryos of pistachio-green broad beans raw from the pod, baking the first gluey-tailed salmon trout from the River Dart.

I also have to bear in mind that, beyond the good home cook, there is a top tier of serious, professional standard cooks who are looking for something more. They might not want the multi-ingrediented, sauce-strewn recipes of the restaurant chef, but neither will they be satisfied with glitzed up versions of bog-standard basics and the classics they have been churning out for years. Somewhere between the Scylla and Charybdis of cutting-edge cuisine and the comfortingly traditional lies this most difficult-to-please reader. They want a challenge, a new take, to at least feel informed about whatever food fashion is current, without necessarily buying into it.

And then there is the question of budgetary restraint; where to pitch the column so as not to insult and exclude people whose means are not consummate with their culinary aspirations. I have always thought of myself as a somewhat extravagant pauper ever since my student days, a committed epicurean with the brakes on. I have never considered economizing on good food a part of my culinary vocabulary, but that doesn't mean to say I condone wanton extravagance. I am committed to the principle of buying and paying for the best; a special offer or a past-its-sell-by-date is just that. I am more likely to think of exotic as a tranche of fallen-from-grace mutton, than some unrecognizable fruit flown in from one or two worlds away.

Truly creative cooking is about plundering the store cupboard and fridge full of last weekend's leftovers, and recycling them as something equally as good as they were in their first incarnation. That, after all, is how the majority of us live, and the column, to be honest, should reflect that, or it merely reflects the aspirational element in all of us to cook how we would cook if we weren't paying the bill. Good cooking is about having the confidence to subtract, rather than add ingredients, about bringing out the essence of the thing itself, and both are elements as indispensable to the alchemy of good food as the most essential ingredient, passion. Nothing is as contagious as passion. If I were to lose mine, the column would be as unthinkable as it would be unwriteable. That, alongside an undimmed appetite and curiosity have been prerequisite to the job.

What has struck me most about the subjects of the pieces, has been the extraordinary commitment and intelligence that they have brought to what it is they are doing, with an equally extraordinary and refreshing lack of greed in the material sense. The majority of those I have interviewed have had the balls to leave extremely high-powered careers for something smaller, infinitely less certain but about which they feel passionate. You will see from the articles just how diverse the skills and experience they bring to their businesses are. Gone are the days of the dippy hippy getting back to nature, growing and sowing for a commune of drop-outs. Here we have Third World agronomists, biochemists, fund managers and advertising executives frayed by the inhuman pressures of their jobs, and bringing their brains and imaginations into fresh pastures that would have been unthinkable at the start of their first careers. No longer does ' being in trade' exude a snobbish disdain from certain quarters; it is as positively admired, envied even, as it was frowned upon. And the producers stand amazed at what is often the most enjoyable bit of their jobs, the bit they dreaded most, selling to the customer. The contact; the establishing of relationships; the pleasure of being praised for their product; even the criticism and suggestion that lead to more and better products is gratifying, satisfying, and essential to understanding how to grow the business.

Ten years ago, I couldn't have conceived of an index such as the one at the back of this book, and I wouldn't presume to call it comprehensive. I have, I am aware, championed the growers in the southwest of England more stridently than those from elsewhere. Microcosmic though this may be to the reader, I think it is important that the column has a regional identity, and the problems that beset farming, the dairy industry, vegetable growers, fishing, are as well reflected here as they are up and down the country. I also feel that to have any contemporary relevance, the column has to address how and from where our food is produced, I could not just write about food if it was merely recipe led. The countryside is in crisis, being attacked from all sides, its way of life questioned by those who very often have no understanding of its everyday realities. City children can grow up without seeing an animal, only the amorphous boneless lump of cling-filmed creature whose provenance and method of rearing is best unknown. My job is to educate the mind as well as the palate, and, in as entertaining way as possible, address the larger issues and concerns that affect the food industry, as well as championing the wave of small, dedicated producers who are radically revolutionizing British food. Even the non-cook can serve wonderful food by learning how to shop for the best.

I have learned more about food with every column I have researched. In fact, my all-time culinary hero George Perry-Smith, arguably the finest restaurateur of the last 50 years, reminded me of something I'd said in a piece I'd written to celebrate his influence: 'The learning has always only just begun.' I feel that every time I cook. The pleasure of cooking is infinite if you have it in you to find it so. First find your passion, then simply remember the learning has always only just begun.

TAMASIN DAY-LEWIS 2001

# SPRING

WHEN I LEFT HOME I COULD COOK AN OMELETTE. It's not that I wasn't fascinated by food, I was, but my curiosity was more to do with greed than fuelled by a desire to cook.

The only time there was a whiff of what was to come, in terms of my future culinary path, was on Wednesday afternoons. It seems the domestic science lesson is almost consigned to history these days, or to those whose academic record is not going to illuminate the firmament. When I was at school, 'Bug' was compulsory, and was conducted in the 'Bug labs'. There, hunger-crazed teenagers were taken through the annals of old-fashioned baking, from rock buns to esse biscuits, Victoria sponges to shortbread.

It is the smells I remember, like I remember all the things I have ever cooked; sweet, yeasty, buttery baking smells, and the gannet-like greed that propelled fingers round bowls of raw cake mixture, the final creations never quite the size or shape they should have been. But talent, originality? Questionable.

Where I excelled was in the greed department, and, mindful of the fact that all offerings, burnt or otherwise, were duly taken back to the dormitory to be shared, I devised a plan. One week it consisted of emptying the sap green bottle into my emergent high-rise Madeira cake. The next it was inky blue meringues. The dormitory declined. For once I didn't go to bed hungry, dreaming of the juicy steaks, the fat, crisp chips, the squeaky, sweet new peas laced with cream and flecks of mint that my grandmother's cook Rhoda cooked for my brother Daniel's and my first lunch whenever we went to stay.

Thinking back, there was one other hint at the future I now seem to be embracing. I staged a hunger strike in the school quad, when the quality and quantity of school food had reached Stygian depths. It was a musical event, with trumpets and chanting, and, since the school was Bedales, there was more bemused anxiety than punishment from the staff. A food committee was set up, and order was restored, but the deprivation that we hard-liners extended through to supper time, was undergone with a kind of missionary determination. I knew better.

At 17, I decided to go vegetarian. Then a stage further. An influential boyfriend persuaded me of the virtues of turning macrobiotic. After a few weeks of unpacking boxes and bottles in the school dining room, and being scrutinized by the unforgiving eye of teenagedom, followed by the clash of pans and tempers in the familial kitchen when I attempted to cook the husky, sprouty, seeded and fermented things I'd bought, the plan was modified, in the non-genetic sense, and incorporated into a passion for eating healthily that has endured. I was the butt of many a jibe, but now the organic movement has taken root, I allow myself a brief sense of smugness: I knew it would happen all along. But before you get the wrong idea, I am not a card-carrying purist. My first and last principle is taste, and I start from the premise that the best ingredients might not make the best cooks, but they can make the best food.

The real transition takes place when you go from being cooked for to being cook. From sweet to savoury. Cakes and baking are followed by learning to cook the dishes that support and nourish one's grown-up culinary repertoire, and give it its foundations. The first dinner party meal I cooked included a richly dark beef stew, embittered with Guinness, then underscored and scented with orange peel, rosemary, bay, garlic and celery. I'd watched it being cooked by my cousin's wife, been her chief chopper and masher, and then cooked it for myself. It is something I still love cooking, and it is the first recipe in my book *West of Ireland Summers, A Cookbook*.

Like a musician learning the repertoire, a large part of my twenties was spent reading cookery books, experimenting, and coping with the exigencies of a series of ill-equipped, undersized kitchens and financial fluctuations. I marinaded haunches of venison in the bath, bargained for cheap belly pork, and cooked huge communal dinners with friends in our college 'gyp' room on a tiny Belling; our staircase eschewed the college kitchen nightly.

Through my working life as a documentary film maker, and as the mother of three young children, I have constantly fed this passion wherever I have found myself. Luckily film crews, like armies, march on their stomachs; children are a different equation. The words 'Children's Menu' have never passed their gaze, let alone their lips. From an early age, my three ate whatever we ate with the requisite compromises in texture and portion size. All three show an unnaturally healthy disrespect of anything they see as obsessional in my approach to food and cooking, have strong likes and dislikes, but share, thank God, a love of good food and an increasing knowledge and concern for high standards and good husbandry.

One of my worries in this age where food fashion has become as seasonal as fashion, is how the new eating-out culture can be translated intelligently into the kitchen. I don't think the strap-a-wok-to-your-back style cookery programme helps, the pleasures and principles of good home cooking are not reinforced by their instant, bite-sized chunks. I speak as a home cook who has also dipped more than the proverbial toe into professional waters. As an avid reader of recipes and food columns, I know what I want to read, and the friends I have asked recently say the following: they want to be made to feel hungry, they want food they can cook, they want ingredients they can find. Those of us who truly love to cook glean recipes like magpies, stealing, albeit lawfully, and using what we've thieved to pass the pleasure on; cooks share their spoils.

I think we've entered a period where food writing is taken more seriously, is not seen as a frivolous occupation, or as an excuse for not writing a novel. I believe food is a profound subject, that there is no aspect of human life that it does not touch, that it exists at the heart of our lives.

We cook differently at different stages of our lives. Right now, since I am relatively confident about my food, I spend the least amount of time I can in the kitchen when the guests have arrived, unless we all hang around the kitchen talking, drinking, stirring. The planning and preparation over, I don't need to feel resentful about barely seeing the people I've invited, as I did a few years back when I struggled with dishes of crazily last minute complexity and critical timing.

Something simple, that tastes of itself, should be left that way, be it the first tiny pebbles of Jersey new potatoes, a sweetly salt oyster, the gluey, stickiness of a slow-cooked osso bucco, the earthiness of a freshly dug carrot. Good cooking is about having the confidence to subtract, rather than add, about bringing out the essence of the thing itself. Striving for originality has got more cooks into trouble than striving for simplicity.

Nothing pleases me more than being reminded of a dish I'd consigned to the deeper reaches of my memory; of reworking something old into something new; of anticipating each breath of a new season, fragile-limbed, day-glo pink rhubarb in a sharply fresh jelly this week, olive-green wands of tight-budded asparagus in a puddle of unsalted butter next. When all this ceases to excite, I guess I will retire from the stove.

# Osso Bucco Milanese

I find myself yearning for veal in the spring and this is a classic dish. Before you say 'I don't eat veal', this is what Charlotte Reynolds of Swaddles Green organic farm has to say. 'Our veal calves are reared in the field with their mothers. It is not white veal, they are not kept in crates, and we keep our calves until they are about five months. They are milk fed and given a bit of hay. We actually need to eat more veal, these calves from the dairy industry do not make good beef because they are from milking herds, so they've got big udders and bony hips; they're short on haunches and well-padded rumps.'

SERVES 8

8 ossi buchi
4 tbsp olive oil
seasoned organic flour
in a ziploc bag
85g / 3oz unsalted butter
1 large onion
16–20 shallots
a heart of celery with its leaves
a generous 300ml / ½ pint
white wine
600ml / 1 pint chicken
or other meat stock

Put a few of the ossi buchi in the bag of flour at a time, shake, then remove them, shaking off excess flour. Tie string around each one so they hold their shape, don't skip this bit, or they'll end up misshapen.

Heat the olive oil in a heavy-bottomed casserole, add a single layer of ossi buchi at a time, and brown on both sides. Remove them to a plate, add butter, then the finely chopped onion and celery and the peeled whole shallots. After about 10 minutes, return the meat to the pan, season with salt and pepper and pour over the heated wine. Let it all bubble together for a few minutes before adding the hot stock.

Turn down to a mere blip, put the lid on, with a sheet of greaseproof paper inside to help seal it, and cook for 1½ hours, turning the veal over every half hour.

You can do all this the night before you want it; I cooked mine in the afternoon and then reheated it slowly for half an hour. The risotto Milanese (see page 18) I also cooked to the halfway point early in the evening before the guests arrived.

# Risotto Milanese

SERVES 8

*a generous pinch of saffron threads*
*soaked in 2 tbsp hot water*
*for an hour*
*2 shallots, peeled and chopped*
*50g / 2oz unsalted butter*
*2 tbsp olive oil*
*675g / 1 ½lb Carnaroli rice*
*300ml / ½ pint red wine*
*125g / 4oz freshly grated Parmesan*
*salt and pepper*
*garlic, lemon and flat-leaf parsley*
*for the gremolada*

Sauté the shallots in the heated oil and half the butter until softened and translucent. Add the rice, stirring to coat it well. Pour over the wine, keep stirring furiously, then add the saffron and half the stock, stir for 3–4 minutes. Cover tightly and switch off until 15 minutes before you want to serve it. Continue cooking if you are not staggering the process. Add the rest of the stock bit by bit until the rice is creamily soft, but not porridgy, then add the rest of the butter and the Parmesan, and stir it in. Season and serve under the osso bucco. Make the gremolada, which consists of the grated rind of a lemon, 2 cloves of finely chopped garlic, and 4 tablespoons of chopped flat-leaf parsley mixed together, and sprinkle on top of the meat.

Serve with a green salad or some braised fennel.

# Rhubarb and Elderflower Jelly

SERVES 6

*1.5kg / 3lb rhubarb. It sounds a lot,*
*but you want an intense juice.*
*You can then use the fruit*
*separately in another pudding.*
*2 tbsp Rock's elderflower cordial,*
*optional*
*the juice of an orange*
*325–450g / 12oz–1lb unrefined*
*sugar. I keep mine in a jar with*
*vanilla pods*
*6 sheets leaf gelatine, dissolved in*
*2–3 tbsp cold water*

Preheat the oven to 150°C / 300°F / Gas Mark 2. Chop the rhubarb into 2.5-cm / 1-inch pieces and place it in an ovenproof dish. Add the cordial, orange juice, 300ml / ½ pint of water, then strew the sugar over it. Cover with a lid, or greaseproof paper and cook until soft, about an hour. Place in a sieve above a measuring jug, and leave until the juice has dripped through. You are aiming for 900ml / 1 ½ pints of liquid, so remember the water from soaking the gelatine counts. Test for sweetness, I like mine quite tart. Add the gelatine to the hot liquid, stir well to dissolve, then pour into the glasses. Cool, then put in the fridge until set to the point at which you can put 4 or 5 pieces of the pinkest rhubarb in the glass at different levels, without them rising to the surface. Refrigerate until needed. A day or two in advance is fine.

# Belly of Pork and Butter Beans

In my impecunious student cooking days I used to make this dish with haricot beans. I couldn't find any in the cupboard, but if anything, the butter beans are an improvement. My hunk of organic belly pork cost £3, the sausages I added to make it more cassoulet-like, and to satisfy my children who are going through a meat-fest phase.

SERVES 6

*450g / 1lb packet butter beans soaked overnight*

*2–3 tbsp olive oil*

*1 large onion, or 8 or 9 shallots which are good in spring*

*6–8 cloves garlic, peeled and whole*

*the heart of a head of celery with its leaves*

*600g / 1¼lb hunk organic belly pork with its rind*

*6 organic pork sausages*

*2 x 240g / 8½oz tins organic peeled tomatoes (Eunature)*

*6 organic tomatoes, skinned, seeded, roughly chopped*

*⅓ jar organic passata*

*3 bay leaves, a bunch of thyme and parsley stalks tied together, and a large handful of fresh, flat-leaf parsley*

*black pepper and salt*

Bring the beans up to the boil in plenty of water, remove the scum, boil furiously for 10 minutes, then simmer with a lid on for 50 minutes. Strain, reserving the water. They will be slightly undercooked. Meanwhile, sauté the chopped onion or whole shallots, with the garlic and chopped celery until softened and translucent.

Add the belly pork in 2.5-cm / 1-inch wide pieces you've cut down to the bone, the bony pieces cut along their length as you would spare ribs. Put them rind side down and cook until browned, with the sausages. Turn them over for 2–3 minutes, then add the tins of tomatoes, chopping as you go, the fresh tomatoes, and the passata. Tuck the herbs in, and throw in all but a few ounces of the beans, which I then mouli through the medium-sized disc to thicken and enrich the tomato sauce. Season with plenty of coarse ground pepper and salt.

Add a little of the bean liquor if the liquid doesn't come above the stew, bring to the boil, then turn down to a gentle simmer, cover tightly with a lid and forget it for an hour.

Sprinkle with flat-leaf parsley and serve with lashings of mashed potato to soak up the juice. I also cooked some freshly cut purple sprouting broccoli from my friend Brigid's garden.

# PHIL THE FISH

WE ARE NO LONGER A NATION OF SHOPKEEPERS, we are a nation of supermarketeers, and the homogenization process has not stopped with the milk. It is not that I am either able, or would want to, bypass them and pretend life would be as easy without them; I am just filled with a sense of gloom and shame at the idea that so many people look no farther than the chilled-fresh aisles of their local supermarkets. That 'produce' is now so far removed from the producers as not to be a subject of conversation or pride, but of head office policy and reward points.

Good food is about a constant dialogue between grower, rearer, maker, seller and customer. It is about loyalty, not to a brand, but to a purveyor of excellence, who understands the term 'provenance,' knows how the changing seasons affect his produce, respects the budget of each customer, and delights in helping the less well-informed stumble without fear into tasting something they would otherwise never have tried.

Good producers and suppliers have transformed my cooking and my knowledge and love of food over the last few years, and I trust their dedication and pride in their product, not unquestioningly, but unquestionably. Assuming this degree of respect, rule number one, be guided by your butcher, your baker, your fish or cheesemonger.

I never walk into Phil Bowditch's fish shop in Taunton and say 'I want,' I always say 'What have you got?' and then subclause it with the size and scale of the occasion and the state of my wallet. He is smart enough and passionate enough about what he's got usually to break through the pain barrier of the latter with an exquisite turbot, or perhaps one of the season's first sea trout from the River Dart: an annual rite of passage to my plate, a streamlined, nose to tail 4½lb beauty in gradations of perfect gunmetal grey with inky constellations of tiny, splattered spots. Caught on Thursday evening, it was Friday's incomparable supper, simply stuffed with fresh, flat-leaf parsley from the garden, anointed with butter and black pepper and doused with a splosh of Chablis, before being parcelled up and baked in a medium oven for 45 minutes. I always let the food drink what I'm drinking, it is rarely superior enough to hesitate.

Phil's mother inspired his love of fish. 'Mum brought me up on fish, and she was a really good cook. She worked in service and the "gentry", as she called them, would bring things back for her, like chunks of salmon from Scotland.' He started with a van and a vision, 'I was determined to break the stranglehold Young's had on supplying caterers with frozen fish in the '70s. I wanted to sell all the local good restaurants fresh fish.'

Driving round Taunton till 9 at night and working his boat catching crabs and lobsters led to the shop, 'The most serious mistake of my life. I thought retailing was the way to go. I'm successful by most people's standards, but it's far easier supplying restaurants, this is darn hard work. I love fish, and I love selling good fish, but I only supply about 2 per cent of the Taunton population. Christ knows what the other 98 per cent live on. Perhaps they're intimidated by too much choice. They'd rather have boards with discounted prices. There's still a resistance to paying for fish, which was historically always seen as a cheap food. They feel they can't afford to cock up £15 worth of fish.' It is not that Phil minds people who are uneducated about fish, it is their lack of adventurousness, 'They stand at the counter, look, ask what something is and how to cook it, and then buy what they've always bought.'

I propose a compulsory school trip for all the local children who believe that fish come in fingers, and their parents, to Phil's shop. Today, among other things, they would have found pale gold smoked haddock from Alfred Enderby in Grimsby, whose fish are still chimney hung to smoke after brining. Not for them the kiln where they are laid flat and the moisture doesn't evaporate sufficiently for them to absorb the smoke properly; red mullet from the English Channel, 'An absolutely beautiful fish, Brixham is the only port you can rely on for them'; a laundry pile of slippery white squid; grey mullet with their trade-mark trellis work of slate grey scales; monk tails, skate, mottled carpet-shell clams, petrolly-glazed mackerel and whiting, 'A must for goujons, and a quarter the price of lemon sole'; and a whole hake, an S-bend coiled sleekly round, scarf-like in its tweedy grey coat. How anyone within a 20-mile radius of Taunton could be one of the 98 percenters, I cannot fathom.

## Grilled Hake Steaks with Spring Herbs

SERVES 3

*three hake steaks about 2.5cm/1in*
*thick*
*good olive oil*
*salt and black pepper*
*1 tbsp each chives, chervil and dill*
*spritz of lemon*

A deliciously underrated fish, even better line caught, since it dies through lack of oxygen, is put in ice, and consequently has a firmer texture than when it has been netted, and effectively drowned because its gills can't flap in the nets. This is the simplest of recipes to inspire the under-confident fish cook. Get your fishmonger to cut each steak thickly, a generous inch. Brush both sides generously with good olive oil, grind on pepper and coarse salt, and grill for 4–5 minutes a side. You can see if the fish is cooked, the translucent raw flesh will be white all through. Finely chop a tablespoon each of chives, chervil and dill, and sprinkle over the steaks with a spritz of lemon and the juice that has escaped into the grill pan.

# Scallop, Squid and Haddock Pie

SERVES 6

*1kg / 2½lb unsmoked haddock,*
*skinned and filleted*
*300–450ml / 10–15fl oz milk*
*1kg / 2½lb potatoes*
*butter and milk for the mashed*
*potato*
*1 tbsp olive oil*
*225g / 8oz baby squid, cleaned and*
*cut into rings*
*the white of two leeks, cleaned and*
*cut into rings*
*a large glass dry white wine or,*
*better still, vermouth*
*a bunch of fresh dill, chopped*
*50g / 2oz unsalted butter*
*25g / 1oz organic white flour*
*a bay leaf, nutmeg, salt and pepper*
*12 fat scallops with their coral,*
*cleaned and prepared*

Preheat the oven to 180°C / 350°F / Gas Mark 4. Bake the haddock in a gratin dish in the oven with 300ml / 10fl oz of the milk and a knob of butter for 15 minutes. Flake it gently into the dish you are going to cook the pie in, in large bits, and reserve the cooking liquid. Boil the potatoes and mash thoroughly with butter and milk.

Heat the oil gently in a small pan and cook the squid briefly until just translucent. Add the leeks and cook a further 2–3 minutes, then add the wine or vermouth, and simmer for 10 minutes. Again, transfer the fish to the cooking dish, and reserve the liquid.

Melt the rest of the butter in a saucepan, add the flour, and when turning nutty, add the fishy liquids, bay, nutmeg, seasoning, and, if you need it, the rest of the milk. You do not want an over-sauced pie. Simmer for a few minutes, then remove from the heat, add the chopped dill, and pour over the fish. Slice the whites of the scallops into three discs and turn them gently into the pie with the corals.

Top with the mashed potato, some tiny bits of butter, and return to the oven until browned and bubbling, about 20 minutes.

# Haddock and Smoked Haddock Fishcakes

A small piece of smoked haddock lifts this dish transcendently, too much would overwhelm.

SERVES 6

675g / 1 ½lb fresh haddock fillet
325g / 12oz natural
smoked haddock
milk
butter
3 medium potatoes, peeled,
steamed and mashed
½ tsp celery salt
a scant fork end cayenne pepper
2 heaped tbsp flat-leaf parsley,
chopped
1 beaten egg
flour, salt and pepper
olive oil

Preheat oven to 180°C / 350°F / Gas Mark 4. Grease a gratin dish with butter and lay your fish fillets in it. Add a splosh of milk, dot with little pieces of butter, season with black pepper and cook in the oven for 15 minutes.

With a spoon and fork, flake away the fish from the skin into large chunks, and pile it on the top of the mashed potato. Add the celery salt and smidgen of cayenne, then scatter on a confetti of parsley. Season, remembering that the smoked haddock is quite salt. Mash together lightly, you want the fish to remain flaky, not pulverized to a paste.

Have three large plates in front of you, one empty, one with the beaten egg, and one with some flour. Flour your hands, and grab a fishcake's worth of the mixture, moulding it before dipping it in the egg, then coating it in flour. Shake off the excess, and place the cake on the clean plate. This quantity should make 12 fishcakes.

Heat a good quantity of olive oil, 6 tablespoons or so, until hot, then cook the fishcakes until well bronzed on both sides. About 5–6 minutes a side should do it. Serve with lemon wedges and a leafy vegetable like purple sprouting broccoli.

# SWADDLES GREEN FARM

IF YOU HAD TO INVENT A PERFECTLY PARADISIACAL SETTING for an organic farm, this would be it. You meander up a lost lane, furrowed like a crease into the Blackdown Hills, until you get to a sign. You take the long track down to Swaddles Green Farm, more cratered than rutted, which finally trails into a thatched farmhouse, a scattering of outbuildings and a farmyard clotted with mud. Regulars broach it be-booted, unless they are not averse to giving their feet as organic an experience as the meat they have come to collect.

It all began 12 years ago, by default. 'Bill's one aim in life was never to run a business' says Charlotte Reynolds wryly of her husband. On leaving Bristol for Somerset, they had armed themselves with a goat to graze the ivy and brambles, and a brace of pigs to rootle over the land, who, before the chop, were tenderly referred to as Bubble and Squeak. By the time they had added a Jersey cow, muscovy ducks and some rare breeds of hen, they were running out of space, and 'The Good Life' was osmosing itself into an experimental business.

So they moved to Swaddles Green Farm, 35 acres of beautiful, unintensively farmed land, with what the estate agents, in optimistic sales-speak, referred to as a 'farmhouse in need of modernization.' In their case it meant windowless, waterless and looless.

Charlotte was undaunted, 'It was totally lunatic, people kept on telling us what we couldn't do, like making sausages without filler, saying they'd fall apart, which they didn't. We had no notion of how to run a business, of profit and loss. I decided to try curing bacon and ham without saltpetre to see if it was possible. No one else seemed to be doing it. The quantity of salt and sugar has to be just right, salty enough to preserve it with the herbs and spices, and with just the right amount of sugar to soften the flesh. At first the brews were either so salty they were unpalatable, or sprouting major whiskers and having fungal attacks. I was doing all the butchery too, hacking about with a ball of string and Jane Grigson propped up in front of me.'

But the first Christmas an ad in the paper was so successful they sold everything. Charlotte, with a background in biochemistry, started a series of organic experiments; ruby-hued salami with thick pearls of fat, chorizo, *jambon cru*, speckled mortadella, shards of richly dense rillettes, potted meats, patés, even organic hot dogs. But with a growing family of animals that now included cattle, sheep, turkeys and geese, and a £100,000 overdraft, it was sell up and pay up time, unless they took the ultimate risk and tried to run it as a business.

Bill gave up teaching special needs children and immersed himself in the carnassial culture that Charlotte was busy apprenticing herself to. 'We were trying to breed, rear, butcher, sell and deliver. We had no proper management accounts, but what we did know was that there was a real market out there for a really fine product, properly raised organic meat.'

I was one of their first customers, have seen things develop, but not change. Bill and Charlotte's purist philosophy is unnegotiable. Simply to 'put only the best in and you will get only the best out. Every ingredient from the sea salt to the organic red wine we put in the jambon cru is the best we can find.'

There has always been an argument that you have to be well-heeled to eat organically, particularly when a chicken can cost four times what you'd pay for an amorphous, frozen lump of knitting-textured flaccid flesh. The Reynolds find it specious. They see shopping for the best as a re-education: 'We sell food to people who think. A lot of our customers are not at all well off, their weekly meat budget is under £10. They eat less of it, and they buy the cheaper cuts.' It is one of Charlotte's major annoyances that so few people buy interesting cuts of meat. The reason, she believes, is that they don't know what to do with them. That the principles of good home cooking are dying a death. 'People are terrified of cooking. I know because of the questions our customers ask us. Although some are keen, dedicated cooks, there are a lot who have no idea. They are the ones who buy fillet steak and chicken breasts. They only want lean meat. They only buy things like hearts for their dogs. Breasts of lamb we'll almost give you, or we throw them away. A culture of cooking and food simply doesn't exist here like it does in Middle Europe and the Mediterranean.

'Everyone wants legs of spring lamb now. But the flavour is feeble and anaemic; the best is the year old, technically hogget, but we sell it as lamb till July. It's not muttony, but it's got the depth of flavour the new season's lamb is too immature to have yet. It is not the fact the meat is organic that intrinsically makes it taste better, it is the breeding and the hanging.'

Charlotte and Bill have five farmers who rear pigs, lambs and beef to their exacting standards, 'beef with fat class four, that's real depth of fat, hung for three weeks. The lambs graze organic grass which is superior in quality to the watery, fertilized grass ordinary lambs get. Organic fields have shorter grass with more interesting plants in it. It grows slowly and more intensely which is passed on into the meat.' I refrain from asking at this point whether she shouldn't introduce redcurrant jelly, mint sauce and wild garlic into the diet.

There is a hitch with the mini-salamis that Charlotte has been experimenting with, 'The new cold store isn't drying them properly, I'm going to have to chuck the whole lot and start again. I can't get the climate right.'

Difficult to believe that a minor detail like the English climate will inhibit Charlotte from producing a perfect salami; indeed, as I leave, she appears to have come up with a solution, 'I need a Tuscan farmhouse.'

# Breast of Lamb cooked in the Daube style.

This is, without doubt, one of the best dishes I have ever cooked. I used two whole breasts as we were eight, and each weighed 1.5kg/3lb. Having abandoned this dish for three hours, I could smell its winey depths three rooms away when I came to take it out of the oven. A sweetly flavoured meat which you could cut with a spoon after its long, slow cooking.

SERVES 8

2 x 1.5kg/3lb whole breasts of lamb on the bone
5 rashers oak-smoked bacon, snipped in 1cm/½ in pieces
5 large carrots cut in 1cm/½in dice
4 sticks celery, chopped
2 onions, chopped
6 cloves garlic
rosemary, bay and parsley stalks tied together with string
1 bottle good red wine
2 x 400g/14oz tins tomatoes
olive oil, salt and pepper

Put the snipped rashers in a large, heavy-bottomed casserole, and heat gently until the fat begins to run. Throw in the carrots, celery, onions and garlic, and sprinkle with a tablespoon or two of olive oil.

Tuck the breasts in next to each other in the casserole, with the bouquet under the flap of one. Season. Heat the wine to boiling point, set light to it, and watch carefully until the flames die down. Pour it over the meat. Add the tomatoes, chopping and sinking them into the wine as you go.

Put a layer of greaseproof paper over the top of the pot, cover it with the lid, and cook in a coolish oven, 150°C/300°F/Gas Mark 2 for 3 hours.

Remove the casserole dish, unlid it, and, with a bulb baster remove the liquid, tomato-coloured fat as far as you dare. I skimmed off 300ml/10fl oz. Don't carve the meat conventionally, it will be so tender that you can cut right through to the bottom in chunks for each portion. Scoop out the vegetables and bacon with the juices, and anoint the meat with them. Is there anything as good as buttery mashed potato with a dish like this?

# Crispy Roast Duck with Turnips

The Reynolds' ducks arrive a day old and live in arks in their fields. They graze freely, eat organic wheat pellets, slugs, snails and worms. They are strong-tasting meaty birds, but not over-fat. There has always been an affinity between duck and peas, but I think the first miniature-lightbulb-sized turnips of the spring are as much of a match.

SERVES 4

*My duck weighed 2.2kg / 5lb*
*2 onions, 1 thinly sliced and the*
*other quartered*
*an orange, quartered*
*bunch of thyme*
*sea salt*

FOR THE SAUCE:
*butter*
*small onion, chopped*
*1 celery stick, chopped*
*duck liver, heart, kidneys and neck*
*1 tbsp pomegranate molasses or*
*squeezed juice of pomegranate.*
*If you can't find either, a sweet*
*orange will do*
*red wine*

FOR THE TURNIPS:
*8 baby turnips, cut into*
*5mm / ¼in dice*
*knob of butter*
*1 dsrtsp brown sugar*

Preheat the oven high, to 220°C / 425°F / Gas Mark 7. This is what I did to really crisp the skin, while keeping the meat pinkly tender. Remove the giblets, prick the skin all over with a fork, and put the duck breast down in the roasting tin on the top of the stove on a moderately hot ring. Leave it as it begins to sizzle. After 2 minutes repeat this on each side, then on the underside. The fat will be beginning to run, and the duck will already have coloured quite deeply. Finally give it another blast breast side down, then remove the tin from the heat, swiftly place a thinly sliced onion under the bird, a quartered orange, onion, and a bunch of thyme inside it, and, still breast up, about 8 generous pinches of sea salt all over its skin.

Roast for 50 minutes, but after 30, remove it from the oven and suck up the fat with your bulb baster, and again prick the skin all over before returning it to the oven. Leave the duck to rest for 10 minutes before carving.

Meanwhile, melt a nut of butter in a small pan, add the onion, celery, and the liver, heart, kidneys and neck of the duck, and brown gently. Then add the pomegranate molasses or juice, red wine to almost cover, and a bit of water, and leave it to simmer for 10–15 minutes, skimming it if you need to. Reheat with the caramelized onions in the roasting tin. Sieve, pushing through as much of the liver as you can, and serve in a *dégraisser* alongside the duck.

I peeled the turnips, cut them into 5mm / ¼ inch dice, and threw them into boiling water until just tender, about seven minutes. Then I tossed them in butter and dark brown sugar with a sprinkling of thyme until soft and caramelized.

# THE BEST CHEESE IN THE WEST

*'You have got to feel passionate. Handmade British cheese is my gospel.'*

IT IS 10.30 IN THE MORNING at The Fine Cheese Company in Bath. It's a 50-mile pilgrimage for me, but supplication is all, in pursuit of the best, and I've been coming to Ann Marie's and Tony Down's shop irregularly ever since I first sniffed it out.

Once you've entered the hallowed ground of the shop floor, I can guarantee you'll never look a pasteurized cheese in the rind again with any degree of pleasure.

It is designed, unlike most shops, with a sort of naughty-child-let-loose-in-a-sweet-shop mentality. You are actively encouraged to step behind the counter, Ann Marie has had labels handwritten in doll-sized scrawl to impel you to inspect closer. You pore over the dresser laden with sheep's, goat's and cow's cheeses ranging from white through pale ivory to buttermilk to deep straw. Soft, creamy, buttery cheeses; melting, crumbly lactic lozenges; pyramids, logs, great cloth-bound drums and truckles; veiny, fruity, moist cheeses, it is an eye's feast of around 150 different types, indigenous British wherever possible.

'British cheeses were on Death Row when we began,' Ann Marie continues, 'Largely brought to their knees by the supermarkets.' So why on earth did she, an account director for a London advertising agency, and Tony, marketing for a big brewery, take redundancy and attempt to become latter-day saviours of an industry perpetually hovering on the brink of extinction?

'Tony was fascinated by cheese, he left first, and went to see the great cheese guru Patrick Rance. Then he started researching, and opened a small shop in Corsham, which proved too small a town to sustain a cheese shop. But he'd built up a large wholesale cheese business by going round all the best local restaurants and making them switch from French to British cheese boards.

'Finally I got tired of takeovers and commuting and resigned. My first job was to find premises. I wanted Bath, it's a hot city, but with premium prices. Luckily we were looking when the recession struck in the mid-eighties, and when we opened we hit the ground running. People were eating out less, but they wanted to eat in better. They wanted treaty things. I thought of this place as somewhere you could come and assemble a really good picnic: cheese, wine, bread, charcuterie, chutneys. You can sample anything you want here. The people of Bath had been starved of good cheese before we opened. I enticed them in by having baskets of wonderful Hobbs' bread in the window. It's the only way with a cheese shop, bread brings in the cheese traffic. Then, when they've bought their Cheddar, Stilton and Brie, I help them extend their repertoire. We took a risk setting up shop opposite Waitrose, but I thought being in their slipstream could be turned to our advantage.'

'People weren't used to seeing the name of the producer. One man looked at the goat's cheese by Mary Holbrooke and said, "Is that the name of the goat?" He saw my face. "It's not is it?" Another, an American asked me whether the unpasteurized cheeses were safe to eat. At my most charmingly aggressive I said, "You're not going to have an immune system left if you don't start eating unpasteurized cheese!"'

There is a growing, greater frustration: increasingly people are buying cheese only for a dinner party or to cook with. They have seen the market decrease by 10 per cent in a year. 'Doctors are forever telling people not to eat dairy whatever's wrong with them, and it's attacked on all sides, food scares have a knock-on effect.' One countermeasure is the new mail order service, an edited version of the shop, more like a larder, from which Ann Marie will select special things to follow meat, fish and the seasons, and send them by 24-hour delivery service. So what does she like best? 'I'm besotted by sheep's cheese. I could live on it. It can cover the whole gamut of cheese experience. People confuse sheep's with goat's cheese, and if they don't like its pronounced goaty flavour assume that they won't like sheep's cheese either. But it has enormous creaminess; Wigmore is incredibly delicate, Lord of the Hundreds is strong and powerful, but has a wonderful creaminess that fills the mouth. Beenleigh Blue is delicious. Tony loves Montgomery, a cloth-bound unpasteurized Cheddar from North Cadbury in Somerset. We have to change the way people eat cheese. It is best with good, crisp things like apples or celery, and you can't beat a good unpasteurized Brie de Meaux served with red cherries, or Mary Holbrooke's Timsboro, a mould-ripened goat's pyramid, slightly flaky, with a rounded creamy flavour, and a bit of walnut bread.'

Ann Marie eats her cheese with a knife and fork, and some salad leaves dressed with their Lapalisse virgin walnut oil, sans bread or biscuits. Even when pushed, she is loath to suggest recipes that involve cooking cheese, other than the goat's one below.

'The theme of the shop is the undiscovered cheese,' she says, 'What people discover with unpasteurized cheese, is how complex the flavours are. The first taste on the palate changes right through till the last. I look forward to things not being so good at a certain time and then hitting their peak; summer's milk can make them blossom. I always advise people to ask what's good when they go into a cheese shop. It puts us on our mettle. If you ask me you're judging me. What I feel more passionately than anything is that we have to fight to keep our unpasteurized cheese alive. We've got to stop the juggernaut effect of the "food police". I'll throw in the towel if we can't sell unpasteurized cheese.'

I rather feel, that as long as Ann Marie and the Fine Cheese Company is in the ring, the food police will be going the full 15 rounds.

# Some do's and don'ts on how to eat cheese:

Do not go for the 'bird table' effect, by serving 6 or 7 cheeses. Ann Marie and Tony suggest a maximum of 4. 'You've got to be really confident to serve just one cheese.' I have to say, that in the late autumn I do just that with a whole Vacherin Mont d'Or, served with only the proverbial silver spoon to help the liquid gold out of its box.

You can achieve all the hard/soft/blue/cow/goat/ sheep combinations with just three cheeses if you buy Beenleigh Blue, Cheddar and a goat's pyramid.

Ann Marie breaks all these rules by serving just 3 white cheeses – with red cherries in summer – Kirkham's Lancashire, an acidic cow's milk cheese with a wonderfully lactic after-taste and crumbly intensity; Spenwood, a fruity, apples and pearsy sheep's milk cheese; and a fresh goat such as Plain Sleight.

Nothing looks prettier than a fresh goat's cheese served with a purple fig on a fig leaf.

They sell a wonderful Membrillo, a pure fruit slab of quince with sugar and lemon. Serve it with Lord of the Hundreds rather than the conventional Spanish Manchego. A perfect pudding. Or try Spenwood with their sweet chestnut honey, instead of the traditional Pecorino.

# Ann Marie's Crostini

*1 thick slice of bread, preferably*
*Pugliese, per person*
*garlic*
*good olive oil*
*Carluccio's black olive and caper*
*paste*
*fresh goat's cheese*
*1 slice prosciutto per person*
*salad leaves*

Squeeze a garlic clove into some good olive oil, and brush it over both sides of a thick slice of bread. Put the bread in a hot oven for 10–15 minutes, turning it once.

Spread a layer of Carluccio's black olive and caper paste over it, then some fresh goat's cheese, which is more moussey than a crottin. Top with a slice of prosciutto, and serve with some dressed salad leaves.

# Kirkham's Lancashire Cheese and Chive Soufflé with Walnuts

The beautiful, lactic taste is not lost in the cooking here, the cheese bubbles creamily without melting. Coat the soufflé dish with ground organic walnuts, and sprinkle some more on top, they enhance rather than mask the flavour as Parmesan might.

SERVES 4–6
DEPENDING ON WHETHER IT'S
A STARTER OR SUPPER

*125g / 4oz Kirkham's*
*Lancashire cheese*
*a dozen or so walnuts*
*50g / 2oz unsalted butter*
*40g / 1 ½oz flour*
*300ml / ½ pint Jersey milk*
*1 ½ tbsp chopped chives*
*salt, pepper and cayenne*
*4 organic egg yolks and 5 whites*

Preheat the oven to 200°C/400°F/Gas Mark 6. Grate the cheese and reserve. Grind the walnuts moderately finely. Butter a soufflé dish that takes at least 900ml/1½ pints, and throw in most of the walnuts, rolling them round the dish till they cling to the butter. Grease a strip of greaseproof paper and place it like a dog-collar 5cm/2in above the top of the dish. Secure with a paper clip.

Melt the butter in a small pan, then make a roux with the flour. Remove from the heat and, with a small whisk, beat in the milk which you have heated to boiling point. Whisk in the yolks one by one, throw in the cheese, then return briefly to a low heat, on no account letting it bubble. Remove, season, and add the chives.

Whisk the whites until stiff. Stir a spoonful of them into the mixture, then lightly and quickly fold in the rest. Spoon into the soufflé dish, sprinkle over the remaining walnuts, and put immediately into the oven. Don't look for 30 minutes. Mine was ready then, puffed up, browned, and with the perfect slightly sad centre. It was an ideal Saturday lunch, served with some peppery rocket leaves tossed in walnut oil.

# THE VEGGIE BOX

WHAT, YOU MIGHT ASK, induced Simon Brooke, a senior chartered accountant specializing in insolvency, seconded to a big job in Bermuda, and his wife Jane, a landscape architect, to throw everything up, pension, partnership prospects, a pretty snug financial future – even an allotment in Epsom – for a small, council farm in Somerset? Unbedazzled by the blue-skied, white-beached island, they plotted not their future tax exile, but their return to England, their dream of running their own organic farm. For two years they saved, fortified by copies of *Farmer's Weekly* sent out by Jane's mother, and between whose covers they delved in search of the ideal, affordable farm.

I am of a firm belief that if any of us could foresee the reality of the hardship years of running one's own business, we would do our best to draw a draught and drink deeply at another well. The fact that, barely five years later, they are muddied yet unbowed, and beginning to see the light from the loam, is a testament not only to their physical powers of attrition.

It is early-ish in the morning, although Jane and Simon are up before the lark in the summer months. We are thrashing through the long grass of their orchard, inspecting raspberries, black, white and redcurrants, and something entirely unbeknown to me, 'God's own barbed wire,' the worcesterberry, a blackcurrant and gooseberry cross with hybrid thorns that look beyond lethal.

Their modest 22 acres, '15 without the lane to the house,' has been newly planted with an amenity woodland stocked with oak and ash, and chestnut and alder for coppicing. They are foster parents to several families of Charlotte and Bill Reynolds' pigs – and, if you count the expectant litters, they look after around 100 porkers, including some rare and beautiful indigenous West Country Large Blacks, in fact, the rarest pig in England. And why have they fallen from favour? Need you guess, the Large Black is an extremely porky porker, and it is black-haired, and the modern consumer likes neither black hair nor fat on his pork.

'We've been growing for five years now, and last year we sort of turned the corner. The first season it was divorce every week. We'd be screaming at each other. It was a nightmare, working all day, waiting till it was cool to pick the vegetables, then packing them at midnight. It was only a trial plot, and we weren't earning anything.'

Two greenhouses nurture Florence fennel, aubergines, chillies, primary-coloured peppers, red, yellow, green and the acid-lime 'banana' kind; there are heritage tomatoes, white, pink and yellow cherry ones, and black, pink and yellow normal-sized ones. Even the Russian Black Krim, a beefsteak tomato coloured like strong coffee, 'our bit of fun,' says Jane, whose preferred territory is the greenhouses, but who has managed to persuade Simon, not unnaturally the financial brains of Merricks Farm, of the necessity sometimes to experiment for the sheer hell of it. They are brutally honest about the state of organic growing when they started, 'The quality was appalling.

The growers hadn't got their act together. Early co-ops and box schemes copied from the originals in Japan and America had started, but they often sold poor quality stuff.' Jane and Simon have gone not just for competitive pricing, but for quality of the highest order, which led to them winning the Organic Food Awards box scheme prize in 1997, the year they finally broke even.

'We are now on a 45-degree learning gradient rather than the 90-degree one we started on,' says Simon. And many myths have been laid to rest in the meanwhile. 'We thought it would be young people buying from us, but the majority are over 50. I think it's because they're a generation who still have strong memories of what good food tastes of.'

'And the young don't know what to do with it,' continues Jane. 'There is a lost generation of 25–35 year olds who don't know how to cook, who had working mothers, fast food, no cookery lessons at school. That's why some of our customers are so unadventurous, still resistant to all sorts of things, even flat-leaf parsley and coriander, that they've seen the trendy TV chefs cooking with. I've had a lady ring me up and say how peculiar her rhubarb crumble tasted. She'd used the red chard! Others believe beetroot comes ready pickled, and they're blown out of the water by our yellow beetroot. But 97 per cent of them stay with us and love the excitement of what's going to appear in the box each week. They're forced to cook food they haven't chosen, they ring and ask what purslane is, go to their cookery books or to the library, and actually say they're becoming better cooks as a result. And we send out recipe leaflets.' 'We're still striving to hit the average wage, but it looks like we'll be able to develop the farm a bit more this year, and take a holiday. And then there's the pension.' It's obvious who's speaking, but Jane says that even after the struggle of the first year they said to each other, 'It can't be as bad as this next year. And we didn't contemplate going back to what we'd come from. We couldn't think of anything we wanted to do more. When you see what you've planted out and harvested all boxed up, and you get customers like the one who burst into tears at the end of February when she knew we were finishing till the new season in May, you forget about things like the slug wipe-out that meant we had to resow all our first outdoor carrots, and you think that maybe we don't take enough time to say, "Look we've done all this in five years."'

I think what has struck me most about Jane and Simon, along with the other producers I've met, is that they share passion without greed, a much under-prized virtue, and one that in their case provides its own reward and, ultimately, defines the word success.

# A Dish of Spring Vegetables

There is nothing as good as a dish of the first, squeaky, sweet peas, thumbnails of broad beans, tight-budded asparagus and the tender hearts of violet-tipped artichokes.

Allow two artichokes each, which you should throw into a large cauldron of boiling water acidulated with a splosh of vinegar or lemon juice. Cook until a leaf will peel easily away from the main stem, then cool slightly, remove the leaves so that you can get to the heart, and carefully cut it away from the woody pulp. While the artichokes are cooking, trim a large bundle of asparagus into 5cm/2in lengths, no woody ends included. Steam, adding the tips about 3 minutes after the wands, until unresistant to the knife. Throw 900g/2lb each of broad beans and peas (unpodded weight) into boiling chicken stock, if you have it, or water, to not quite cover, in two small pans, and cook briefly, but slightly more than *al dente*. Remove the broad beans from the stock, and when slightly cooled, pop them out of their grey wrinkly jackets. It really is worth it, and it isn't that much of an effort. Melt a generous lump of butter in a pan, and add the four vegetables. Toss briefly, do not stir or you'll break up the asparagus, sprinkle over some finely chopped mint, season and add some cooking stock if you feel like it. This amount serves four.

# Leek and Parma Ham Gratin

The new season's leeks are young, long and tender; they can be steamed, wrapped and cooked under a bubblingly rich gratin of buttered breadcrumbs and Beaufort cheese.

SERVES 4

*2 leeks per person*
*6 slices Parma ham, cut in half*
*600ml/1 pint béchamel sauce,*
*made with 25g/1oz each of butter*
*and flour, and 600ml/1 pint milk,*
*salt, pepper and nutmeg*
*2 handfuls breadcrumbs*
*25g/1oz butter*
*125g/4oz Beaufort, or the best*
*Gruyère you can find*

Preheat the oven to 180°F/350°C/Gas Mark 4. Strip the leeks of their tough outer skins and dark green ends and wash well. Steam them until tender, then leave them to cool while you make the béchamel.

Wrap the leeks in the strips of Parma ham, then place them in a row on the bottom of a buttered gratin dish. Pour over the béchamel.

Briefly fry the breadcrumbs in butter until golden, then sprinkle a thin layer of them over the surface of the béchamel. Add the grated Beaufort or Gruyère, and put the dish in the oven for about 25 minutes, or until the béchamel begins to bubble through the golden crust. Serve with a salad.

# Beetroot and Apple Salad with a Horseradish Dressing

SERVES 4

3 or 4 medium-sized beetroot
2 good-flavoured eating apples,
peeled
best olive oil
Aspall's organic cider vinegar
1 tsp grated fresh horseradish or
English Provender Company's
freshly grated hot horseradish
salt and pepper
chopped coriander leaves

Cook 3 or 4 medium-sized beetroot, skins on, cleaned, but with whiskers still attached to stop them bleeding, in a pan of boiling water, until a knife can easily pierce them. Cool slightly, then skin and grate them on a coarse grater; I also tried the fine grater of the food processor but the texture was too pulpy. Grate the peeled apples into the beetroot, then make your dressing with best olive oil, Aspall's organic cider vinegar, and a teaspoon of freshly grated horseradish. Season, pour over the salad, and scatter a handful of chopped coriander leaves over it.

If you can't stand the heat, I tried another version with half an organic pink grapefruit. I made a dressing with 2 tablespoons of its juice and the same of olive oil. It was delicious and astringent, and the grapefruit flavour came through.

# Braised Fennel with Olives and Cardamom

SERVES 4

4 bulbs fennel
2tbsp olive oil
2 cloves garlic
8 black olives, stoned
3 cardamom pods, crushed
a bunch of thyme
a scant 600ml/1 pint chicken
stock or half water, half white wine
salt and pepper

Preheat oven to 180°C/350°F/Gas Mark 4.

Once you have removed the tough outer layer, cut vertically down the fennel bulbs, quartering each one. Sweat them gently in the olive oil in a heavy-bottomed casserole.

Add the garlic, olives, cardamom and thyme, and the liquid, season, and bring to the boil. Cover with greaseproof paper and then with a lid, and bake in the oven for 1¼–1½ hours. Particularly delicious with pork or fish.

# ROB MANN'S ASPARAGUS

'LAST YEAR WAS A DISASTER, and this year we've been washed out so far, we've had 7 inches of rain in the last month,' Rob Mann tells me from the warmth of his farmhouse kitchen. He and his wife Rebecca farm 30 miles from me at Rodney Stoke, in the heart of Cheddar. An acre and a half of their land is given over to asparagus, and the conversion to organic will be complete this September. Unearthing an organic grower of these precious, fragile green wands has taken some time; the Manns appear to be the nearest to growing it on a commercial scale.

The frustrations of the long fallow period from seeding to sparse first crop two years later; the abruptness of the cropping season, so easily marred by our inclement climate; and the sheer toil of weeding and hand-picking all conspire to discourage the grower from growing this most highly prized and highly priced vegetable. But imagine May passing without a plate of warm, olive-green asparagus, bending like a bow to the tightly furled spear tips as you dip them in a glossy puddle of hollandaise, or dribble them with clear primrose-coloured unsalted butter, a spritz of lemon and a scrunch of black pepper. Unthinkable.

At the moment, the constant rain has lowered the temperature of the soil, so the asparagus is just not growing, as is apparent when the three of us set off across the farmyard through liquid mud to the wetly clogged fields above. Rivulets of water course down the field's edge, and a damp stain across the clayey red soil suggests an underground spring is leaking into the bare, sodden earth. Not a solitary spear breaks through the blank red canvas of soil. We climb higher to the second asparagus field, and there we see, erratically dotting the dark earth, the first tender violet tips poking through like tightly closed fists. 'Some swear by the superiority of the white-stemmed French asparagus, but I maintain our native green is incomparable. In Germany, Belgium and France they grow it under the soil, and earth it up because they prefer it white. Our green asparagus tastes unique because of the rich Cheddar soil; there's no comparison between our's and the Spanish stuff. I pick mine at 9 inches – trim off an inch, and you can eat all of it. I pick the night before market and keep the bottoms in water with a tiny bit of sugar overnight. You can do it in your fridge at home and it will keep fresh for 2–3 days in half an inch of water.'

On a warm sunny day, asparagus can grow between a foot and fifteen inches, and Rob and Rebecca have to pick at twice, at 6am and 4pm. Somehow, the frustrations, the back breaking, sheer hard graft are converted, if not into pleasure, at least to satisfaction. 'Fanatical is a bit strong a word, but it's very addictive growing asparagus, it's a satisfying crop to grow, and you get a lot of feedback. I'm never going to get rich, but it is a short, concentrated season, and I do enjoy it in a masochistic way.' Rob adds, 'I've even begun to acquire a taste for it. When I first grew it I thought it was like glorified cabbage.'

# Asparagus with Hollandaise

I am of the firm opinion that asparagus needs dressing down rather than dressing up, and that its most compatible partners are butter and eggs. Choose the freshest asparagus you can lay your hands on, any sign of dried, withering, scaly stalks and it's not worth buying. Simply dressed, with butter, vinaigrette or hollandaise, asparagus should be eaten warm, and in the fingers. 450g/1lb will do two people. Trim the bases if the spears need it, then either stand the bundles upright, tied with string, in a lidded pan with 8cm/3in of boiling, salted water, or lower them diagonally into a steamer, leaving the tips to just poke out from the semi-closed lid, so they don't overcook. Check with the point of a knife after 5 minutes, and if it slips in unresisted, the asparagus is cooked. The fattest stems will take up to 5 minutes longer. Drain well. Cook the new potatoes for your next course around the asparagus; it will scent them deliciously.

SERVES 4

3 egg yolks
2 tbsp dry white wine
2 tbsp lemon juice
225g/8oz best unsalted butter
salt and cayenne pepper

Clarify the butter first, by simply melting it gently in a pan, letting it cool slightly, then pouring the clear liquid into a jug, leaving the curd-like solids in the pan.

Put the yolks, wine and lemon juice in a bowl and set it over a barely simmering pan of water. The bowl must not touch the water.

Whisk with a balloon whisk until it begins to thicken, then start to add the melted butter, drop by drop at first, then in a steady trickle, whisking all the time. All you need is patience to achieve a glossy, satiny sauce. Season, and pour a deep yellow puddle on to the plate.

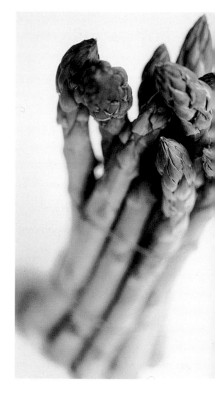

# Asparagus, Fennel and Red Pepper Salad

Loath as I am to eat asparagus in any form that isn't as near as damn it *au natur*, this salad, which my friend George Morley suggested we make one greedy weekend, quite converted me. It makes a brilliant starter, but allows the asparagus to play the starring role, so the peppers don't overwhelm.

SERVES 6

2 organic red peppers

2 large bundles of asparagus, 450g / 1lb each

2 bulbs fennel

olive oil, lemon juice, salt and pepper, and a sprinkling of chervil if you have it to hand

Grill the peppers on all sides and put them in a bowl under clingfilm so the skins begin to steam off. Skin, de-seed and cut them into thin strips. Cut the asparagus into 5cm / 2in chunks, and steam the stalks on their own for a couple of minutes. Add the tips, and steam until cooked, about another 3 minutes. Remove the outer layer of the fennel bulbs down to the firm heart, and slice them as thinly as you can, with a mandolin if you have one. Put all the vegetables into a bowl, then pour in your oil and lemon dressing, and mix together gently by hand. Serve with a good crusted bread like *Boule de Meule*.

# Frittata Stuffed with Sprue

Dipping verdant green spears of asparagus into runny boiled egg yolks is a real post-nursery delight, as is throwing the violet-tinged tips into a sea of creamy scrambled eggs. But try these little bundles of sprue wrapped in a basil-scented frittata.

SERVES 4

6 large organic eggs

1 bunch basil, roughly torn, a few leaves set aside

1 clove garlic, peeled and finely chopped

2 tbsp freshly grated Parmesan

225g / 8oz sprue, or fine-stemmed asparagus

olive oil, salt and pepper

Beat the eggs in a bowl then add the basil, garlic, Parmesan and seasoning. Allow the mixture to rest a bit if you have time, for the basil to permeate the eggs. Cook the sprue as in the recipe above, although it won't take so long, then drain, season, and dribble over a bit of olive oil. Put a couple of tablespoons of olive oil into a frying pan on a medium heat, then pour in a quarter of the egg mixture and swirl it around as you would for a pancake. When it turns opaque, flip it over and cook the other side briefly. Cook the remaining frittatas. Put a little bundle of sprue at the edge of each frittata and roll up. Sprinkle on the remaining basil and a bit of extra Parmesan and serve.

# SEGGIANO, THE OLIVE OIL

CROSSING THE TARMAC TO THE WAITING 727, I look skywards to the cockpit. Simultaneously the pilot looks down, waves, gives me a thumbs up. I am not in the habit of picking up Ryanair pilots, but my Mayo friend Michael Tom Durkan, who had been on standby, had suddenly been scheduled to fly and managed to swap flights. Minutes later I am in the cockpit, harnessed like a baby in a buggy, watching the rubber-streaked runway run away beneath us. Once we are cruising at 10,000 metres, everything quietly, impeccably under control, Michael Tom turns to me, 'You can see the feverish pace we work at up here.' We arrive early in Pisa after the best flight ever, but of course I am biased.

Three hours later, with the gloom gathering, I can just begin to decipher the surrounding hillscape as we arrive at Seggiano, a medieval hilltop village clinging to the sides of Monte Amiata, an extinct volcano. I am spending a couple of days with David Harrison and Peri Eagleton, who started their eponymous company, Seggiano, six years ago, producing and selling their own and their neighbours' olive oil. More recently they have added pecorinos, *sott'olios*, vegetable creams and coarse patés, honey and handmade biscuits to their list.

Dawn reveals the silvery-leafed olive grove their farmhouse sits in, vines below, roan-tipped chestnuts girdling the hills above, and a necklace of beeches and black, tapered tongues of cyprus trees at the summit. We set off early to a nearby farm to collect the new season's olive oil for bottling. '*Contadinos* are the bedrock of Italian society,' David tells me, 'They are not peasants, they are small farmers who live as self-sufficiently as possible off the family smallholding.' Firewood is stacked in an elegantly graded still life. There are netted runs for hens and rabbits, rows of artichokes. We enter a cool, dark barn under the house where the two men begin pouring the viscous green liquid into huge containers. A few remaining jars of summer-bottled fruits grace the shelves, *pomodori*, *sugo*, chopped peaches and capers. 'There's a renaissance of olive producing here, and I feel quite proud we've been part of it. We're trying to get everyone to go organic,' David says. 'I knew nothing about olives when I came here first,' Peri tells me, 'But in 1992 there was a glut of them, neighbours came to me on their knees begging me to do something, to start selling them in England. The Olivastra Seggianese we grow locally is a female tree. Its unique feature is that it withstands the cold better than any other variety. Up here we're at the highest altitude they can grow, 450 metres, and the olive fly can't survive the winter, it's too cold. Lower down and all over Europe they've got infestations. We don't need to treat our trees, so they are mostly organic, although a lot of our neighbours haven't bothered with certification.'

Seggiano olive oil is quite unlike the classic Tuscan olive oils with their pepperiness, their *amaro* – bitter – aftertaste, their robust, more masculine flavour. 'The olivastra has a creamy texture, a delicate flavour, no bitter finish. It has its own subtle identity, but it's too delicate to waste on strong flavours. You wouldn't want to roast with it, but it's great with vegetables, potatoes, rice, fish, pasta,' Peri says.

In the autumn, David and Peri's olives are hand-picked, then taken to the local olive mill. Here they are slow crushed under a huge granite wheel. 'Heat and air are critical, too much air at this stage causes oxidation. You get rancidity if you ill-treat your oil,' Peri continues. 'I can tell customers whose olive trees the oil is from, who's looked after them, what they've done to them, where the olives have been milled and stored. Just being organic means nothing. Organic industrially made products taste awful and have no virtues. If there isn't some little person like us who really cares, who's really proud of their product, it's no good. We care passionately about what we are doing.'

## Cannellini Beans with Garlic, Sage and Seggiano Olive Oil

In this most famous of Tuscan dishes, it is the libation of olive oil poured over the warm beans just before serving that makes it. It is as delicious made with the chalky textured, speckledy borlotti beans. Serve with roast pork or lamb, or on its own if you prefer. The tomatoes are optional, I prefer the dish without their distraction.

SERVES 4 AS AN ACCOMPANIMENT

225g / 8oz dried cannellini beans, soaked for at least 8 hours
sprigs of rosemary and sage
1 medium onion, and a couple of celery stalks
2 or 3 garlic cloves
6 tbsp Seggiano olive oil
3 fresh or tinned tomatoes, skinned, seeded and chopped (optional)
salt and fresh black pepper

Cook the beans in plenty of water, with a sprig each of rosemary and sage, the onion and celery and a clove of garlic, until tender. Drain the beans, discarding the other vegetables, but keeping the cooking liquor.

Saute another sprig of fresh sage in 3 tablespoons of olive oil with the two bruised cloves of garlic. When the garlic begins to frizzle, remove it. Add the tomatoes if you are using them. Add the beans, and turn them in the oil, then pour over enough of the bean stock to cover the base of the saucepan. Season with salt and pepper – never season dried beans with salt during the initial cooking stage, it will merely toughen the skins to husks – and cook until most of the liquid has evaporated. Transfer to an earthenware dish to cool and pour over a good glug of olive oil, about 3 tablespoons, just before serving. Best served warm.

# White Tuscan Salad

SERVES 4

2 whole fresh buffalo mozzarella,
the best you can find
2 bulbs fennel, the woody leaves
and stalks removed ruthlessly down
to the firm bulb
1 celery heart, the white only
salt and fresh black pepper
125 ml/4fl oz Seggiano olive oil
juice of a lemon

This is a perfect antipasto. Drain the mozzarellas and cut them into thin slices. Arrange them in a single layer on a large, dark plate. Halve the trimmed fennel bulbs and remove the triangular cores. Slice them wafer thin on a mandolin or by hand, and chop the celery hearts into small diagonal slices cut on the cross.

Strew the vegetables over the mozzarella, season, lash on the olive oil and the juice of a lemon, and serve. Wonderful with Baker and Spice's baguette rolled in fennel and poppy seeds, warmed in the oven.

# Spaghetti Aglio e Olio

The simplest of foods demand only the absolute best of ingredients. For this use fresh spring garlic with Seggiano's new season's olive oil. The chopped red chilli pepper you must use according to your taste.

SERVES 4

450g/1lb spaghetti or spaghettini
6 tbsp Seggiano olive oil
2–3 tsp finely minced new garlic
finely chopped red chilli pepper
a large handful flat-leaf
parsley, chopped

Cook the pasta according to the instructions, in plenty of boiling, well-salted water.

Meanwhile, put the olive oil, garlic and chilli in a saucepan and heat very gently. You want the garlic to colour, but barely. Drain the pasta, return to the pan and toss it with the olive oil mixture, coating the pasta thoroughly. Add the parsley, toss again, check the seasoning and serve.

# Shoulder of Pork Braised with Bay, Milk and Potatoes

SERVES 6

1.6 kg / 3½lb shoulder of pork
a large onion, sliced thinly
a branch of bay with 10–12 leaves
900g / 2lb potatoes, peeled and
sliced into thin discs
600–900ml / 1–1½ pints creamy
milk
salt and pepper

Preheat the oven to 220°C/425°F/Gas Mark 7. Lay the sliced onion on the bottom of a roasting tin, put the joint on top of it, and scatter a good sprinkling of coarse sea salt over the scored fat. Roast in the oven for an hour.

Heat the milk, remove the roasting tin from the oven, and strew the bay leaves on the base of it. Arrange the potatoes in layers around the meat, seasoning as you go, then pour on milk just to cover. Return to the oven; check after 30 minutes that the potatoes aren't drying out. Replenish with milk if you need to. Fifteen minutes later, pierce the potatoes with a skewer, and if they are soft right through to the bottom, all is ready. Let the meat stand for 10 minutes before carving, keeping the potatoes warm while you do.

# Baby Artichokes Marinated in Seggiano Olive Oil

SERVES 6

1.5 kg / 3lb small artichokes
4 lemons
150–175ml / 5–6fl oz
extra virgin olive oil
2 sprigs each thyme and
parsley
bay leaves
a stalk of celery
a dozen black peppercorns

Have a large bowl of cold water with the juice of half a lemon squeezed into it to hand while you trim the artichokes. Snap off and discard the dark outer leaves, trim the base and the stalk, and rub the other half of the lemon over the cut surfaces as you go. Cut the top 1cm/½in off the remaining leaves, and throw the artichokes into the acidulated water to prevent discoloration.

Bring a large pan of water to the boil, add salt, and boil the artichokes until just tender. Drain well, and place in a bowl. Make the marinade by putting all the other ingredients into a saucepan, with the juice of the three remaining lemons and 900ml/1½ pints of water. Simmer uncovered for 20 minutes, then pour the hot liquid over the artichokes and leave to cool. Cover and refrigerate for at least 3 days.

When you want to eat them, remove the artichokes with a slotted spoon and serve with an extra splash of olive oil.

# MAURO'S HONEY

'There is no point in being an intellectual bee,' Mauro Pagliaccia, beekeeper and biology teacher informs me. We are sitting looking out across his terrace, dazzled by the early spring glitter of Lake Bolsena in the near distance. From 2 to 10, from 10 to 20, to 100, to 500, Mauro's hives have grown like Topsy, each of the 500 demanding 12 hours of his time a year.

Consider the toil of the average worker bee and you will realize that the pursuit of amber nectar is as refined and high-tech an art, and as artful an industry, as you have ever encountered. The binding force, gluing the whole enterprise of each hive's fragile eco-system together, is the queen. 'If you lose the queen, the bees are headless,' Mauro tells me, 'She produces hormones which keep the family together, bonds them; if she goes, they throw in the towel.'

In the winter, each family of bees, up to 15,000 a hive, is coiled up tightly into a sort of bee ball. By the summer, there will be up to 100,000 in each hive. The workers live for about 40 days, frenziedly departing and returning to the hive with propolis, pollen and nectar, and with water, which they evaporate with their wings to keep the temperature inside constant when it gets too hot. When the virgin queen takes her virgin flight, three or four kilometres up into the air, she is pursued by the drones, the fastest and fittest of whom gets to cover her. Cruelly, his tackle is ripped away from him, 'but she's got the goodies'.

The hive is like a miniature court, 'the queen can neither cook, clean nor wash up. Everything is done for her, even the removing of the dead drone's genitals. She is covered by several bees during the season, then she returns to the hive and doesn't do it again.' Miraculously, the sperm lasts for five years, but each year the quality goes down. In a good season, a queen can lay 4,000 to 5,000 eggs a day between May and September.

Once the queen is spent, Mauro introduces a new one to the hive. New queens are sent through the post, and are bred to arrive in peak reproductive condition. They come with a retinue of serfs, the old queen is removed from the hive, and the new incumbent is enthroned. Nothing is left to chance, with bee security guards posted near the hive entrance, as much to keep their monarch from straying as to prevent the hard-pressed occupants from buzzing off. Even the queen's diet is controlled, her court feeding her on royal jelly, vitamins and salts.

The hives set amid the heather towards the sea produce a honey redolent of caramelized barley. Along the coast where the eucalyptus trees grow, the honey tastes 'like cheese, gorgonzola, it makes you think of pig, it smells of animal. There are palely gold honeys from abandoned valleys of wild acacia and clover; intensely burnished liquid-toffee honey from the sweet chestnut trees above, which straddle the hills with the black, tapered tongues of cyprus. There is a thick, fudgy depthed sunflower honey as yellow as lemon curd. And there is Mauro's *melata* – honey dew – which is not made from nectar. 'The aphids suck sap from the trees and secretions from the plants, ingesting the salt and minerals and excreting the sugars. The bees come and eat these secretions and turn them into honey dew.' This liquid mahogany, heaped with minerals, salts and enzymes, is, Mauro believes, a powerful force against osteoporosis. 'Honey is full of antibacterial properties; it's also an expectorant, good for the throat and chest.'

The oldest written reference to honey is thought to be Egyptian, from around 5500 BC. Some 7,500 years later, Mauro employs the same ancient techniques for its gathering, driving the bees away from the hive with smoke so that he can remove the dripping frames; he is as proprietorial about building up his hives, and the sacred principles of good husbandry, as the bees are of their queen.

## Honey-Blackened Duck Legs

The mahogany-dark chestnut honey turns to black when you bake these duck legs, and spoons of lumpy bitter marmalade give the dish a sweet-sour taste. Honey used in place of sugar always darkens the food, because the single sugars in it caramelize so readily.

SERVES 6

6 organic duck legs

FOR THE MARINADE:
2 heaped dsrtsp Seggiano chestnut honey
2 dsrtsp chunky bitter marmalade
1 tsp star anise, pounded in a mortar then sieved
juice of a lime
2 dsrtsp Tamari sauce
a glass of whatever red wine you happen to be drinking
8–10 black peppercorns, cracked and scrunched a little in a mortar

Preheat oven to 200°C/400°F/Gas Mark 6. Mix the marinade ingredients together in a bowl, stirring well, then pour over the duck legs, and either leave for a couple of hours or cover and put in the fridge overnight.

Place the legs in an earthenware dish, spoon the marinade over evenly, and bake. After 20 minutes turn the legs over, the top side will already be a wonderful molassey colour.

After another 20 minutes, throw in the glass of wine, scrape all the dark, sticky juices into it, and turn the legs for a final 20 minute blast.

I served mine on rice, with purple sprouting broccoli.

# Rhubarb, Ginger and Acacia Honey Ice Cream

SERVES 12

15 wands of rhubarb

4 heaped dsrtsp acacia honey or

2 heaped dsrtsp acacia honey and

2 of sugar

2 globes of stem ginger, finely
chopped

2 x 284ml/10fl oz cartons of
cream

Chop about 15 wands of rhubarb into short chunks, throw them into an earthenware dish, trickle over 2 heaped dessertspoons of acacia honey and 2 finely chopped globes of stem ginger. Bake in a moderate oven until cooked, about 25–30 minutes.

Whisk the cartons of cream together with 2 tablespoons of the ginger syrup, and either two more dessertspoons of honey, or the same of sugar, depending on how honeyed you like things, until thick but not stiff. Stir in the cooled rhubarb and its juice and taste for sweetness. Churn in an ice cream machine, or turn into ice trays and put in the freezer in the usual way. This quantity made one and a half pails in my machine.

# Honey Spiced Madeleines

Serve with ice creams, fools, a fruit compote, or warm for tea.

SERVES 6

25g/1oz sultanas

15g/½oz flour

65g/2½oz caster sugar

15g/½oz ground almonds

½ tsp each of ground ginger,
cinnamon and liquorice

pinch each of ground mace
and 5 star spice

a suspicion of nutmeg

50g/2oz unsalted butter

1 tbsp acacia or other runny honey

2 egg whites

Preheat oven to 180°C/350°F/Gas Mark 4. Soak the sultanas in hot water for 20 minutes to plump them up.

Mix all the dry ingredients bar the sultanas together in a bowl. Melt the butter in a pan until it turns nut brown, then remove from the heat and stir in the honey.

Cool slightly, then add to the dry ingredients. Beat together in an electric mixer. Gradually add the egg whites until well mixed, the consistency should be like runny paste. Cover and chill for 30 minutes.

Chill a 12-mould madeleine sheet – a Yorkshire pudding one will do. Brush the moulds with melted butter, dust with flour, shaking out any excess, and scatter the sultanas over the bases. Spoon in the mixture, and bake for 10–15 minutes until golden and just firm to the touch.

# THE CIDER HOUSE RULES

'WE'RE AFTER ANYONE WHO DOESN'T DRINK CIDER, and that's 80 per cent of the country.' Brothers Barry and Henry Guild, 32 and 31 respectively, are swift to reveal their intentions, as we stand quaffing their fine, newly launched extra dry straight from the Aspalls vat. I was born a committed 20 percenter, in fact, one of my earlier memories, not unnaturally a pretty hazy one, is of 'scrumping' for apples in the school orchards and fermenting a lethal liquid in a bucket behind my locker in the dorm. Strained through a pair of tights into Ribena bottles, the contents exploded like a geyser on opening, the blossom pink brew fizzing delectably as we sampled it late at night by the swimming pool with the boys. The cider house rules at Aspall House are somewhat bigger on quality. The Chevallier Guild family arrived at their beautifully moated Suffolk house at the turn of the 18th century, and by 1728 Aspalls was launched. Nearly 300 years later, it is still a family business, still making cider, and still bottling by hand in the only thatched bottling factory in the country. Do not be lulled into thinking that they are ripe for a Sir John Harvey Jones makeover though, Barry and Henry's somewhat unorthodox style of management is anything but flaky or antediluvian. While their father John concentrated on turning apple juice into a household staple in the '70s, after an enlightening trip to Switzerland the boys are on the cusp of instigating a cider renaissance, having spotted a gap in the quality end of the commercial market.

'We've got 90 acres of our own orchards, things like bittersweet Kingston Blacks, and a very rare breed that my great-grandfather planted at the turn of the century called Medaille d'Or,' says Barry, 'My favourite is called Slack my Girdle – we've got to grow them. Occasionally the cider can get tainted by what is known as "mousiness." It's like licking the floor of a budgerigar's cage, but luckily we've got two people working here who can pick up the faintest hint of it, so we lock them up in the lab to test for it! We designed our own label and bought beautiful antique green bottles from Italy, and we've spent the last six and half years since we joined the business playing around with the cider.

'The basic philosophy hasn't changed at all, we're only modifying what was here. We were the first firm to be given a Soil Association label. Grandfather loved it, the crop sprayer had broken down and, being Scottish, he didn't want to buy a new one.'

The apple-a-day adage is sacrosanct with the Guild family. They drink a capful of organic cider vinegar three times a day to fend off arthritis. The boys' grandmother is 97 and 'fully on the spot, she's really got her wits about her.' Their father John says it's brilliantly cooling in the summer, and a natural diuretic, and their mother Jenny uses it as a hair rinse. Medicinal, cosmetic, preprandial or whatever, I am not sure as I leave whether the feelgood factor is attributable to the cider or the vinegar, but fully intend to carry on taking the medicine.

# Cod, Fennel and Smoked Bacon Pie

A classic fish pie is hard to beat, except where my elder daughter Miranda is concerned. This is sufficiently different to warrant her approval, with a hint of smoked bacon, the cod cut into chunks and not precooked, and quarters of steamed fennel. Accompany with copious quantities of Aspall's cider.

SERVES 6

*1 and a bit kilos / 2½lb boned, filleted cod, cut a good 2.5cm / 1 in thick*
*4 bulbs fennel*
*3 slices organic smoked back bacon, I used bacon from Swaddles Green Farm*
*béchamel sauce made with 50g / 2oz each butter and flour, and 600ml / 1 pint milk*
*2 tbsp each flat-leaf parsley and chives, finely chopped*
*900g / 2lb potatoes, steamed and mashed with butter and milk*
*salt and pepper*

Preheat oven to 180°C / 350°F / Gas Mark 4. Cut the cod into the same sized chunks you would for a meat stew, and put them in the bottom of a deepish ovenproof dish. Season. Trim the fennel, removing any faintly stringy, woody layers, and cut into quarters vertically. Steam the quarters of fennel until just unresistant at their base, and add them to the fish. Snip the bacon into fine strips, and fry until browned in a small pan, drain and add to the dish. Any more than 3 rashers would, I feel, overwhelm the pie.

Pour in the seasoned béchamel sauce, into which you have stirred the fresh herbs off the heat. It might not appear to be enough, but remember that cod exudes quite a bit of juice while cooking.

Cover with mashed potato, furrow the surface with a fork, dot with butter, and cook for 35–40 minutes until browned and bubbling.

# Trinity Burnt Cream

Whatever anyone says, this is easy to make as long as you have the patience to keep stirring. I feel it needs a good eight hours in the fridge, and that on no account should it be made in the oven in a *bain-marie*. The consistency will never have that satiny finish of a properly stirred all cream custard. The other mistake is to oversweeten; remember, the top is pure caramel.

MAKES 8 RAMEKINS

*900ml / 1½ pints organic double cream, Jersey if you can get it*
*1 vanilla pod*
*7 large organic egg yolks*
*3 dsrtsp vanilla caster sugar*
*demerara sugar*

Chill the ramekins in the freezer while you make the custard. Split the vanilla pod, extract the seeds, and put them in a pan with the cream and the pod. Bring to scalding point, then remove from the heat and leave to infuse for 10 minutes. Whisk together the egg yolks and caster sugar, then strain the cream into them through a sieve, and return to the pan.

On a low heat, stir the mixture continuously, until you can feel it thickening with your spoon. This takes 10–15 minutes. On no account turn the heat up, you will end up with scrambled eggs. Eventually you will find a jelly-like trail left behind your spoon as you stir. I use a little balloon whisk as the custard begins to thicken, which I sort of worry quickly across the custard.

Remove from the heat, and pour into the chilled ramekins. Place in the fridge for a good 8 hours. Remove half an hour before you want them, scatter a thin layer of demerara over the surface with your fingers, followed by a tiny sprinkle of water, then blast with a blowtorch or under a very hot grill until the sugar has caramelized.

Return to the fridge for 30 minutes before serving.

# BAKER AND SPICE

RUNNING DOWN THE HILL THE HALF MILE to our local bakery on a Saturday morning is as enduring a memory of childhood as any I have. At the counter, conspiratorially, I would ask for 'Joan's Dad,' and be sent down a narrow corridor to the floury heat of the bakery. There, he would be fielding a paddle with the grace of a pole vaulter, atop which, rafts of battered baking tins were perched ready for the flames, or extracted with a flick of the wrist, their damp, steaming heat and yeasty smell the one I would hold on to if all others were denied. There is nothing as fearsomely evocative as the smell of baking bread.

Doughy cottage loaves, their topknots splattered with poppy seeds; hot meat pies, mince, gravy and an unfashionable lardy crust, that he would give me, to be eaten through palate-searing heat so as not to be discovered before I got home; sugar-coated doughnuts with their hidden trove of lumpy strawberry; these are the things that have led me, many years and many countries' bakeries later, to the doors of Baker and Spice. This is where I come for the best croissants this side of the Channel, sandy, grainy, buttery strata of flaky dough with a shell of crispness and a secret, stretchy, lycra-like middle, that melts on contact with the tongue. Here too, are biscuits, tarts, cakes, a traiteur, and loaves whose brilliance serves to further undermine the woefully poor pap we put up with from supermarkets and bakery chains. If you go to Baker and Spice, like a voyage of discovery, you will start to learn just how much you didn't know; to understand that the staff of life can be the stuff of dreams.

Their bread baron, Dan Lepard, arrived there circuitously via cooking for Alastair Little; being a pastry chef; making flat breads all over New York; working on sour dough in the restaurants of LA; and setting up the bakery and patisserie for Fergus Henderson's restaurant St John in Smithfield. Frustration drove him to bread scholarship, 'I wanted to learn more, but there was nowhere to learn. I went to the British Library and combed through all their books on baking over the last 200 years. They were mainly in French, so I sat there with a dictionary. I was looking for something more, something vibrant, something good at it's heart. I didn't realize I was doing anything unusual until I started working at Mezzo. British bakers were very sceptical. They'd ask me what was wrong with a crusty white loaf, why I didn't use yeast, why I used French flour – it's the speed of the milling, they mill it slower than us.'

And then Gail Stephens offered Dan a job at Baker and Spice. 'She had all the equipment, everything I would have chosen, and better than in any restaurant I've worked in.'

We have passed through to the back of the shop, where Sami, the Israeli traiteur, is cooking troughs of huge artichokes, and broad beans to spike with smoked paprika, fresh coriander and preserved lemon. Through the patisserie, into the cool of the *viennoiserie*, where Elan is stretching and rolling up the triangles of dough for the croissants, straight off a mini conveyor belt of flat paste. Dan unlatches the heavy, black door of the bread oven, which, like the doors of Hell, open to reveal a gas jet blasting flames into its low-ceilinged depths. The brick floor is stamped 1902, the oven has been going, with few modifications, since then. Out of this come the breads of his imagination. My favourite is a flat, furled, giant's foot of a loaf, wrapped like *calzone*, and constellated with buds of bronze roasted garlic. 'Alastair Little was always roasting garlic. To begin with we hand-peel the cloves, then I pin out the dough, spread the garlic and herbs over it, then fold it up. We leave it to ferment for 45 minutes, so layers of garlic juice leak into the dough, then we cut it all the way down and fold it. It's made with French and English flour, and based on a *focaccia* dough I made at Alastair's.' 'Where did you get the idea for it?' 'I read a piece Zoe Heller wrote about eating bread with chunks of garlic in it, and it inspired me. I think of the finished thing, then work backwards, work sympathetically with the ingredients, and see what they want to make. You've got to excite people.'

Far from disparaging the in-store apologies for bakeries that so many supermarkets have, Dan looks at their influence more elliptically: 'They have helped. They've opened people's eyes to different flavours in the same way as cheap travel. We have to be excellent, the supermarket can't be, they have to turn out the cheapest possible food. What we do is expensive. Good bread takes time. We can't compete on price, we can on quality.'

There are speckled cannonballs of bread perched on a rack in the shop, made with organic potatoes roasted in their skins with fresh Italian rosemary, olive oil and mavrococos seeds. Below it are batons rolled in poppy, sesame, fennel and aniseed with a fresh almost medicinal flavour; great bricks of *Pain de Mie*, 'the bread of the crumb'; paniers of almond-shaped mahogany hued hazelnut and raisin sourdough made with a rye starter and organic apple juice; and *Boule de Meule*, the traditional *pain levain* generated with fresh orange juice and no yeast. 'Flavours should work in harmony, should be mellow and not too acidic.'

In the shop window, black chocolate cookies, cracked like parched earth; foot-long cheese straws crusted with Parmesan; cakes oozing sticky juices; tarts of plum, pear, apricot, the fruit plunged upright up to its middle in frangipane. If there is an earthly paradise, this is as close as it gets. Here, no ingredient is too good, and it takes as long as it takes. If you, like me, live several counties away, you will never get enough; desire, after all, is always maddened by inaccessibility. You have to abandon self-control at the door here.

# Orange and Pine Nut Cake

SERVES 8

6 eggs, separated
190g / 6 and a bit oz caster sugar
275g / 10oz pine nuts
175g / 6oz flaked almonds, toasted
and roughly ground
zest and juice of two oranges,
keep separate
2 tbsp runny honey

This recipe comes from James Webb, head pastry chef at Baker and Spice.

Preheat the oven to 180°C / 350°F / Gas Mark 4. In a bowl, whisk 85g / 3oz sugar with the yolks, until thick and pale. Fold in the ground almonds, whole pine nuts and orange zest.

In another bowl, whisk the remaining sugar with the egg whites to a thick, glossy meringue. Fold, a third at a time, into the orange and pine nut mixture, then pour into a buttered cake tin, with a buttered greaseproof paper lining. My loaf tin was just too small, I will try a springform tin next time.

Bake in the centre of the oven for about an hour, or until a skewer comes out clean. Leave to cool for 15 minutes. Warm the honey until it thins, mix with the orange juice, and pour this mixture over the cake in the tin.

Leave to cool, then remove from the tin and serve with thick cream and fresh fruit. The children adored it as much as the grown-ups.

# Guinea Fowl with Preserved Lemons and Broad Beans

SERVES 4

1 guinea fowl, quartered
by your butcher
10 tbsp good olive oil
1 large onion, peeled
and finely chopped
500g / a generous pound broad
beans after podding
500ml / 16fl oz water
1 large bunch coriander, stalks
removed and roughly chopped
the juice of a lemon
1 preserved lemon (available from
some supermarkets and good delis)
salt and pepper

Another Baker and Spice recipe, this time from Sami Tamimi, the chef. In a large, non-reactive saucepan, put half the olive oil with the chopped onion, and sauté over a medium heat until soft and transparent.

Scrape the onion out of the pan into a small bowl, and add the remaining oil to the pan. Add the jointed guinea fowl and fry until the skin has browned, turning it as you go. When it has coloured, return the onion to the pan with the broad beans and water. Simmer for 20 minutes, then add the coriander, lemon juice, strips of peel, thinly sliced, from the preserved lemon, salt and pepper. Simmer for a further 10 minutes, then remove from the heat and serve with good bread and salad.

# REZA, STAR OF INDIA

WHEN REZA BRINGS THE GALOUTI KEBAB TO THE TABLE, I am more than prepared to be underwhelmed. Flat, grey discs of meat, they look about as appetising as a Wimpy, and culinary appearances, in my opinion, are seldom rather than often deceptive. Carolyn and I take a bite, almost disbelievingly, as an explosion of ginger, mint, coriander and the dusky traces of cardamom, cumin, star anise and saffron burst unconstrained on to our tongues. The meat, softly spoon-tender, has been turned to velvet with fresh pineapple juice. A dish of purity and perfection. We progress to more of the same, including an outstanding Khubani Gosht, a traditional Parsee dish of lamb cooked with apricots. 'Surely it's a Persian dish Reza?' 'Yes, but remember the Zoroastrians were originally from Persia.'

The Star of India in the Old Brompton Road has been in Reza Mahammad's family for 46 years. Reza's father was one of the first Indians to come to England before the war, becoming the chef at the Veeraswamy, and then running the Indian kitchen at the Cumberland Hotel. The eldest of five children, Reza was sent to India to be educated, but, in the middle of his 'A' Levels, his father dropped down dead. Reza had set his heart on reading History of Art and Music at university, but 'I was brought back immediately, at 16, to run the family business. If you were Asian, you had to become an accountant or a solicitor, the arts were not the done thing. I did hotel management, then went to L'Escargot as a waiter, but I was the head of the family, it was expected that I should come back and run the restaurant. I did resent it at the time, but we don't talk about that.'

Quite what Indian food tasted like in the 1950s, I can do no more than imagine, but Reza is convinced that the ubiquitous high street Indian restaurant has been hugely influenced to this day by the food his father began to serve in London all those years ago. 'My father was an incredible chef. The food was very different then because so few of the ingredients we take for granted were available, and people weren't used to real Indian food. At the Star we served a mixture of Bombay, Madras and Ceylon dishes, our chef invented the European style of Indian food. Before that, he'd cooked for the Maharajahs of Mysore.'

At 11am the following Thursday, I arrive at Reza's flat, a bhajee throw away from the restaurant. He has promised to cook some of his favourite dishes, including the ambrosial galouti kebab. The kitchen is a trove of half-recognizable, half-obscure delights, the rows of sealed jars an inventory of exotica. As I point, Reza dispenses titbits of information like juicy morsels: 'angelica powder, I use that in a Persian dish of lentils and orange juice. Whole angelica, that's for broad beans. Dried rose petals, I put them in the grinder with cumin and cinnamon, and add it to cooked rice, or stuff quails with a rice and rose petal mixture. Orange peel, fennel seeds, carrom seeds — they're from fresh lovage — we use that for our crème caramel in the restaurant.'

Reza started cooking 12 years ago, 'I taught myself. In the restaurant in the '80s, I'd started to integrate the old and the new styles of Indian food, then I thought it was time to move on, so I started experimenting, and seven years ago I went to Bombay to the Oberoi Hotel to meet Vineet, a chef I'd heard about. The restaurant was brilliant, prawns cooked in coconut shells, traditional Indian food that was so innovative I wanted to bring it back here. He got very inspired, adapting and inventing new dishes, but we did things gradually, radical change might have alienated our customers.' Recently a new chef took over, and together they try out new dishes and constantly change the menu, but keep the signature dishes that the customers wouldn't countenance losing.

Reza slaps the galouti kebabs – little flat meat patties that the two of us have been shaping with wetted hands so that they shouldn't stick – on the griddle, and minutes later we are pulling the black-crusted flesh apart, hot, spicy mouthfuls with each taste taking its turn to be discovered. It is perfectly clear to me that the real star of India is its owner, Reza.

# Galouti Kebabs

SERVES 4

450g / 1lb lean minced lamb
65g / 2½oz ghee or clarified butter
1 onion
1cm / ½in piece of fresh ginger
4 cloves garlic
6 mint leaves
½ bunch fresh coriander
1 tbsp fresh pineapple juice
a few strands of saffron soaked in milk
salt and chilli powder to taste
2 cloves
4 cardamom pods
½ a blade of mace
1 tsp cumin
1cm / ½in of a cinnamon stick
1 star anise

Peel and finely chop the onion. Dry roast the whole spices in a pan for a few seconds, then grind them in a coffee grinder or pestle and mortar. Sauté the onion until softened in a tablespoon of ghee. Put all the ingredients except the mince and ghee in a food processor, and blitz to a paste.

Spread the meat out on a flat tray, and pour over the paste of spices. Lightly mix them together with a spoon, then leave covered in the fridge for 4–6 hours to soften. Keeping your hands dampened, shape the meat into patties, each about 6cm / 2½in in diameter.

Heat some ghee in a heavy-bottomed pan or on a griddle, then cook the patties for a couple of minutes or so a side, until cooked through, with a slightly blackened crust.

Serve with cucumber you have peeled into ribbons, grated carrot, and a spritz of lime juice.

# Haveli ke Kofta

These are the most delicious parcels of shredded vegetables and spices formed into miniature aubergine shapes around a green chilli, coated in cornflour, briskly deep fried, and dunked in a spiced tomato sauce. If you think it sounds complicated, don't, it's no more so than making a stuffing.

SERVES 8

*4 small courgettes*
*4 small carrots*
*1 floret each of cauliflower and broccoli*
*50g / 2oz fine green beans*
*50g / 2oz baby corns*
*50g / 2oz cooked, peeled potato*
*1 tbsp sunflower oil*
*2.5cm / 1in piece of fresh ginger*
*½ tsp black mustard seeds*
*16 small green chillies*
*½ tsp turmeric*
*½ tsp chilli powder*
*salt*
*1 bunch fresh coriander*
*2 tbsp cornflour*
*25g / 1oz breadcrumbs*

Grate the courgettes on the coarse side of the grater, then do the same with the carrots. Grate the broccoli and cauliflower, then shred the beans finely. Grate the baby corns. Slit and chop 3 of the chillies.

Heat the oil in a heavy pan, add the mustard seeds and wait until they crackle. Add the chopped ginger and the chopped green chillies, stir for a moment, add the salt, turmeric and chilli powder. Add the grated vegetables and cook until they begin to soften, then remove from the heat and leave them to cool. Grate the potato, mix it into the vegetables, then add the chopped coriander and breadcrumbs. Slit the remaining chillies down the middle and briefly fry them.

Shape the koftas by flattening each one into a 6cm / 2½ inch disc in the palm of your hand, lying a chilli across the middle of it, stalk sticking out, then shaping it into a mini aubergine. Dust all over with cornflour, and deep-fry in a flavourless oil until golden brown, about 1–2 minutes.

Serve with the sauce opposite and sprinkle with chopped fresh coriander. You can do all the preparation up to the deep frying part in advance.

# Kofta Sauce

MAKES ENOUGH FOR 8 TO GO
WITH THE HAVELI KE KOFTA

*750g / 1¾lb tomatoes*
*50g / 2oz unsalted butter*
*2 medium onions, peeled and*
*chopped*
*2 green chillies*
*2.5cm / 1in piece of fresh ginger*
*4–5 cloves garlic*
*1 tbsp vegetable oil*
*1 tbsp tomato paste*
*salt and white pepper*
*½ tsp garam masala*
*½ tsp dried fenugreek*
*(kasuri methi)*
*½ tsp chilli powder, or to taste*
*50ml / 2fl oz single cream*

Skin, seed, chop and salt the tomatoes. Purée the peeled ginger and garlic in a blender or pestle and mortar with a tablespoon of water to make a smooth paste. Melt the butter in a pan, add the onions, sprinkle over a bit of salt to get the full impact of the flavour; do the same with the chopped green chillies, and sauté for a minute. Add the tomatoes, reduce the heat, and let everything simmer until the tomatoes are soft. Blitz in a food processor.

Heat the oil, add the ginger and garlic paste, cook for a minute, add the tomato paste and the remaining spices, and stir for 30 seconds. As you add the spices, sprinkle over a bit of water, Reza believes this burning then sprinkling releases the flavours.

Add the tomato sauce, and simmer until it thickens. Carefully place the koftas in the sauce, and simmer for 2–3 minutes. Remove them to a heated serving dish, add the cream to the sauce, stir to amalgamate, and pour it over the exotic koftas. Sprinkle over a few chopped coriander leaves and serve.

# CLARENCE COURT EGGS

'THE KING' IS STRUTTING THROUGH THE YARD, his regal head supporting a shaggy, cream-coloured mane, '50s-style side-whiskers, a beard and a pair of searching, owl-like eyes. A radio blares near by to fend off marauding foxes; wearily, he picks his way through the dirt to give it a nonchalant clout, and turns away to puff up his considerable chest, a feathered waistcoat streaked with shades of tawny, roan and straw. 'He,' says Philip Lee Woolf, 'is definitely the king in the pecking order, the others all show respect for him, particularly the cockerels who keep well clear.'

Our subject, the Dom of the poultry world, is an Araucana, originally from South America. This particular gentleman was brought back from America in a friend's suitcase – in egg, not feathered form – and when the chicks hatched out, Philip began crossing them with other rare breeds. 'Somebody had asked for blue eggs, so I got to work. You've got to breed your own flock, there are too many problems if you buy in. Rare breeds are less resistant, they've less immunity to disease because there are so few of them the gene stock is really small. That means the stock gets weaker, so you start breeding with as wide a variety of blood lines as you can.'

Arriving at Clarence Court, a small farm a whisker over the Gloucestershire border into Worcestershire, I am introduced to the birds by Philip, who offers me his observations on the temperament, characteristics and character of each individual breed as though they were his own offspring. 'Philip know his hens individually,' his wife Janet comments later. 'He lives for them.' 'It's very important you like the bird, not just the eggs,' Philip insists. 'We started off with Marans, and gradually built up a free-range flock of them. They're a lovely placid bird with a personality all of their own, quirky, very laid back, nothing flusters them,' which, in the hen house, and subsequently the market place, does not exactly equate with Keynsian economics, (as in: aggregate demand determines the level of output and employment). 'They're a business disaster,' Philip continues, 'They come out in the morning, and if they don't feel like laying they won't, but when they do, the eggs are all the more special. They feel like silk, there's a sheen to the shell, and they've got a superb flavour, denser and richer than most eggs, with a nice natural yellow yolk. But they don't exactly wear themselves out, so they go on laying. With 200 birds, you're lucky to get 90 eggs a day. That's the difference between the old breeds and the modern hybrids, which are bred to produce like machines and after seven or eight months they're worn out. All these 'special value' supermarket eggs are watery. If you break them on a plate they'll spread out flat, they're absolute rubbish. Our eggs stand up on the plate, if they don't, it means they've got no substance to them.'

This month, Philip is launching a new breed, the Old Cotswold Leg Bar. Their painterly eggs range from duck egg and sky blue through turquoise, peachy pink and white to olive green, each box a palette of different colours. 'It's taken nearly five years, I was determined to breed in more vigour to create a better layer, but something that's got all the qualities of an old breed and isn't a modern hybrid. The eggs are as good as the Marans', all richness and hardness of shell.' After working seven days a week with only one holiday in ten years, Philip is optimistically end of termish: 'The Cotswold is the magical bird that's going to lay the golden egg. By the end of next year I'll be able to take a holiday.'

## Baked Eggs with Spring Vegetables

This is an all-in-one supper, the scarlet and green vegetables flecking the yellow and white eggs like a primary-coloured picture.

SERVES 4

*1 large onion, finely chopped*
*2 cloves garlic, finely chopped*
*4 tbsp olive oil*
*125g / 4oz small chorizo, well-spiced sausage*
*or smoked bacon, cubed*
*2 red peppers, skinned and chopped*
*325g / 12oz tomatoes, skinned, seeded and chopped*
*1–2 tbsp Fino or Amontillado sherry*
*125g / 4oz each of small new broad beans and young peas*
*8 large eggs*
*salt and cayenne pepper*

Preheat the oven to 180°C / 350°F / Gas Mark 4.

Warm a shallow terracotta baking dish. Heat the oil in a pan, and add the onion, cooking gently until it softens. Add the garlic, cook for a minute, push aside, add the meat, and fry until coloured, then remove it.

Add the peppers and tomatoes, and cook until reduced and softened, adding the sherry when it starts to look dry.

Briefly steam the broad beans and peas until just tender, and add them.

Transfer the mixture with the meat to the casserole, whisk the eggs together briefly — you are looking for an egg white and yolk contrast, not something that looks like an omelette — and season. Pour over the vegetables and bake for about 10–15 minutes, when the eggs are just set.

# Polenta, Almond and Lemon Cake

I have adapted this from the original *The River Café Cook Book*. Janet Lee Woolf believes their eggs make all the difference to cake baking, adding flavour and lightness to the sponge. This golden-crusted cake should ooze a slightly sad, grainy, almondy centre.

SERVES 12

325g/12oz softened, unsalted butter

325g/12oz golden caster or icing sugar

325g/12oz organic ground almonds

2 tsp vanilla extract

4 large eggs

zest of 3 lemons and juice of 1

225g/8oz organic polenta

1½ tsp baking powder

½ tsp sea salt

Preheat oven to 160°C/325°F/Gas Mark 3. Butter and flour a 22cm/9in springform cake tin.

Beat the butter and sugar together in an electric mixer, or by hand, until light and fluffy. Stir in the ground almonds and vanilla. Beat in the eggs, one at a time. Fold in the lemon zest and juice, the polenta, baking powder and salt. Spoon into the cake tin and bake.

I kept checking mine from 45 minutes, but it wasn't ready until it had cooked for an hour. I served it with the ice cream on page 79.

# Caramel Ice Cream

This is from Simon Hopkinson's wonderful book *Roast Chicken and Other Stories*; it is a wickedly rich, bitter and thoroughly decadent ice cream.

SERVES 4

*250g / 9oz caster sugar*
*1 vanilla pod, split lengthways and chopped into small pieces*
*200ml / 7fl oz organic double cream*
*350ml / 12fl oz milk*
*8 egg yolks*

Heat the sugar gently in a heavy-bottomed pan until melted. Do not stir during this time, though you might like to tilt the pan from time to time.

Once it is completely melted and golden brown, add the vanilla pod and stir gently with a wooden spoon until the caramel is a deep mahogany colour. Wait a moment longer or until you think the caramel might smell slightly burnt, and then add the cream off the heat. There will be an instant eruption, so keep stirring.

Heat the milk, then beat the egg yolks, pour the hot milk over them, and whisk together. Add to the caramel mixture and cook gently, as though for custard, stirring with a wooden spoon. I find the mixture thickens almost immediately. When it does, remove from the heat and strain through a sieve into a cold bowl. When cool, freeze in the usual way.

# THE MODEL VILLAGE POST OFFICE

INSIDE THE DOOR THERE IS A FRAGRANT CRATE OF SEVILLE ORANGES lurking below the creamy cauliflowers, parsnips, leeks, peppers, root ginger and chestnuts. I snoop along the shelves, taking surreptitious notes like a private dick, eyes scudding from shelf top to shelf bottom, patum pepericum, fruit compotes, semolina, camomile and Earl Grey teas, coarse and fine sea salt, Mancha saffron. Oddities and exotica brashly arranged next to the store cupboard staples. Tabasco, Aspalls' cider vinegar, chickpeas, Thai green curry paste, fish sauce and lemon grass. There are old-fashioned cottage loaves with headmistressy top-knots, knife-bending Devon honey, whole nutmegs, cinnamon and shiny vanilla pods, clotted cream and crème fraîche, Cointreau and Glenfiddich, amaretti, Roquefort, and home-crimped pasties. And there are no yellow lines outside the door.

I am not in a swish food emporium, or an upmarket delicatessen. I am in a sub-post office in the Devon village of Willand, where my friend Gale has suggested I pay a visit. If you lived here, you would genuinely never have to enter a supermarket again, and you wouldn't be consigned to a diet of pot noodles and Borrower-sized tins of treacle puddings. There are no anaemic apples and pallid pears here; no curled-up-and-died vegetables and tired, wan tomatoes.

So how have Sue and Roger Lane managed it? 'I thought we were just a normal post office,' Sue says disingenuously. 'We've trebled the turnover. It's only common sense. You've got to have a shop that looks bright and uncluttered. We'd no idea what we were taking on or what people would like. You can't do a lot of specialist things, but I know my customers, I get things they want, and I get them to try things. I got one old lady to try clam chowder soup, and she has it every week now. As soon as people come through the door I say "Good morning." A lot of our elderly don't see anyone, they come in every day even if it's just for a loaf or a stamp. We keep their keys and we deliver free of charge every day even if it's just a pint of milk. That way we can check on them. They come here for a giggle, a gossip, it's all part of the countryside experience.'

Sue is also passionate about local produce. A nearby farm supplies organic vegetables. She stocks Peverstone Cheese Company's unpasteurized Tiskey Meadow and Hunting Pink, and a nanny goat's cheese from Dartmoor. Culm Valley Bakery bring fresh bread every day. Eggs are from free-range hens in the village. People can order organic meat here, and organic turkeys at Christmas. In the summer I sell fresh herbs, flowers and plants, and local children bring me field mushrooms for pocket money.' She would sell more local producers' wares, but for the fact that Devon County Council, who she approached for help seven months ago, have done nothing about it.

Sue estimates there are 70 or 80 people who 'do everything here, as well as the regulars and the passing trade. The food is over 50 per cent of the business, but we are under threat when pensions and benefits will be sent direct in 2003. I see my customers every day, and I know a lot of them don't have bank accounts and they wouldn't use a hole in the wall. The most important thing is the caring side, it's what people come for. If someone has lost a loved one we take them through to the sitting room for a cuddle, and help with the things they don't know how to do.

It is shaming to think of the recent 476 closures of sub-post offices in the light of my conversation with Sue. Not only are she and Roger running a first-class shop and post office, they are cutting down the local Social Services bill. Can the government afford to ignore that?

# Chickpea and Chorizo Stew

SERVES 6

*375g/13oz chickpeas, soaked and cooked in 750ml/1¼ pints stock and 300ml/½ pint organic tomato passata until tender. You can do all this the night before if it makes life easier*
*600g/1¼lb or so good-quality fat spicy chorizo, cut into hunks*
*2 medium onions, chopped*
*3–4 cloves garlic, finely chopped*
*olive oil*
*225g/8oz jar Navarrico wood-roasted piquillo peppers from Brindisa, or grill and skin ordinary red ones if you can't get them*
*a heaped tsp smoked paprika*

Fry the onions gently in a good glug of olive oil in a heavy-bottomed casserole until softened and translucent, then throw in the hunks of chorizo. Cook for about 10 minutes, turning them as you go. Once they exude some fat, add the garlic, then add the chickpeas and their liquor to the pot. Cut the peppers into strips and add them with the paprika, simmer for another 10 minutes, ladle into bowls and serve. Just as great the second day.

# Vanilla Castle Puddings with Raspberry Jam

Nostalgia for these little golden turrets, turned out like golden sand castles with a trickle of hot, seedy raspberry jam slipping from their roofs, led me to reconstruct this sublime nursery pudding. My father adored them when he was alive.

MAKES 6–8 DARIOLE MOULDS

*175g / 6oz unsalted butter*
*150g / 5oz vanilla caster sugar*
*the scraped-out insides*
*of a vanilla pod*
*3 eggs*
*175g / 6oz plain organic flour*
*1 rounded tsp baking powder*
*a jar of the best*
*raspberry jam you can find*

Set the oven to 180°C / 350°F / Gas Mark 4. Grease the dariole moulds. Cream together the butter and sugar with the vanilla until soft and pale. Beat in the eggs one by one. Stir in the sifted flour and baking powder until amalgamated.

Fill the moulds three-quarters full, any more and you will witness an eruption. Place the moulds on a baking tray and bake for about 25 minutes until gloriously golden and risen. Turn them out with a palette knife, and pour over copious quantities of hot raspberry jam.

# PETER WHITEMAN, 'ALOOWALLAHSAHIB'

PETER WHITEMAN IS STRIDING TOWARDS ME THROUGH HIS VEGETABLES, be-shorted, be-bearded, be-booted, his garb and mien that of a 19th-century explorer or mountaineer. The overall impression is of someone who belongs to the landscape, and has been tested by the sort of physical rigours that most of us admire but tend to observe from a distance.

When Peter came down from Oxford, where he read Botany, his modest ambition was to reclaim deserts. He spent six years in the Kalahari, followed by Ethiopia, Nepal, Kenya and the Hindukush, before returning to England after 17 years. 'What brought you back?' 'I got married. I thought I'd haul my wife back to Nepal, but it wasn't to be.'

As a Third World agronomist, Peter spurned the convention of 'research then persuasion,' adopting a more immediate approach than the proscribed scientific model. 'We were devising, running, testing and demonstrating improvements for the farmers for their main crops. When the rainfall is limited, you have to maximize the efficiency of the water you've got and conserve and choose the best crops to retain moisture. Each green leaf is like a hole in a bucket.' In Hunza, a mountain oasis irrigated by glacial melt-water high in the rainshadow area of the Hindukush, Peter's extraordinary expertise and fascination for the potato led to the title *aloowallahsahib*, or 'the man who knows about potatoes' being bestowed on him. 'The British took potatoes out there at the turn of the century. At 10,000 feet there are no aphids, cool nights and warm days with lots of sun, no shortage of water and lower humidity, so tuber multiplication is brilliant. There's a high yield of 50 tons an acre. I taught the farmers how to farm a higher yield. They're so hungry at the end of the winter they peel the eyes out of the potatoes to plant them!'

*Aloowallahsahib* returned, to the wettest corner of England, Devon. 'I'd spent all my time telling people what to do, I thought now I ought to have a go myself. I found a 20-acre farm, so by Third World standards I'm a very rich man. I reacted strongly against the agriculture here, so I chose the organic way as the right way to use the resources we had.' We sit and inspect the earthy, mottled tubers Peter has laid out in home-made baskets, and he proceeds to compare the life cycle of one of his spuds with that of an average, unorganically grown one. 'I spray nothing. I plant early in March, the seed potatoes are well chitted — the little eyes have opened and sprouted which you can't do with machines. Blight is the scourge of organic potatoes, especially in the southwest, the muggy mild days of June cause the spores to germinate. You risk frost by planting early, but I just knock the tops off and they come back again. Without blight, I harvest 25 tons an acre, once it comes, I chop the tops off immediately to stop growth, and achieve most of the potential yield from starting early. Slugs are a problem, but I encourage frogs, toads and slow worms. If you don't grow organically, roughly a ton of fertilizer per acre is spread in the seed bed,

and the soil is pulverized, which destroys its structure and discourages worms. After planting, a pre-emergent herbicide is sprayed, then, in blight weather, a systemic fungicide is sprayed weekly. Prior to mechanical harvesting, sulphuric acid is sprayed to get rid of the tops so they're not in the way, and when they're stored another vapour is sprayed on to stop sprouting. You can sink your teeth into one of my potatoes and know there are no hidden nasties.' Which is precisely what we do.

Peter has built a huge terracotta igloo of a field oven, fashioned from straw, clay and cow dung, and from its smoky, oaky depths he rescues a clutch of potatoes whose floury, creamy centres we break into, adding a splurt of butter and some finely chopped landcress. At the heart of Peter's philosophy is stewardship; a sense that he is a tenant, a servant of the land, and that what he ploughs into it in his lifetime will be reaped by the next generation. He looks no farther than his borders, utilizing, crafting everything. Chairs from logs and willow poles, hurdles from the hedgerows, a tautly bent yew bow and arrows for pheasant control. His vegetables are sold at 80 per cent of the supermarket price, nothing picked until it is ripe. 'When you pick ripe fruit and vegetables they are full of sugar from photosynthesis from the sun; they use sugar to breathe, and when they've breathed it away they become starchy. I pick the potatoes the day before market, it gives me a real kick. I'm really a very rich man with 20 acres, I'm so lucky, I've got immense resources. I stand amazed, I've got milk, meat, manure, timber, hedgerows, fruit, veg and nuts, and I'm working with raw resources and making something people really value.'

## Gratin of Potatoes with Mustard and Crème Fraîche

SERVES 6

12 medium organic, waxy potatoes,
1 clove garlic
butter
chicken stock to cover,
about 600ml/1pint
salt and pepper
200ml/7fl oz organic
crème fraîche
2 dsrtsp seeded mustard
1 dsrtsp Dijon mustard

Preheat the oven to 200°C/400°F/Gas Mark 6. Slice the potatoes into thin discs.

Grease a gratin dish with a bit of butter, and put in your potatoes in layers with one finely sliced clove of garlic, seasoning as you go. Pour on the hot stock to nearly the level of the top layer, cover with greaseproof paper, and cook for 45 minutes.

Mix the crème fraîche and mustards in a bowl. Pour and spread over the top of the gratin, and return to the oven until the potatoes are tender right the way through, about another 15 minutes. Do not add the cream mixture earlier, mustard turns bitter when cooked for too long.

# Braised Veal with Fennel and Paprika

I will repeat my anti food-police mantra from Charlotte Reynolds' Swaddles Green Organic Farm: 'Our veal calves are reared in the field with their mothers. It is not white veal, they are not kept in crates, and we keep our calves until they are about five months. They are milk fed and given a bit of hay. We actually need to eat more veal; these calves from the dairy industry do not make good beef because they are from milking herds, so they've got big udders and bony hips, they're short on haunches and well padded rumps.'

SERVES 6.

*1kg / 2½lb braising veal,*
*cut into 2.5cm / 1 in squares*
*flour*
*olive oil*
*2 onions and 4 cloves garlic, peeled*
*and finely chopped*
*4 bulbs fennel, all tough layers*
*removed, quartered carefully to*
*keep them attached at base*
*2 celery stalks, finely chopped with*
*their leaves*
*1 heaped dsrtsp paprika,*
*Hungarian if possible*
*300ml / ½ pint white wine, I used*
*a Riesling*
*2 x 400g / 14oz tins organic*
*tomatoes*
*salt, pepper and 2 or 3 bay leaves*

Preheat the oven to 150°C / 300°F / Gas Mark 2.

Put a few tablespoons of flour in a ziploc bag and shake the veal, a few cubes at a time, to coat it. Brown the veal gently on all sides in 3–4 tablespoons of fruity olive oil in a heavy-bottomed casserole. Remove the meat, add more oil if necessary, and gently sauté the vegetables, keeping the fennel quarters intact. Sprinkle the paprika over the vegetables, return the meat to the pan, add the bay leaves and white wine. Bring to the boil, add the tomatoes, chopping them down as you go, season with salt and pepper, bring up to boiling point again, then cover with a piece of greaseproof paper before putting the casserole in the oven for 1½–2 hours.

I served this stickily piquant stew with a baking tray of Peter's Roseval potatoes rolled in olive oil in their skins in the tray, sprinkled with coarse sea salt, and scattered with whole garlic cloves and branches of thyme. They need a hotter oven, 200°C / 400°F / Gas Mark 6 for up to an hour. You could use Pink Fir Apples, Linzer Delicatesse or Anya, all of which are in the supermarkets at the moment. Something fine-skinned and waxy anyway.

# Halibut in a Green Sauce

A dish of distinction and simplicity, good enough to show off with.

SERVES 6

*6 halibut steaks,*
*2.5cm / 1 in thick, on the bone*
*olive oil*
*salt and pepper*

FOR THE SAUCE:
*2 tbsp each of flat-leaf and curly*
*parsley, finely chopped*
*2 tbsp mint, finely chopped*
*1 tbsp each of dill and chervil,*
*finely chopped*
*6 cloves garlic, almost minced*
*12 salted anchovies, desalinated,*
*despined and almost*
*minced, anchovies in olive oil will*
*do if you can't get the salted ones*
*2 tbsp chopped capers in olive oil;*
*if in brine rinse carefully*
*6 or 7 cornichons, finely chopped*
*at the last minute*
*1 hard-boiled egg, finely chopped*
*olive oil and black pepper*

Preheat oven to 200°C/400°F/Gas Mark 6. If you have a mezzaluna it is easy to chop the herbs finely enough, if not, be patient. Do not do this in a blender or it will look like gunged up grass mowings. Add the garlic, anchovies, capers and black pepper to the herbs in a bowl, then dribble in your best extra virgin olive oil until amalgamated, but not oily or too thick. Stir in the egg and cornichons and taste, this is a strident sauce and might need more cornichons or garlic.

Heat a film of olive oil in a heavy-bottomed, ovenproof frying pan or gratin dish, and when hot put the pieces of fish in for about a minute a side just to seal and turn opaque. Turn carefully so they don't flake. Transfer the pan to the top of the hot oven for 6–8 minutes, test with a skewer, the fish should not resist. Put a steak on each plate, and pass round the sauce for everyone to dollop on. Serve with a green salad and the Gratin of Potatoes on page 86.

2

# SUMMER

IT IS AN UNWRITTEN BUT OFT-SPOKEN LAW, that other people's picnics always taste better than one's own. It was not until I turned to *Larousse Gastronomique* that I began to understand why that should be. It describes the picnic as 'a meal taken in the open, or a meal to which each participant contributes a dish.' I am not so sure, this being England, that 'the open' need always apply. One evening, I found myself with my two daughters, transporting a semi-constructed Salade Niçoise to the scene of Miranda's chiropractic appointment in Exeter. As she was returning to sing in a school concert, there was no alternative but to shake engine-lubricant quantities of a chivey, garlicky dressing from a tightly lidded jam jar on to a bowl of glossy olives, green beans, waxy potatoes, tomatoes and fresh tuna, and peel the eggs before tucking into a front and back seat supper that had all the ingredients of a good picnic, even the discomfort. As for the dictum that each participant 'contributes a dish,' I can only marvel at the revelation, and hurriedly set about finding the perfect picnic partners. The next stage will be dinner parties cooked entirely on this principle.

It speaks well of the national character, if one is inclined to believe in such a thing, that in a country where climatic inclemency and unpredictability are depressingly predictable, we battle, tease, conquer and ignore the elements and have our picnics regardless. We sit dripping, freezing, windswept, damp-bottomed, but would consider abandoning the pleasure principled picnic unthinkable. Some of us even eat things out of doors that we wouldn't have in the house.

Impromptu or highly organized and planned, there is nothing like the thought of a picnic for engendering a spirit of almost infantile excitement. Eton's celebrated '4th of June' was more than a wash-out last year, it was a drench-out. I was an ingénue, unaware of the complicated rituals engaged in just to ensure that picnic partners achieve confluence in the picnicking field, mobiles, helium balloons and marquees being the most obvious methods. What amazed me further, as I was waved into a field of liquid mud past an avenue of dripping canvas, was how the scale of potential disaster inflicted by the weather rose in direct proportion to the scale of grandness of the picnic. Picture this: under the sodden canvas of the smartest structure, a whole lamb was turning wearily on a spit, supervised by several uniformed staff, who busied themselves butling, and holding down acres of damply flapping linen and flower arrangements. A sight that somehow made me feel wickedly grateful for all the soggy tomato sandwiches leaking their juice into inferior white bread; for the slabs of railway cake, the stone-hard boiled eggs with their halo of black orbiting their crumbly, yellow planet of yolk; the lard-slicked chipolatas, we consumed as children on Irish beaches where the elements and the sand invaded eyes, mouths, food. We paid no heed to the weather. Without the sun, or at least the absence of wind and rain, the most lavish preparations become ridiculous. My smorgasbord of ready-made Planet Organic food — I had been working away from home, so had to cheat — consumed in the car and under the dripping tail-gate of the boot, were what picnics are all about. More trying than the weather, is having to do it all dressed up.

This year, relieved of novitiate status, we played by *Larousse*'s rules. Dividing the labour between two families, my responsibilities were the meat, the bread, a spiced puy lentil salad, puddings and our side of the drink. Spurning throwaway barbecues and the lingering taste of paraffin, it consisted of cooked and easily assembled and transported foods, and things that are easily eaten regardless of the weather, in one's finery. We decided against a cold fish and mayonnaise. Consider not just the oily wreckage of this most unctuous of sauces, separating and liquefying like eye ointment in transit, but also its potential to ruin best frocks. Meat, even creamy sauces, are less hazardous. Consider also, that you are catering for children and the ravening maw of the teenage appetite, and what they want is meat, and Charles Atlas style quantities of it.

First I make a killer of a sumptuously rich Green and Black's chocolate cake, stuffed with raspberries and heavily, chocolately iced. Then some giant meringues, to be served like a deconstructed Eton Mess with strawberries and cream. The eponymous 'Mess' can be made with the leftover slightly crushed strawberries, bashed up meringue and lightly whipped cream the following day. Our fellow picnickers are bringing cheese, a salt, hard lump of Desmond's, smoked salmon sandwiches, potato salad, and a flagon of roast tomato soup.

A night of thunder and lightning bodes ill. At 7.30 am I put the chicken in to cook, basking dreamily in sesame oil, tamari sauce, root ginger, garlic and orange juice. The sausages bake, then are coated in seed mustard for the last few minutes, the two dishes swaddled in enough foil to insulate a mountaineer, and we head for school. Under the dripping chestnut tree we lay out our joint offerings. Our respective mothers look on approvingly, mine savouring the picnic partner's soup in true other-people's-picnic style, theirs, despite erring on the nona side of octogenarian, literally spooning the chocolate and raspberry cake straight from the tin.

Of that there is no doubt, lack of sunshine dampens neither spirits nor appetites, that is the nature of the picnic. It has been as enjoyable to plan and prepare, and as delicious to eat, as we could have hoped for. So I would like to think that it is mere champagne-sodden rhetoric that induces my picnic partner to declare, 'Next year we'll order an Indian take-away from Slough.'

## Spiced Puy Lentils

SERVES 8–10 AS A SIDE DISH

225g / 8oz puy lentils
2 tsp ground cumin
large handful of fresh coriander,
chopped
the juice of a lemon
150ml / 5fl oz olive oil
salt and pepper

Hardly a recipe, but one of the few salads that travels well. Throw the puy lentils into a large pan of boiling water. They don't need soaking, they are the delicious speckledy, earthy blue-black ones. Cook until tender, about half an hour, and drain. Cool and refrigerate in a bowl overnight if you need to. Before setting off on your picnic, stir in the ground cumin, a large handful of fresh, chopped coriander, the lemon juice, olive oil and sea salt and pepper. Taste and make sure it is lemony enough.

When you arrive, add more olive oil if it has all been absorbed. So much better than wilted lettuce or leaking tomatoes.

# Chinese Chicken Drumsticks

Allow two per person. The great thing about swaddling the cooked drumsticks in foil is that, even five hours after cooking, the memory of warmth still clings to them. Marinade them overnight if possible, but even 30 minutes is better than nothing.

FOR THE MARINADE:

125ml/4fl oz organic tamari soya sauce, made by Sanchi, and available in healthfood shops
2 tbsp sesame oil
5cm/2in piece of fresh ginger, peeled and grated
4 cloves garlic, crushed to a paste with salt in a mortar
juice of an orange
2 tsp molasses sugar

Preheat the oven to 180°C/360°F/Gas Mark 4.

Simply mix the marinade ingredients in the dish you are going to cook in, in my case a terracotta one, and turn the chicken drumsticks in it. Cover and leave in the fridge.

Bring back to room temperature before cooking. Place in the oven and cook for about 30–40 minutes basting occasionally. A skewer will tell you they're cooked when the blood no longer runs from them. You could reduce the stickily browned juices if you want, but tamari is salty, so be careful. I covered mine in foil and put them straight in the boot.

# Overnight Meringues

Baker and Spice make them larger than life, about six inches by four. They are plaster-of-Paris outside, with a middle my younger daughter describes as 'marshmallowy.'

MAKES 12

6 egg whites
500g/1lb 2oz caster sugar
flaked toasted almonds

Preheat the oven to 150°C/300°F/Gas Mark 2. Cover a large tray with nonstick baking parchment. Over a simmering pan of water, place a bowl with 6 egg whites and the caster sugar. Stir until the sugar has dissolved and the mixture is very warm. Beat with an electric mixer until thick and cool, then spoon large mounds on to the tray, 3 across and 4 down. Lightly sprinkle with flaked toasted almonds. Place the tray in the oven, turn off the heat, and leave overnight.

# Vanilla Cheesecake with Summer Fruits

This is the first proper pudding I learned to make when I left home. It does not demand huge feats of technical wizardry, just good ingredients, and is the sort of food that teenagers love. Infinitely superior to the claggy, gelatine-stiffened manufactured version with its livid fruit glaze.

SERVES 8

1 packet Dove's organic digestives,
available at supermarkets
85g / 3oz unsalted butter
450g / 1lb organic cream cheese,
Sainsbury's sell 150g / 5oz tubs
2 eggs and 1 egg yolk
175ml / 6fl oz organic double
cream
50g / 2oz vanilla sugar
the inside of a vanilla pod
1 carton (150ml / 5fl oz) soured
cream
1 dsrtsp vanilla sugar
some raspberries, redcurrants
and strawberries
1 tbsp redcurrant jelly to glaze

Preheat the oven to 190°C / 375°F / Gas Mark 5. Put the digestive biscuits in a ziploc bag, seal, and crush to crumbs with a rolling pin. Tip into a bowl and pour over the butter which you have melted. Stir to amalgamate. Press into the bottom of a loose-bottomed cake tin, 20cm / 8in diameter and 5cm / 2in deep, with the back of a wooden spoon. You don't want too thick a base; if necessary, discard a tablespoon of mixture, or eat it! Put in the centre of the oven for 10 minutes. Meanwhile, tip the cream cheese, eggs and yolk, double cream, sugar and seeds from a split vanilla pod into the bowl of a blender and whizz until smooth, or whisk by hand. Pour into the cake tin and return to the oven for 25 minutes, or until still slightly trembly in the middle when nudged. Leave to cool.

Turn out, and spread the soured cream that you have whisked with a spoon of sugar over the surface with a rubber spatula. Decorate around the edge only with strings of redcurrant, and a few raspberries and strawberries. The middle is not solid enough when you cut it to support the weight of the fruit. Melt a tablespoon of redcurrant jelly with a teaspoon of cold water, and brush over the fruit.

Still good the next day. I am eating some as I write, so don't assume it's just for teenagers!

# BASIL, TARRAGON, LOVAGE AND THYME

MY FRIEND GALE, SELF-APPOINTED ROVING CULINARY SLEUTH, is on the telephone from wettest Devon, 'I've found an organic herb grower in Tiverton Market.' The following Tuesday I enter the pannier market and am transported, momentarily, to a Ligurian basil field. What I am not prepared for is quite how extensive my ignorance is about this herb, the high priestess of the Mediterranean, whose omni-presence is in danger of eclipsing our cold-climate cuisine. The truth is, food always tastes better eaten where it is indigenous, no amount of modification other than the climatic sort will change that. But here, in a not too far distant small-town market, the heady, nosey pungence of several hundred basil plants is beginning to tell me otherwise.

I introduce myself to the stallholders, Mike and Sylvie, and so beginneth the first lesson. I was aware of only three types of basil, the verdant-leafed ordinary sort we all make pesto with; 'Genovese', the more minimalist bush basil, soft skinned, frail limbed, perfect for strewing over tomato salads; and a wine-dark purple basil, 'Rubin.' Here there are 17 different kinds, including a huge, palm-of-the-hand sized 'Napolitana' basil with a skin like bubble wrap; the grape-skinned 'Rubin' which I seize in pot loads for my first purple pesto – Sylvie tears it raw into steamed rice – and an intense, rough tasting 'Holy' basil, grown around the Thai temples. My later research tells me that this last was regarded by the Hindus with such reverence, that when the British required them to take an oath in court, it took the place of the Bible. Sylvie says it is best used in combination with other spices, 'It gives an extra kick, it's the same principle as the clove, disgusting on its own, but great in a sauce.' Here in the West, sanctity replaced by fecundity, basil is the symbol of fertility. There is spicy 'Green Globe', brilliant at surviving the cooking process, 'It is extremely strong,' Sylvie says; lime and lemon basils, the lime sharply, astringently sherbetty and citric on the tongue; 'Cinnamon' and 'Anise' basils with echoes of tarragon.

'We're still small enough to have time to talk to people, they can touch and smell the herbs and get hooked.' If there is one thing that sums up the difference between French and English market culture, it is this. In France you touch, squeeze, taste, in England prohibition is an unspoken rule. Sylvie says, 'We also rely on our personalities. Being French, I have to take English taste into consideration.' It is clearly another country to her, 'You don't use tarragon. At home we put a sprig of it in our bottles of oil and vinegar, and we don't cook chicken without it. And the English don't use chervil. We use twice as much of it in salads and with fish as we would parsley. It is a traditional component of our bouquets garnis.' Get Sylvie on the subject of parsley, and there is clearly a La Manche-sized gap between us and them. 'The English want curly parsley, not flat-leaf, and they haven't discovered how to cook with it. I stir-fry it in huge branches until it goes black and crispy, and mix it with rice. It looks like burnt grass to people here.'

# Fresh Thyme Soup

This is an intensely flavoured, beautiful soup to make in summer, when the thyme flowers have turned into new growth. It is simple, aromatic, and needs no embellishment.

SERVES 4

a whole handful of thyme, as much as you can wrap your fist around

1 small onion, finely chopped

2 small new potatoes

a knob of butter

olive oil

750ml / 1 ¼ pint strong chicken stock, i.e. strong enough to jellify in the fridge

450ml / ¾ pint Jersey milk

salt and pepper

Strip half the thyme stalks, about 10 or 12 twigs, of their leaves and chop to release the oils. Melt a knob of butter and a couple of tablespoons of good olive oil in a heavy-bottomed casserole, then add the finely chopped onion, the diced potatoes and the thyme. Stir to coat for a few minutes, then ladle in the stock. Bring to the boil, add the milk, bring to the boil again, turn down to a lazy simmer, adding the rest of the thyme stalks tied in a bundle like a bouquet garni, salt and pepper.

Put the lid on, and continue to simmer for about 20 minutes. Remove the bouquet, check the seasoning, and put the soup through the thinnest of the three discs of a mouli-legumes. The result is utterly white, with tiny flecks of thyme.

Do not add cream, or you will dilute the magical flavour, the essence of the herb.

# Lovage and Potato Soup

The Greeks and the Romans used lovage, as did the Tudors and the Stuarts, who also bathed in it. It has a sort of musky flavour redolent of old spice and underscores a dish in just the same way as celery. If you grow some, you will use it – it's good with smoked fish and on salads.

SERVES 4

50g / 2oz lovage leaves after stripping them from their stalks

1 medium onion, finely chopped

3 medium potatoes, diced

1.2 litre / 2 pints chicken stock

a knob of butter and 2 tbsp olive oil

Heat the butter and oil together in a heavy-bottomed casserole, add the onion and potato, and stir to coat. Add the finely chopped lovage, stir for a couple of minutes, season, then add the stock. Bring to the boil, then turn down to a blip of a simmer, and put the lid on the pan for 15 minutes. Liquidize thoroughly, add salt and pepper to taste, and heat to scalding point again. I also ate this soup cold the next day, jellied and straight from the fridge, and it was delicious.

# SPANISH FISH STEW

I FIRST ATE *BRANDADE DE MORUE* IN PROVENCE, unsurprisingly, where it is something of a national dish. The morning markets in the glorious towns of Apt, Cavaillon, Carpentras and Isle sur la Sorgue, where the summer heat filters down through huge plane trees, and all life is brighter, slower, more headily scented, are the place to buy salt cod. Huge dirty cream triangles hang out to dry like old, bald sheepskin rugs, their curious fishy-salt smell hanging in the air; you point, you insist on a piece from the middle, not the tail – the bottom handkerchief corner is more salt, less succulent. Then you take it home and launder it, like sheets, before tucking it snugly into the pot.

It wasn't until I went to Spain that I realized they too had incorporated this North Atlantic fish into their diet, and have done since medieval times. The Catholics in particular devour it on their meatless days. There, these sweet-salt softened blankets are stewed with the *piquillo* pepper, a long, red, spicy kind of pepper, in Spain's most famous salt cod dish, *bacalao a la vizcaina*.

I cannot fathom why we have largely given up the practice of salting cod, the fish that we eat as a nation as hungrily as we do chips. Phil Bowditch, my Taunton fishmonger, still salts his, but won't have any before mid-July, so I've been to Garcia, a Spanish delicatessen in London's Portobello Road. I find it just as mysterious that we do not tend to slow-simmer summer fish stews with anything like the brio and alacrity with which we turn to their meaty winter counterpart. A barely bubbling stove-top thing, reeking of red wine, garlic, thyme and meat juices is synonymous with the more robust dishes we crave as the year cools and dwindles.

A fish stew in summer is as vibrant, as equable, as complementary to its season as its winter-comforter cousin. It demands the strident primary colours of scarlet and yellow peppers, green peas straight from the pod, flecks of courgette and aubergine, and the meaty-textured, firm-fleshed fish that don't desiccate in the stewing. Rose-pink tuna, bright white swordfish, transparently tiny squid, coral-coloured crustacea. The essence of summer nursed in a single pot, an easy marriage of vegetable, fish, olive oil and herbs stewed until each exudes its juice for the others to stew in. Unless you have grandiose notions of langoustine and lobster tails, you cut your fish according to your purse; a small piece of salt cod surrounded by a jammy heap of vegetables; a seam of tuna and squid lurking under layers of chick peas, tomatoes and peppers.

Last September I went to southern Spain for the *vendimia*, the grape harvest, to write about sherry. Four days in the magic, sherry-making triangle of Jerez de la Frontera, Puerto de Santa Maria and Sanlucar were enough to convert me to the joys and subtleties of good sherry, but I was as seduced by the piscatorial splendour of the region, starting with the Saturday morning fish market in Jerez. Great tuna lay stranded on their sides on trolleys; old ladies guarded the entrance, sat sentinel with dishes of tiny shrimps hopping and gavotting through their fingers, and in four days I tried more undiscovered fish and fish recipes than I would in an average year at home. Mantis shrimps with black-eyed tails; sea anemones spotted ten minutes earlier in their seawater bath in a fisherman's car boot, like lumps of bottle green jelly, before being pulled through a plate of batter and deep fried; baby squid stuffed with more baby squid; tuna slicked with a fine film of lard – pig fat and olive oil are a standard combination for cooking in in Spain.

On the final night, a banquet had been prepared by José Antonio Valdespino at his restaurant La Mesa Redonda. His brother Miguel presides over the last of the family-owned bodegas, his sherry some of the greatest I tasted. The Valdespino family wanted us to try the ancient cooking of Jerez, the thing I most want to do whenever I travel anywhere, but am usually unable to achieve as a mere tourist. There was no hint of the dreaded 'international kitchen' about this dinner, each of the 12 courses, we were told, were things they ate at home. The simplest carrot salad was marinaded in olive oil and oregano; bay-leaf-sized red mullet were deep fried; there was the succulent oiliness of salad *ventresca*, belly of tuna with sherry vinegar and red pimentos slow-simmered in olive oil; *crujente*, filleted anchovies cooked over sliced fried potatoes; *mojama*, dried tuna marinaded in olive oil; sweetbreads stewed with sherry; and then the Moorish-influenced spicing and combined sweetness of turkey breasts cooked in cinnamon, almonds and honey. Each course was accompanied by a different sherry from the Valdespino bodega, and as we walked the few hundred yards to the *buleria*, in the city widely believed to be the home of the flamenco, I vowed I would do better the following summer, with whatever good fish I could lay my hands on. I never slavishly reproduce, both climate and ingredients forbid it, but I do re-create the feel and mood of a dish when the time and my mood feel right, and I think they just about do.

# Hoi Sauce

SERVES 6 TO ACCOMPANY
ZARZUELA

2.5cm / 1 in of fresh ginger, grated
olive oil
2 tbsp capers
juice of a lime
6 tbsp fish stock
3 tbsp white wine
a spoonful of Harissa

Fry the chopped ginger in olive oil for 2–3 minutes, add everything else, and cook for 5 minutes on a high heat.

I leave the size of the spoon used for the Harissa to your desire for heat, but start with a teaspoon and test.

Serve the sauce separately for people to spoon over the Zarzuela on page 102.

# Zarzuela

*Zarzuela* is the name of a type of Spanish operetta. It was first performed in the Zarzuela Palace on the outskirts of Madrid. When the palace was built in the 17th century, the whole area was covered in brambles, or *zarzas*, so it was effectively christened 'Little Bramble Palace'. *Zarzuela de Pescado* or *de Mariscos* translates as an operetta of a fish stew, or seafood stew! It is the most versatile of dishes, on which you can improvise according to your taste, your budget and what is in season.

SERVES 6

*1kg / 2½lb mixed fish, tuna,*
*swordfish, squid, monkfish*
*the pulp and juice of two limes*
*4 cloves garlic, chopped*
*4 medium onions, peeled and*
*chopped*
*4 bulbs fennel, thinly sliced*
*6–8 skinned, seeded and*
*chopped tomatoes*
*225g / 8oz soaked, cooked*
*chickpeas*
*2–3 seeded and finely*
*sliced yellow peppers*
*450g / 1lb cherry tomatoes*
*generous pinch of saffron threads*
*300ml / ½ pint each of dry white*
*wine and fish stock, mixed with the*
*juice of two limes,*
*infuse the saffron in the liquid*
*olive oil, salt and pepper*
*a handful of fresh coriander*

I always include squid. If the squid are large, blanch them in the pulp and juice of two limes, then slice into rings. Cut the other fish into 8cm / 3in pieces.

Fry the garlic, onions and fennel in olive oil until softened and translucent, it takes about 20 minutes. In a large, heavy-bottomed casserole, put a layer of half this mixture, followed by the firmer fish and the skinned, seeded and chopped tomatoes. Then a layer of chickpeas and squid, followed by another layer of the onion mixture. Top this with the yellow peppers and the cherry tomatoes. Pour the saffrony liquid over, it will not cover, then bring the whole dish very slowly up to the boil.

I find if you have completed this process slowly enough, it will be cooked when it reaches boiling point, but test the peppers to see if they're soft. A sprinkle of chopped coriander completes the dish, unless you feel like a hot sauce to accompany it (see Hoi Sauce on page 101).

# Bacalao en Samfaina – Salt Cod in Summer Vegetable Sauce

You cannot buy fresh *piquillo* peppers here, but Brindisa import 'El Navarrico' organic *piquillo* peppers in jars, which you could add at the end of the vegetable cooking time. Or simply use ordinary red peppers. This is a luscious dish, intensely flavoured by the salt cod, but you could add a teaspoon of harissa or a bit of chilli if you want a bit of additional heat.

SERVES 4

*450g / 1lb chunk from the middle of the salt cod*

*2 or 3 rashers organic green back bacon*

*2 small aubergines, peeled*

*1 large onion, peeled and chopped*

*2 cloves garlic, finely chopped*

*2 red peppers, seeded and cut into small squares*

*750g / 1¾ lb skinned, seeded tomatoes, and a teaspoon of molasses sugar*

*2 small courgettes, cubed with their skins on*

*a bay leaf*

*175ml / 6fl oz dry white wine*

*olive oil, salt and pepper*

Soak the salt cod, split into 3 or 4 pieces, for at least 24 hours in several changes of water.

Cube the aubergines, sprinkle them with salt, and leave in a colander for 30 minutes. Remove all the skin and bones from the salt cod, then cut it into fish fingers.

Heat some olive oil in a heavy-bottomed casserole, and fry the bacon in strips with the onion and garlic, until the onion is translucent. Add the peppers, tomatoes, sugar, wine and bay leaf and simmer gently for about 25 minutes, until the tomato has collapsed into the sauce.

Fry the fish separately in olive oil for about 2 minutes a side, until golden. Put it in the tomato sauce. Wipe the aubergines dry, and fry them gently in the fishy oiled pan with the courgettes until softened. Turn into the tomato sauce and simmer gently for about 15 minutes.

Check the seasoning and serve with good crusty bread.

# Squid Braised in its Ink with Fennel, Peas and Oloroso

SERVES 4

600g / 1 ¼ lb squid, cleaned, plus
the ink sacs, or two sachets of ink
3 small bulbs fennel
3 small organic onions
3 cloves garlic, finely chopped
175 ml / 6fl oz Valdespino, dry
Viejo Oloroso, or a similar sherry
4 large tomatoes
1 tbsp tomato paste
2 bay leaves
2 strips of orange rind
salt and pepper
225g / 8oz fresh peas,
shelled weight
olive oil

Preheat the oven to 150°C / 300°F / Gas Mark 2. Slice the fennel bulbs thinly and finely chop the onions. Skin, seed and chop the tomatoes.

Heat some olive oil in a heavy-bottomed casserole, then add the fennel, onions and garlic, and cook gently until softened a bit. Add the squid and stir to coat. Then add the sherry, and bring to a simmer.

Add the tomatoes and tomato paste, the bay leaves and orange rind, and season. Squeeze in the squid ink, stir, and cover with greaseproof paper and a lid. Put in the oven for an hour, then remove and add the peas. Stir, cover and return to the oven for a further hour. Eat hot or warm out of soup bowls.

This dish is is full of strong flavours, beautifully green and black, and perfect as a starter or a main course. It can be made the day before and reheated. Accompany it with a glass of cold Fino or Manzanilla. Lee and Sandeman and other good wine merchants and off-licences stock Valdespino.

# THE SPIRIT OF THE FRUIT

I ARRIVE EARLY AT A SMALL, SECLUDED TRADING ESTATE in the tiny village of South Brent in Devon. Opening an unmarked door, I see a man in a white coat bent over four huge glass jars, inside which are lurking a cornucopia of citrusy bits, spices, herbs and murky-looking liquor.

Edward Kain looks up, slightly startled, disturbed in the privacy of his early morning calculations. It is an exacting business, perfecting a new fruit liqueur, and the one in question, based on an old Italian recipe called *Centerbe,* is already approaching maturation in its fourth incarnation. The pursuit of post-prandial pleasure, as is the way of good things, 'Is great fun in the trying, but whether it will work or not who can say? I am upping the citrus element with clementines, lime and lemon peel.' I cast an eye down a spell-length list of ingredients that include cinnamon, cardamom, juniper, saffron, coffee beans, cloves, rosemary, dried lime flowers, sage, thyme, fresh ginger and China tea. 'I started experimenting last October. It's three months between macerating and tasting the finished infusion.'

Edward spent 25 years in the steel industry, as general manager of a foundry. 'I was working with nickel and chromium, the exotic end of metallurgy. It was 13 hours a day, six and a half days a week. In a good year we made a lot of money, in a bad one we broke even. We bought and sold in dollars, and our profitability depended on the exchange rate. I couldn't get my superiors to understand this. One day I just quit, and went home to tell my wife.' 'What did she say?' 'Oh good, you've been heading for an early grave.'

They bought a fruit farm in Dittisham, famous for its plums. If you've never heard of the rare Dittisham plum, you won't know of the legend that has it that the fruit arrived there by sea. A German ship's captain, unable to sell his cargo, dumped it on the village foreshore, and the plum stones germinated. The villagers planted the seedlings in their gardens, and the trees have thrived ever since. Attempts to grow them outside the village have been unsuccessful.

Whether there is even a kernel of truth in this, I can't say, but unplug a bottle of Dittisham Plum Liqueur, sparklingly clear and coloured like a slow-baked quince, raise it to your nose, and you will sniff an almondy-sharp scent that is all fruity tartness on the tongue.

When Edward started the business proper two and a half years ago, he was as clear in spirit as his product about what he was trying to do, 'The philosophy is that all the liqueurs are based on locally grown English fruit. We pick the plums in Dittisham from the trees of ten friends, the first week of August. The strawberries and raspberries come from Kenton; I first started with raspberries in vodka 12 years ago.'

You can choose from the deepest, darkest, purplest blackberry to a fruity, dry for your white wines or Kir Royales; there is a palely delicate quince; a throbbingly syrupy, sticky strawberry, which could slalom successfully down the white slopes of vanilla ice cream, or be poured into the oases of Galia or Charentais melons. The raspberry I found myself carrying around in my bag last week, even producing it unashamedly at tea with my son's tutor. Well, I did have to test it. When I asked Edward how he tested each new concoction, he confessed it was in church. Not in the soporific depths of a sermon, but, 'When I'm close to getting it right, I take it up the church tower. I'm a bell-ringer. You get reactions from 0–100. The plum is wonderful with duck, the quince in a pork stir-fry, and the blackcurrant in game or sorbets; it's not nearly as sweet as the French cassis, it's got a cleaner flavour.'

## Cassis Syllabub

You can use raspberries, redcurrants or blackberries in this stratospherically light syllabub, seamed with deep purple fruit.

SERVES 4–6

125ml/4fl oz Cassis or blackcurrant liqueur
2 tbsp Cognac
pared rind and juice of a lemon
50g/2oz caster sugar
300ml/10fl oz double cream
450g/1lb blackcurrants
light muscovado sugar to taste and a squeeze of lemon

Macerate the Cassis, Cognac, lemon rind and juice together for a few hours, or overnight. Strain into a bowl and stir in the sugar until it has completely dissolved. Stir in the cream slowly, then beat everything together with a balloon whisk until it has cohered and thickened. You want it to hold its shape, but softly; if you overbeat, it will begin to curdle and separate.

Swirl the raw blackcurrants in a food processor until puréed, then push them through a nylon sieve. Add sugar to taste, and a squeeze of lemon juice to bring out the flavour. You will probably have too much here, but it is not worth making less; you can use the leftover blackcurrant purée in a wonderful fool or ice cream.

Spoon a layer of syllabub into individual glasses, or one glass bowl, then add a stratum of the raw blackcurrant purée. You want it to look like thin seam, not a thick stripe. Repeat with a layer of each, then add a final layer of syllabub. Keep cool, but do not refrigerate. It will keep well for a couple of days. You can add a little twist of lemon peel or a tiny sprig of rosemary to the top of each glass.

# Blueberry Genoise with Blackberry Devon Liqueur

This is an airily light sponge with a seam of blueberries cooked into it. When you turn it out, it is mottled purple and yellow, the fruit bleeding into the sponge.

MAKES 22CM/9 INCH CAKE

4 organic eggs
125g/4oz vanilla caster sugar
rind of an orange
125g/4oz organic flour and a
pinch of salt
50g/2oz melted butter
275g/10oz blueberries, and a
spoon or so of sugar

Preheat the oven to 180°C/350°F/Gas Mark 4. Brush melted butter over the base and sides of a 22cm/9 inch springform cake tin. Cover the base with a circle of baking parchment, also buttered, and sprinkle flour over it, shaking off the excess. Beat the eggs, sugar and rind together until trebled in volume, light and foamy. The beaters will leave a trail. I did it in the Kitchen Aid, otherwise beat over a pan of barely simmering water, and when expanded, remove and beat until cool.

Sift half the flour on to the egg mixture, and fold it in gently with a metal spoon. Sift over the rest and the salt, then pour the warm butter, without its white sediment, around the side, and fold them both in thoroughly but lightly.

Pour half the mixture into the tin, throw in the blueberries and sprinkle them with a dessertspoon of sugar, then cover with the other half of the mixture. Bake for about 40 minutes. The top should spring back to the touch when cooked.

Cool for 10 minutes, then turn out onto a wire rack. The blueberries will be uppermost. While still warm, brush with blackberry liqueur and serve. Pass the bottle around for people to pour on more liqueur.

# Peach and Raspberry Trifle with Devon Raspberry Liqueur

This is no mere trifle. It is wondrously rich, fruity and full of hidden depths.

SERVES 6

*5 macaroons*
*250ml/8fl oz white wine*
*4–6 tbsp raspberry liqueur*
*600ml/1 pint organic double*
*cream*
*300ml/½ pint milk*
*2 eggs and 2 yolks*
*1 tbsp sifted cornflour*
*vanilla caster sugar to taste*
*325g/12oz raw raspberries*
*icing sugar to taste*
*5 ripe peaches*
*juice of a lemon*

Put 5 macaroons into a large glass bowl and pour over 125ml/4 fl oz of the white wine and 2–3 tablespoons of raspberry liqueur.

Now bring the milk and 300ml/10fl oz of the double cream to scalding point, and pour them over the two eggs and two yolks which you have beaten with the sifted cornflour. Return to the pan and whisk until thickened. Add vanilla caster sugar to taste, and pour over the macaroons.

Purée the raw raspberries in a food processor, sieve and add icing sugar to taste. Pour this mixture over the cooled custard. Scald 5 ripe peaches, skin and slice them, and place them on the raspberries.

In a bowl, put the juice of a lemon, the rest of the white wine and raspberry liqueur, and stir in 25g/1oz sugar until dissolved. Taste for sweetness. Pour over the remaining 300ml/10fl oz organic double cream and whisk with a wire whisk until thickened but not stiff. The mixture will have a lovely peachy blush to it. Top the peaches with it.

Sheer hedonism. My next door neighbour snuck in for some at tea time because she'd spotted it before lunch.

## Summer Pudding with Devon Raspberry Liqueur

I happen to believe that Elizabeth David and Jane Grigson got it right, the best summer pudding is made with raspberries and redcurrants only — about 4:1 rasps to reds.

SERVES 6

*675g/1½lb raspberries*
*200g/7oz redcurrants*
*125g/4oz vanilla caster sugar*
*1–2 tbsp raspberry liqueur*
*white bread cut into slices, the crusts removed*

Put the raspberries and redcurrants in a heavy pot with the vanilla caster sugar. Heat gently and briefly until the fruit begins to bleed and the sugar is dissolved. No more than about 3–4 minutes, the fruit must not lose its shape or cook.

Line a pudding basin with slices of day-old good white bread. There should be no gaps.

With a slotted spoon, pile in the fruit, leaving some of the juice in the pot. Sprinkle a tablespoon or two of raspberry liqueur over the pudding before finishing with a top layer of bread. Cover with a plate that just fits, weight it, and put the basin in the fridge overnight. Turn it out just before you serve it onto a not completely flat plate, and pour over the rest of the juice to which you've added more raspberry liqueur to taste. You should still pass round the bottle too!

# FRANCE

THE INVENTORY READS LIKE THIS: one wonky one-armed colander, one grater, one spatula and two wooden spoons, three or four lidless 'heritage' pots of the sort of dubious non-stickery that I fear even Oxfam might reject, a green plastic salad bowl that the *femme à menage* has been seen shaking bleach into, and a large pyrex dish. This is the holiday house we are sharing with our friends Peter and Susie Ibbotson, their three children, and Susie's parents, so the ages range from Charissa at ten, to Susie's mother on the cusp of octogenarianism. We are in a large, stone house, perched on one of those precariously terraced hillsides where the black figs plop from their sprawly-leaved boughs, and the silvery grey olive trees, their fruit still hard and green pea sized, twist out of the ground black barked, snakily, their branches wrapping around some imaginary object. There is a red squirrel in the nearest walnut tree, whittling away in the early morning, and behind, a densely treed mountain that separates the edge of our village, Seillans, from the next, Mons, 13 kilometres away.

I am not planning on becoming a candidate for martyrdom, and cooking for the dozen of us on a daily basis, but have promised a *grande bouffe* after the Saturday market in neighbouring Fayence. In the gathering heat, I walk past the first stall with its great cartwheels of Provençale tarts and ridged brioche tins, with family-sized brioche sneaking over the top, all yellow and yeasty. A brief circumambulation, and I feel I have sniffed out the most promising stall, where the produce has clearly been reared, grown and cooked by the husband and wife stallholders. Tiny ducks and chickens, their heads and necks wrapped scarf-like around them, next to fists of basil, mint and parsley. The tomatoes are cracked and redly plump cheeked, the courgettes squeaky, glossy and firm, alongside violet-skinned onions, great buds of new garlic, lettuces still damp from being eased out of the earth. On the Saturday I return to Fayence to meet Gilles, the photographer, who tells me to look out for a man built like a rugby player and carrying a camera. Buttressed like a prop forward, there is no missing him. At Madame's stall, he inspects all my chosen ingredients with the wary eye of a Frenchman incredulous that anyone from the wrong side of La Manche should actually recognize a good dinner, let alone know how to prepare one. He pulls, pummels, scratches, sniffs, and turns over everything, giving Madame the Spanish Inquisition as he goes. By the end of our marketeering foray I have been lectured on such diverse subjects as the relative merits of the sausages he uses for a cassoulet – he is a native of Toulouse – to the way in which Moroccan girls are taught how to kiss by biting the end off a fig and sucking out the flesh. When he sees the kitchen he falls silent. There isn't even a lemon squeezer. He attacks the ducks with the bread knife, cleaving them with a single blow. We make a tomato salad, then briefly fry slices of courgettes in olive oil, and spritz them still warm with lemon and basil. Next, a garlicky, oily dressing for a pile of knitting-needle-width green beans, and a cooling cucumber salad with a yoghurt, fresh mint and garlic dressing. Then we marinade shavings of fennel in olive oil, lemon juice and the juice from the tomatoes. I have bought slippers of *fougasse* and *fougassette* in the local boulangerie. The *fougasse* stuffed with anchovies or lardons, the *fougassettes* with Roquefort and walnuts or ham and mushrooms. We have icy slices of melon, fresh goat's cheeses and salty dry crottins, and blue-black figs. The barbecue is kindled, lit and ready-to-char, and the duck is dried and placed skin down to frazzle and crisp. The marinade meets the giblet stock, and in the absence of Cognac an Irish measure of whiskey, and the whole is reduced, with the livers mashed into the juice. By half past one we have our groaning board, and are pulling the crisped, pinkly bloody flesh from the bones and dunking the *fougasse* into the sauce. The salty anchovy and sweet-fleshed duck are an unsuspectedly delicious partnership, and the assembled crew fall on the assembly job with scant thought of the exigencies of the holiday kitchen.

# Balsamic Tomato Chicken with Basil

I cooked this delicious, summery dish after I had interviewed Lindsey Bareham on publication of her wonderful *The Big Red Book of Tomatoes*. Lindsey likes this dish because it is full of flavour and quick to make, as easy for one as for six.

SERVES 4

500g / 1lb 2oz vine tomatoes
50g / 2oz butter
1 tbsp olive oil
1 garlic clove, crushed to a paste with a pinch of salt
450g / 1lb organic chicken fillet
2–3 tbsp good balsamic vinegar, gran reserva if possible
salt, pepper and sugar
a squeeze of lemon juice
a knob of butter
a handful of basil leaves

Core, blanch and seed the vine tomatoes, and dice them small. Tip all the seed debris into a sieve above a bowl, and press with the back of a wooden spoon to extract all the liquid. Set aside. Melt half the butter gently in a pan, add the oil and garlic and cook until aromatic.

Cut the chicken into strips 5 x 1cm / 2 x ½in and put in the pan, turn up the heat and fry briskly until it is plump and springy. Pour over the balsamic vinegar, stir, then add the rest of the butter, the tomatoes and seed debris liquid. Season, and simmer for about 15 minutes until the tomatoes have turned into a sauce and the chicken is completely cooked.

Taste, adjust the seasoning with salt, sugar and a squeeze of lemon, and stir in the knob of butter until it has dissolved. Shred the basil leaves over the top and serve with rice, potatoes or pasta.

# Lindsey Bareham's Iced Roast Tomato Soup
## with Fresh Tomatoes and Basil

SERVES 6

*2 tbsp olive oil, plus a little extra*

*20 medium tomatoes, (approx 1.2kg / 2¾lb)*

*4 medium onions*

*2 large cloves garlic*

*400ml / 14fl oz iced water*

*salt and pepper*

*Tabasco*

*juice of ½ a lemon*

*1 tbsp tomato ketchup, optional*

*6 vine-ripened tomatoes*

*18 or so basil leaves*

*cream, optional*

Preheat the oven to 200°C/400°F/Gas Mark 6. Line a baking sheet with a layer of foil and brush over a thin film of oil. Stand the tomatoes, core side down, in the middle of the sheet. Halve the onions through the middle, leaving only 2–3 layers of skin, and put them cut side down around the edges. Cover the cloves of garlic with the flat of a knife, and press hard until you hear a crack.

Bake in the middle of the oven for 15 minutes, lower the heat a bit, and continue to cook for about 30 minutes until the skin of the tomatoes has split and is starting to weep, and the onions are tender when pierced with a knife. Add the garlic cloves 20 minutes before the end of cooking.

Cool slightly, skin, and tip everything into the food processor bowl, with the juice. Liquidize, then sieve, pressing hard to extract every scrap. Add half the iced water, then adjust the flavour with salt, pepper, Tabasco, lemon juice, ketchup, and more water if it needs it. Cover and put in the fridge to chill. Meanwhile, core, blanch and seed the vine tomatoes and dice them small. Tip all the seed debris into a sieve above a bowl, and press with the back of a wooden spoon to extract all the liquid. Add it, with the diced tomato, to the soup, stirring well. Serve chilled with torn basil leaves strewn over the top. A splash of olive oil or cream looks very pretty.

# Bruschetta with Pistou and Tomato.

good bread
olive oil
pistou
tomatoes

Like the *daube* and *aioli*, *pistou* is as indigenous to Provençale cooking as you can get, despite its origin in Genoa. The word itself means pounded basil. It is a richly verdant racing green emulsion of fresh basil, garlic and olive oil, and without the benefit of a pestle and mortar.

I bought a freshly made jar of it from Fayence market. The evening of the *grande bouffe* we toasted *pain à l'ancienne* cut in thick slices and daubed with olive oil, then crisped it on both sides in a hot oven, before spreading on the pistou and sitting tomatoes from the salad on top.

# Soupe au Pistou

I usually make this with some cannellini or haricot beans and the last minute addition of some vermicelli, but you can also use cooked green beans. The French, locally, use their fresh coco beans straight from the pod.

SERVES 6

1 medium onion, chopped
1 leek, chopped
olive oil
a few tomatoes, skinned and chopped
1.7 litre / 3 pints stock or water
3 potatoes, cubed
5 or 6 tomatoes, halved, seeded and grilled
a handful of green beans
pistou

After sweating the chopped onion and leek gently in olive oil, add the chopped tomatoes, stock or water and the potatoes, and cook until tender. Throw in the beans, chopped if necessary, and if you like some halved, seeded, grilled tomatoes to give more depth and resonance. Pass around the pistou for everyone to stir in a great green-oiled slick of it.

Pistou is also wonderful stirred into an iced pea soup. Stew a couple of pounds of freshly podded peas with a generous lump of butter, a finely chopped onion, two small torn up lettuces and a scattering of mint. A ladle of water is all you need at this stage. When cooked, add a further 5–6 ladles of water, liquidize, sieve and season. Refrigerate for a few hours, add a squeeze of lemon, and stir the dense green liquid. Serve with a spoon of pistou plopped into the middle of each bowl.

# FRANCE II

WE ARE SITTING BETTERAVE-HUED AFTER THE WALK, ordering lunch at Le Petit Bonheur. 'What is *salade de gesiers?*' demands Harry. I don't know. A couple sitting behind us proceed to tell me, showing me the bits, courtesy of their necks and stomachs, and I relate the detail: chicken crops, and all the bits around the stomach bar the actual offal itself. We get talking about food, regional French food, and after the dubious flattery of being told that I know far too much about food to be English, I summon up the courage to air my theory. We have, I explain, been in the area a scant week, eating only in local villages and towns, but it is as though the thing that has cemented French life, preserved its culinary character, through strong, regionally based ingredients and cooking, *la vraie cuisine du terroir*, is slowly becoming unmortared. Nothing as drastic as the ubiquitous three-continents-on-a-plate kind of food, but a sort of fuzzing at the boundaries.

Not quite knowing the depth and intensity of national pride, I have to say I am feeling the *terroir* under my feet is distinctly dodgy, but the couple agree. They are on their annual three-week biking tour of every gastronomic region, and are profoundly worried. Madame, I am informed is a superlative cook. They live in Paris. *Salade de gesiers* is not a Provençale dish. Nor is the *veau à la crème*, the semi-preserved morilles, indeed, half the menu. Pah! You must have the *côte d'agneau* grilled with Provençale herbs I am instructed. It is the only really local dish. I know when not to argue, and order it. I go further. The best meal we've had so far was when we crossed the border to Italy for a simple plate of seafood spaghetti, sweetly softened octopus, clams, mussels and prawns in an oily, tomatoey, garlicky slather of sauce. And a plate of incomparable wood-grilled *gamberoni*, which the children unfurled out of their bendy carapaces with incredulity. So, what of the famous bouillabaisse, I demand, for that is my end of week, end of holiday holy grail?

Conspiratorially I am informed that they do likewise every year in St Raphael in a tiny restaurant whose name has slipped their memory. Madame telephones her friend, who isn't there, and agrees to call us later. By the next morning, I am beginning to take my disappointment like a man, even when I discover that she wasn't told she'd have to dial the code for England to get the mobile.

We set off for St Raphael. I will find this place, and partake of the ultimate fish dinner – which, after all, is what a bouillabaisse is – come what may. Scanning every restaurant menu I begin. It is hot. Getting late. The children edging towards mutiny. I see a sign for the *vieux port*. Follow it. The fish market is being hosed down. I accost the broad-hipped, black-dressed old lady in charge of the hose, ask for the best bouillabaisse in town. She laughs and points. Yards from where we are standing, across the street, a huge gnarled tree bends into an old house, its branches shading the tiny terrace below. It is called La Bouillabaisse!

We sit down, a menu arrives. There is no messing here, there are only four things on it: bouillabaisse, paella, langoustines, sole. When the great black pot is brought from the kitchen, with great black, steep-sided dishes and a great black platter of steaming fish, we gasp. A whole wooden mortar of fiery red rouille, thickly glossy is accompanied by a pannier of toasted baguettes. The daurade and rascasse are tenderly filleted before our eyes, there are heaps of crabs and shellfish, and a saffrony, tomatoey broth to ladle over it. We eat until every bone and shell is picked and sucked clean and dry. I presume the debris will be returned to the bowels of the pot for recycling. We have just eaten our truly memorable meal of the trip; absolutely no lip-service to faddism or food fashion has been paid, and I am happy and grateful for it. I will be back.

# Vitello Tonnato with Green Olives

A classic summer dish, relying on an olive oil-based mayonnaise for strength of flavour, that can be made, unbelievably, up to five days before you want to eat it. I do not, as is conventional, poach the veal, I roast it.

SERVES 8

1.2kg / 2¾lb boned loin of veal
1 onion, finely sliced
flat-leaf parsley

FOR THE FRESH TUNA SAUCE:
225g / 8oz tuna steak
6 anchovy fillets
3 tbsp drained capers
3 tbsp lemon juice
250ml / 8fl oz olive oil
salt, pepper
12–15 green olives, stoned and roughly chopped
mayonnaise, made with 2egg yolks, 300ml / 10fl oz olive oil, the juice of a lemon and salt and pepper

Grill or griddle the tuna steak until just tender, about 2–3 minutes. Process all the tuna sauce ingredients, bar the mayonnaise and the green olives, until creamy and smooth, but do not overdo it. Stir in the green olives, then fold in the mayonnaise.

Roast the veal for an hour on a finely sliced onion in a hottish oven, 190°C / 375°F / Gas Mark 5. Cool, slice, and add the warm meat juices to the tuna sauce. Spread a layer of tuna sauce thinly on a serving dish, top with slices of veal, spread another layer of sauce, and repeat until the final layer of sauce. Scatter some chopped, flat-leaf parsley over the top, and decorate sparingly with a few anchovy fillets and black olives. Refrigerate for at least 24 hours.

# Fish Stew with a Rouille

Not *la vraie* bouillabaisse, but a delicious, simple-to-make stew on the same principles.

SERVES 8

FOR THE FISH STOCK
*1.5–1.8kg / 3–4lb fish bones*
*4 litres / 6¾ pints water*
*2 fennel bulbs, chopped*
*2 stalks of celery, chopped*
*with leaves*
*2 onions, chopped*
*6 quartered tomatoes and 1 tbsp*
*tomato purée*
*saffron and a splosh of Pernod*
*are optional*

FOR THE ROUILLE
*150g / 5oz roasted, peeled peppers,*
*1 seeded red chilli*
*a crustless slice of day-old bread*
*5 small cloves peeled garlic*
*125–175ml / 4–6fl oz olive oil*

FOR THE FISH STEW
*675g / 1½lb filleted, boned weight*
*of red mullet*
*675g / 1½lb boned monkfish tail*
*450g / 1lb squid, cleaned and cut*
*into rings*
*450g / 1lb large prawns in shells*

First make an intensely flavoured fish stock with the fish bones, sole and turbot are good, and I add prawn or crab shells to enhance the flavour and colour. Add the water, bring to the boil, remove scum and simmer for 30 minutes. Sieve and discard the bones. Simmer for a further 30 minutes. Add the other ingredients. Simmer until softened, press through a sieve and season. You can refrigerate this overnight, then the stew will take a mere three minutes to cook after reheating the soup.

*The Rouille*
Process together the roasted, peeled peppers – if you are feeling lazy, the supermarkets sell a good brand imported by Brindisa called *pimientos asados del bierzo* – with the chilli, a crustless slice of day-old bread soaked in water and wrung out, and the garlic. Pour the olive oil in a steady stream into the processor until you have a sumptuously thickened vermillion ointment. Taste and season.

*The Fish Stew*
I used the fish listed, but you can improvise. Cut the fish into generous, 5cm / 2in chunks, and throw them into the barely simmering pot of fish soup. They are ready as soon as they lose their translucence, about 3 minutes. Put in the peeled prawns, and serve with toasted slices of baguette and rouille.

# Tonno e Fagioli

This is a lovely, simple summer dish, to which the addition of fresh lime juice, such a friend of tuna, brings out the true flavour.

SERVES 8–10

450g / 1lb cannellini beans
2 large tuna steaks
1 large red onion
juice of up to 2 lemons and 2 limes
olive oil, salt and pepper
flat-leaf parsley, chopped

Soak the cannellini beans overnight. Cook until tender, about 40 minutes. Pour some of the olive oil on to the hot beans once you have drained them. Grill or griddle the tuna steaks until barely cooked through, about 2–3 minutes.

Slice the onion into the finest circles you can muster. When the beans are still warm, add the tuna, more oil, the citrus juice to taste, and the onions. Amalgamate gently and season. Sprinkle with a large handful of chopped flat-leaf parsley.

# How to cook a salmon

The method I use of cooking at a very low temperature retains all the moisture and vibrant flamingo-pink colouring of the fish. I find most people overcook their fish to a sort of dry, desiccated pale pink flesh to which the bones seem to weld themselves.

one wild salmon
dill, fennel, parsley and chervil
about a glass of white wine
a lump of butter or splosh olive oil
salt and pepper

Preheat the oven to 150°C / 300°F / Gas Mark 2. Put the fish on a large piece of foil on a baking sheet, raising the edges of the foil a bit so you can anoint the fish with a libation of white wine, about a glass. Add a splosh of olive oil if the fish is to be eaten cold, or a lump of butter for hot. A few branches of any combination of dill, fennel, parsley and chervil stuffed into the cavity will add to the flavour. Scrunch over some salt and pepper, and seal your fish into its baggy parcel. Up to 2 and a bit kilos or 5lb, the fish will take an hour, and can then be cooled in its parcel to tepid, when you can skin it most successfully. If it is any larger, allow 12 minutes to the 450g/lb.

# Seafood Plate

Stephen Markwick, whose eponymous restaurant 'Markwick's' is Bristol's best, serves the following five fish dishes together as one incredible starter. You can pick my combination or serve one element.

FOR THE CRAB:
*125g / 4oz white meat*
*50g / 2oz brown meat*
*dill, lemon juice, olive oil*

### Crab
Simply pick the meat from the crab, and dress it with some fresh dill, lemon juice and olive oil.

FOR THE SQUID:
*175g / 6oz squid, sliced thinly*
*1 clove garlic, finely chopped*
*1 red chilli, finely chopped*
*a handful of flat-leaf parsley*
*2 tbsp olive oil*

### Squid
'Wok' or pan fry all the squid ingredients over a high heat in the hot oil until tender, about 1-2 minutes. Season. Serve warm.

FOR THE SALMON:
*125g / 4oz wild salmon*
*4 thin slices of smoked salmon*
*juice of half a lemon*
*a large spoonful of tartare sauce*

### Salmon
Cut the salmon into fine dice and marinade briefly with the juice of half a lemon for about 15 minutes to start the cooking process. Drain well and mix with the tartare sauce. Tear each smoked salmon slice into two, place a spoon of the salmon and tartare sauce mixture in the middle and roll it up like a miniature pancake.

FOR THE TARTARE SAUCE:
*homemade mayonnaise*
*1 tbsp each of gherkins and capers*
*1 chopped anchovy fillet,*
*1 tbsp chopped shallot*
*1 tsp French mustard*
*dill, chervil and tarragon*

### Tartare Sauce
Homemade tartare sauce is easy. To your homemade mayonnaise, add chopped gherkins and chopped capers, a chopped anchovy fillet, chopped shallot and a teaspoon of French mustard. Then throw in some finely chopped dill, chervil and tarragon.

FOR THE SCALLOPS
*4 scallops*
*olive oil*
*vinaigrette*

### Scallops
Slice each scallop into 2 or 3 discs, and fry briefly in hot olive oil with the corals; 30 seconds a side should do it. Dress them while still hot with vinaigrette and serve warm.

**FOR THE CEVICHE**

*125g / 4oz lemon sole fillet*

*juice of half a lemon*

*olive oil*

*a handful of flat-leaf parsley*

**FOR THE TOMATO CHILLI**

**SAUCE**

*2–3 ripe tomatoes*

*1 red and 1 green chilli*

*half a small red onion*

*1 tbsp each of chopped red and*

*yellow pepper*

*1 tsp chopped garlic*

*1 tbsp chopped coriander*

*dash each of Tabasco and*

*Worcester sauce*

*olive oil*

*salt and pepper*

*Ceviche*

Cut the sole fillet thinly on the diagonal into strips, marinade for at least an hour in the lemon juice, drain well, and dress with olive oil, parsley and seasoning. Serve with a tomato and chilli sauce.

*Tomato Chilli Sauce*

Chop the onion and chilli finely, and mix with the skinned, seeded, diced tomato and chopped peppers. Add the garlic and coriander, and mix with enough olive oil to loosen. Add salt and pepper and adjust the chilli to taste.

Depending on how dressed up or how dressed down you like your food, and on how many of the above you are gracing each plate with, you might like to add the following accompaniments: some sliced avocado with the ceviche; a cucumber and fennel sambal with the crab, which means a spoonful of doll-sized diced cucumber and fennel dressed with a bit of olive oil and some dill; some cucumber pickle with the salmon, which, once made, is better left for a month before using, so think ahead!

# Cucumber Pickle, adapted from Joyce Molyneaux's recipe

*4 cucumbers*
*450g / 1lb finely sliced onions*
*40g / 1½oz salt*
*275g / 10oz brown sugar*
*40g / 1½oz mustard seed*
*1 tsp ground turmeric*
*1 tsp ground mace*
*600ml / 1 pint white wine vinegar*

Cut the cucumbers in half and slice them on the fine shredder of a mandolin, so you get 15cm/6in ribbons. Mix with the onions and salt, and put into a colander with a weighted plate for 2–3 hours to drain off the excess water.

Put the sugar, spices and vinegar in a pan, bring to the boil to dissolve the sugar, and simmer for a few minutes to amalgamate the flavours. Wash the salt out of the cucumber and onions and drain again. Put them into the liquid, bring back to the boil, and simmer for several minutes.

Drain in the colander and then reduce the liquid to a syrup. Pot the cucumbers into jars and then add the reduced liquid. Leave for a month if possible before using.

# Leeks Vinaigrette

A perfect summer starter, with the new season's taut white wands of leek, and that magical combination of chives, mustard and chopped egg. A real classic.

SERVES 4

*12 fine leeks*
*2 tbsp Dijon mustard*
*4 tbsp warm water*
*2 tbsp red or white wine vinegar*
*150ml / 5fl oz olive oil, or more to taste*
*salt and pepper*
*2 softly hard-boiled organic eggs*
*a handful of snipped chives*

Wash the leeks very well and trim the green leaves to about 2.5cm/1in. Steam them until collapsed and tender. Drain, and allow them to cool, then halve them lengthwise.

Blitz the mustard, water, vinegar, salt and pepper in a blender, then, with the motor running, gradually pour in the olive oil until you have a thick, mustardy emulsion. Taste and adjust. You might need a little more water if it is too thick.

Irrigate the leeks, which you have laid regimental-style in a flat dish, then sprinkle over the finely chopped egg and the snipped chives.

# Pork Fillet en Papillote with Dijon, Fennel and Black Olives.

Inspired by my earthenware pot of Maille mustard after a trip to Dijon, I stuffed some tender, organic pork fillet with a delicious *duxelles* of vegetables bound with mustard, and breathing aniseedy Pernod fumes, and baked them in foil in the oven.

SERVES 6–7

*1 kg / 2½ lb pork fillet*
*2 bulbs fennel, with frondy bits*
*2 red onions*
*2 sticks celery, with their leaves*
*12 good black olives*
*olive oil and butter*
*salt and pepper*
*a good slug of Pernod, say 2 tbsp*
*2 heaped dsrtsp Dijon mustard*

Preheat the oven to 180°C/350°F/Gas Mark 4. Slice the pork fillets almost in half lengthwise, then open them out like butterflies and flatten them slightly with your hands. Trim the bulbs of fennel and onion rigorously to the point of wastefully – you want the tenderest, juiciest parts of both – and chop into a fine *duxelles*, which means smaller than dice by quite some way. String the sticks of celery and chop as for the fennel and onions.

Stew all the vegetables together in a little olive oil and butter until softened and translucent, season, add the halved, pitted olives, pour on the Pernod, allow it to bubble briefly, dollop on the mustard, and stir it into the mixture to bind it off the heat. Cool slightly. Spread it in the centre of the pork fillets, then simply press them together, and fix with string, which I tied in a sort of large, raggedy blanket stitch.

Place each fillet on its own bit of foil, and seal loosely. Place all the fillets on a flat baking tray, and cook in the oven for 35 minutes. Test with a skewer. In this time, mine were cooked through, with a tinge of pink, and had created a good puddle of juice. Serve with new potatoes and something simple like broad or runner beans, or fresh peas.

# Chicken Thighs Stewed with Summer Vegetables

A simple summer dish that I made with peas picked from the garden seconds before. It can be left to cook for nearly an hour, then brought to the table in the pot.

SERVES 6

*6 plump, organic chicken thighs*
*1 large onion, peeled and chopped*
*2–3 new potatoes per person,*
*cleaned, scraped and left whole*
*chicken stock to cover*
*6 carrots, cut in thinnish discs*
*450g / 1lb shelled weight fresh*
*peas*
*225g / 8oz broad beans, steamed*
*briefly and skinned (optional)*
*a large handful of fresh mint*
*olive oil*
*salt and pepper*

Heat a couple of tablespoons of olive oil in a heavy-bottomed pan. Sauté the onion gently with a bit of salt until softened and translucent, then add the chicken thighs skin side down, and brown for a few minutes. Season. Turn them over, and brown the flesh side briefly.

Remove the chicken from the pot, and gently turn the potatoes in the oil and chicken fat for a few minutes. Lay the thighs on top of the potatoes, pour over hot stock to cover, then throw in the carrots, bring just to the boil, turn down to a bare simmer, and put the lid on.

Come back in 50 minutes and pour in the fresh peas. Ten minutes later add the cooked broad beans, season to taste and add the freshly chopped mint off the heat. With a skewer, test that the potatoes are cooked through, skim some of the chicken fat from the surface if you feel it necessary, and serve.

# Homemade Chicken Nuggets

SERVES 8

750g / 1¾lb minced chicken,
brown meat
175g / 6oz brown breadcrumbs
175g / 6oz grated mature Cheddar
1 tbsp mayonnaise to bind
1 clove garlic
salt and pepper
beaten egg and some fine toasted
breadcrumbs to coat the nuggets

Preheat the oven to 180°C/350°F/Gas Mark 4. Mix all the ingredients up to and including the seasoning together. Form into golf-ball sized nuggets with damp hands to prevent sticking, and roll each one first in beaten egg and then in the toasted breadcrumbs. You can freeze them at this stage if you want to, or if you need only a few of them.

Place on a greased baking sheet, and cook for about 25 minutes if fresh, and for 45 if frozen. Ketchup is inevitable for the children, but if you find it resistible, add some finely chopped cornichons, capers and anchovy, with a sprinkling of chives and dill, to your mayonnaise to make a sauce tartare.

# Fresh Pea Masala

A lovely summer side dish to accompany a spiced lamb, chicken or prawn dish.

SERVES 4

2 tbsp olive oil
2 tsp black mustard seed
1 tsp fennel seeds
2.5cm / 1in of fresh ginger, grated
1 onion, thinly sliced
1 tsp ground coriander
1 tsp turmeric
cayenne pepper to taste
a large tomato, cut into chunks
1 ladle of water
salt and pepper
275g / 10oz fresh peas
a bunch of coriander, chopped

Heat the oil in a pan, add the mustard and fennel seeds, and when they begin to pop, after about 30 seconds, add the ginger and onion and sprinkle on some salt. Cook until softened, then add the ground coriander, turmeric and cayenne. Stir together, add the tomato and water, and cook for a couple of minutes. Stir in the peas and season with salt and pepper. Cover the pan and cook until the peas are tender. Adjust the seasoning, throw the coriander over the dish like confetti, and serve.

# Swaddles Shepherd's Pie

SERVES 6–8

900g / 2lb minced lamb
1 large onion
6 cloves garlic
sunflower oil
5cm / 2in fresh ginger, grated
1 red chilli
⅓ tsp each of ground allspice,
cinnamon, nutmeg and turmeric
1 tbsp tomato purée
1 tsp fresh thyme
1 tbsp lemon juice
salt and pepper
fresh coriander, chopped

Preheat the oven to 190°C / 375°F / Gas Mark 5. Peel, chop and sauté the onion and garlic gently until softened in a couple of tablespoons of sunflower oil, sprinkling a bit of salt on to help release the flavours.

Add the chopped chilli and ginger and the spices, then add the meat and brown it. Add the tomato purée, lemon and thyme and simmer gently for about 40 minutes. Season with salt and pepper and throw in a couple of tablespoons of chopped fresh coriander.

Cover with mounds of mash made with 900g / 2lb potatoes, and dot with extra butter for the top. Bake in the oven for 30–40 minutes. You want a bubbling, crustily browned top. Serve with Cumin Spiced Carrots.

# Cumin Spiced Carrots

I cooked these, thinking they might work perfectly with the Swaddles Shepherd's Pie. Charissa and Harry were unanimous in their approval. Curiously, the cumin seemed to add sweetness as well as muskiness.

1 large organic carrot per person
1 heaped tsp cumin seeds for
3 carrots
15g / ½oz unsalted butter
salt and pepper

Cut the carrots into thin discs, what my children call money carrots. Steam them until on the point of tenderness when spiked with a knife. Toast the cumin seeds in a dry frying pan until they begin to exude their signature smell, 1–2 minutes should do it. Crush them coarsely, not to a complete powder, in a pestle and mortar.

Melt the butter in a pan, throw in the cumin, stir, then throw in the carrots and toss vigorously to coat; you might need a smidgen more butter. Season with salt and pepper and serve.

# MEN AND THEIR BARBIES

WHAT IS IT ABOUT MEN AND THEIR BARBIES? Like some echo of a primeval ritual, man, robbed of his daily meat-seeking mission, cannot wait to find grill, griddle, rusty rack and tongs and set fire to a pyre of spherically cloned charcoal. It takes only the wateriest hint of summer sun before the fire is laid, lit, or, in true Betjemanesque-style, switched on, and even the most confirmed kitchen shirkers – the kind who act dumb when you ask them where they keep their whisk or potato masher – are out flaying, torching, turning whole sides of meat, cremating them out of their tiny skins. No man I know favours French-style pale flesh oozing its bloody juices on to the plate; nothing less than a burnt offering will do, and by that I mean Dickensian charnel house, a graveyard of blackened, sepulchral bones encrusted with charcoal, piled into a famine heap, to be ripped by teeth and fingers, every bone picked clean. And then there is the look, don't touch element. A man in charge of his barbecue is not looking for help, he's looking for an audience, preferably of eager, half-starved children, eyeing up the meat like a crow would carrion, then swooping down for the first scorching morsel.

It is a cool evening when we arrive at Mark's. We sit tight in the kitchen, threading spicy lamb, peppers and mushrooms on skewers, and hungrily trowelling hummus on to pitta bread. Mark throws us thick jackets and we head out into the dusk. His barbecue is bricked into the garden wall, smouldering with logs, the meat juices mingling with the damp, woody scent. We pull the hot flesh from the sticks, and tuck into comically elongated sausages; the children huddle round the table conspiratorially, Mark, Yseult and I atop the wall around the dying heat and light.

Two days later it is Harry's birthday. We leave for Ireland in the morning, but tonight there's a barbecue for 14. It is the afternoon before I have time to marinade the meat. Chicken thighs in fresh coriander, ginger and garlic, dowsed in a milky paste of coconut and Greek yoghurt. Cubed leg of lamb on a cocktail of roasted, ground spices scented with chilli and sticky lumps of lime chutney. Griddled, baked aubergines are turned into a smoky dipping sauce with roasted sesame paste, garlic, lemon juice and olive oil. Too late to soak the chick peas, I bring them to the boil, discard the water, and pour on more cold. Two hours later I will mulch them in their gluey liquor with more tahini, garlic, lemon juice and olive oil, then add a film of oil and smoked paprika to the top. Harry has ordered my white chocolate and raspberry tart, and I've made a flourless chocolate and raspberry cake. There is distant thunder, followed by a summer storm, the rain lashing down in vertical stair rods. When it clears, the children man the barbecue and the lager. The five teenage boys wrap the meat into wads of soft white roll, and fire ketchup into them. They eat as though it were the last supper, but that is a thrice daily occurrence. Miraculously, there is some of everything left to eat cold on the Irish Sea the next day. Thank God for a calm crossing.

# Curried Lamb Kebabs

MAKES 14 SKEWERFULS

1.5kg / 3lb lean cubed leg of organic lamb
1 tbsp cumin seeds
2 heaped tsp fennel seeds
2 heaped tsp coriander seeds
1 red chilli, seeded and finely chopped
3 cloves garlic
salt and pepper
1 whole jar of Geeta's lime and chilli chutney
2 large onions
4–5 dozen cherry tomatoes

Roast the three seeds together in a frying pan until they exude their characteristic toasty smell, a couple of minutes should do it. Throw them into a mortar, and grind them into a coarse powder, then add the chilli, garlic, salt and pepper, and grind them all down together.

Pour into a bowl with the lime chutney, stir together, then mix thoroughly into the meat. Leave covered with clingfilm in the fridge to marinade for as long as you have.

Peel the onions and cut them into chunks. Bring the meat to room temperature before you skewer it alternately with the onions and tomatoes. Barbecue according to your taste. The chunks of lime will crust delectably over the fire

# Smoky Aubergine Dip

This will make enough to accompany the lamb. If you don't have a griddle, just bake the aubergines in a hottish oven in their skins until soft when pierced with a knife, about an hour.

SERVES 6–8 AS AN ACCOMPANIMENT

2 large aubergines
2 tbsp tahini paste, I favour the organic Meridian one
olive oil
juice of one and half lemons
2 cloves garlic
salt and pepper

Griddle the aubergines until charred on all sides, then finish them off until softened in a roasting tin in the oven.

Skin them, and blitz them in a food processor with the tahini, a good 2–3 tablespoons of olive oil, the lemon juice, and the chopped garlic. Season and add more lemon juice, tahini or olive oil according to taste.

Turn into a small terrine to cool, then add a good splosh of green olive oil over the surface.

# THE PERFECT PEACH

Ask yourself this, how often is the gap between what you expect of a peach, a nectarine, an apricot and the thing itself, as yawning, as chasmic as the Channel Tunnel? We buy with our eyes, so the deception appears even more cruel. The beautiful, fecund fruit with its wine-dark skin, its velvet fuzz, striations of yellow, pink blush, conceals a dry, woolly interior that makes a mockery of the word ripe. And it probably declared itself Ready to Eat on the packet. Yet from Virgil's search for the 'downy peach' to the yearnings of Eliot's Prufrock, this is the fruit that has been most celebrated in the literature of both East and West.

Marks and Spencer's stone fruit buying policy sets exemplary standards; ripeness, flavour, quality, are all. If you happen upon a quartet of bullet-hard, juice-free fruit after reading this, I suggest you storm the portals and shout. There is one man responsible for peaches, apricots and their filial, fuzz-less side-kick, the nectarine, food technologist Peter Village. We meet at Marignane Airport, and it becomes immediately apparent that I am in the hands of that rare breed, the passionate expert. Peter has bought stone fruit for M and S for 30 years from all over the world, and has built up a network of outstanding growers from California to Canada, across the Antipodes, India, southern Europe and beyond to Morocco. 'I bring a world-wide view to the individual growers, and I bring the customers' view to them; that is the most important thing really. I am quite convinced that we operate the highest quality standards.'

Sixteen years ago, nobody in England bought peaches from France. Then Peter discovered Estagel, the Bois family's business, and they have worked together ever since. The Bois, fourth-generation fruit farmers, who followed the sun from their beginnings in a small, Ardèche valley to the flat, hot and Mistral-blown landscape of the Camargue at Nîmes, were 'looking for discerning customers,' Henri Pierre Bois tells me. His brother Christian continues, 'Marks and Spencer want the best peaches for the longest time possible. The climate and *terroir* are better here in the south, with the dryness and the heat; you need well-controlled irrigation, the Rhône valley descends right to Nîmes. We've just bought some more orchards in Portugal, so we can compete with Seville for early peaches now.'

We leave the lofty awning of ancient parasol pines, an avenue of which carves through the Bois orchards to the beautiful 17th-century stone house built round a central courtyard. Christian decants us into their experimental apricot orchard, where 1,700 varieties are being nurtured in short, squat rows, each tree different from the last. They vary from luminous scarlet and orange to pale gold with a speckled blush, from dry, tasteless, acid, tart – if an apricot feels hollow it will be dry – to one whose acid-sweet intense apricotness does it for my taste buds. Number 2458, I am promised, will be named after me if it lives up to its early promise. Time and fashion will tell.

So why is your peach, nectarine or apricot so often unyielding when it has left its golden bough? Simply because it has not been ripened for long enough on the tree. Why? Because most growers pick and pack by machine; it is quicker and cheaper, but it is at the expense of that most important element, flavour. The longer the fruit is left on the tree, the higher its sugar level, the better it will taste. Simple? Not quite. It can't be left until fully ripened, or it would get to the customer too late. 'We try to live dangerously,' Peter tells me, 'By picking when the fruit has the optimum sugar level, but you can still handle it without bruising. Its eating quality is established, but it will go on ripening.' Here at Estagel, the pickers pick each breed up to nine times over a ten-day period. That way you get the peach that splurts juice when you bite into it. Below the trees is a carpet of abandoned fruit, a glut of wasted beauty that didn't make the grade.

# White Fruit Summer Pudding

I dreamed this up on my return from Nîmes, a pudding glowing white and pale gold with waxy Napoleon cherries from Marks and Spencer, their white-fleshed nectarines and peaches, and some tart jewels of white currants, milky like moonstones. I made an intense raw raspberry sauce to pour over it.

SERVES 10

*450g / 1lb white cherries, pre-stoning weight*
*225g / 8oz white currants stripped from their stems with a fork*
*4 white nectarines and 2 peaches, or any combination thereof, plunged into boiling water for 30 seconds, skinned, then cut into about 6 slices per half*
*125g / 4oz vanilla sugar*
*thick white sliced day-old bread, the crusts removed*

Start the night before. Stone the cherries, and throw them into a heavy-bottomed pan with the white currants, nectarines and peaches. Strew over the sugar, turn the fruit gently, then let it bleed over a gentle heat until the juices run. About 2–3 minutes. The fruit should not begin to collapse or cook. Remove from the heat. Test the juice for sweetness, you may need a little more sugar, but do not over sweeten.

Line the bowl with the bread, fitting it tight as slates on a roof to prevent leaks. Spoon in the fruit, leaving the pink juices that collect at the bottom. Pour them into a jug to be kept for later. Cover with a layer of bread cut out to fit exactly, then fit a plate inside the top of the bowl, and put some weights on it to press the fruit down. Refrigerate overnight. Take the pudding out an hour before you want to eat it. Just before serving, turn it out on to a large plate, and pour over the peachy juices. Serve with the raw raspberry sauce on page 135 and cream.

# Baked Stuffed Peaches or Nectarines

I use white nectarines for this delicious dish. The gooey, almondy stuffing puffs up and spills out of the fruit cavity, then dies down to look like a peach stone.

SERVES 4

*4 nectarines, steeped in boiling water for a minute, then skinned and halved*
*65g / 2½oz amarettini de Saronno or amaretti*
*1–2 tbsp vanilla sugar*
*1 egg yolk*
*butter*

Preheat the oven to 160°C/325°F/Gas Mark 3. Enlarge the stone cavities, keeping the extra pulp and juice in a bowl. Crush the amarettini in a pestle and mortar, or in a plastic bag with a rolling pin. Tip the crumbs into the bowl with the extra fruit pulp, add the sugar and egg yolk, and pound together until it is a damp, coherent mass of stuffing. Heap it generously into the nectarine cavities so that it mounds over the fruit, then set the fruit halves in a greased gratin dish and bake for 45 minutes. Serve either warm or cold. I served mine warm with some cold raw raspberry sauce dribbled over the summit.

# Raw Raspberry Sauce

SERVES 10

*640g / 1 lb 6oz raspberries*
*2–3 tbsp golden icing sugar*
*lemon juice to taste*

Liquidize the raspberries thoroughly in a food processor, then put them through a nylon sieve. Sift over the first couple of spoons of icing sugar and whisk it in well. Add a good spritz of lemon, taste, and adjust sweet and sour accordingly.

# GOING HOME TO IRELAND

WHEN MY FATHER FIRST BROUGHT US HOME TO IRELAND, it was in one of the huge old tubs that plied its trade between Liverpool and Dublin, rolling uncontrollably across the Irish sea: my brother Daniel and I tramping the deck whey-faced until dawn as we shuddered through the swell. Our childhood summers in County Mayo were spent at the incomparable Old Head Hotel. We braved the icy Atlantic breakers, picnicked in the dunes of deserted strands on densely damp slices of soda bread and thick butter, shrimps we'd netted and cooked in sea water in old tin cans, and we fished, walked, rode and later danced in the parochial halls the length and breadth of the county. The place left its mark indelibly on both of us.

My father had left County Laois, his birthplace, as a young boy when his mother died, and had been reared in England; our introduction to his native land was to shape our childhood and our adulthood too. My brother's home is in County Wicklow now, and eight years ago I bought a cottage overlooking the still empty, desolate beaches of our childhood. An awesome, granite mountain behind, and a track up to it is flanked by densely hedged fuschia, dripping gouts of crimson petals through July and August, buzzing with bees and butterflies. The water comes from a turfy mountain stream across a field behind the house, and I have spent several years ridding the house of such delights as a fungus-filled bath planted straight on an earth floor, a leaky flat-roofed extension, and fighting an unwinable war against the salt and damp that blows straight off the Atlantic and raids and invades, despite dehumidifier, central heating and turf fires.

No one holidays here for the Mediterranean climate, for the predictably clear blue skies. The unpredictable weather is as unchangeable as it ever was, but what has changed, dramatically, is the food. Twenty years ago all that grew or could be bought was heads of cabbage, turnips, carrots, potatoes and onions, local mountain lamb, and whatever fish you could catch. The lorries from Dublin brought anaemic apples, pears and oranges and little else besides, but now there is a renaissance of growers and producers who neither discard the age-old traditions of home baking, butter churning, curing, brining, salting and preserving, nor remain stuck in a sepia-toned time warp. There is a vibrant culinary enterprise culture here in the west that friends tell me exists across the country. It is vibrant in terms of its energy, its originality and its cross pollination, the result of the 'blow-ins'– foreigners who have moved here from Germany, Holland, France and England – meeting the natives and espousing each other's food traditions, adapting them, changing them, refining them.

Of course there are other important factors. Ireland is still a largely rural population. Many areas are isolated, miles from villages let alone towns. Providing the ingredients for food for the family table is still part of the way of life, shopping for it subsidiary. Cakes of soda bread and scones are baked daily with buttermilk from the kitchen pail. Cheese making has begun to flourish again over the last 20 years, most producers starting in their kitchens. In a land where famine haunted generations, where there was never enough food to preserve for the lean months, the new culture of abundance is hard to adopt, memories of the lean years hard to shrug off.

The climate makes one crave carbohydrates and large quantities of meat. Sweet mountain lamb, fattened on the lusher pastures of the midlands; beef with its crust of ivory fat; the most traditional meat of all, the pig – few families were without one pre-famine times, but the house pig has become a thing of the past, an exception rather than a rule.

Westport being 25 miles away, the weekly shopping trip is supplemented by the generosity of my neighbours. This morning a bounty bag of freshly dug tiny carrots and onions from Tommy and Mary next door – they had my strawberry tart a couple of days ago. Mary has instigated a tradition that we would be loath to give up. After heaving across the Irish Sea in the new fastest ferry we regulars call the vomit comet, and the long drive either side of it, we head straight for her house where there's a vat of boiled bacon and cabbage awaiting us, blipping gently on the stove, the cabbage stewing gently in the juices from the meat. The potatoes are mashed in the pot on the floor, and Mary cuts juicy thick tranches of tender meat, and builds a Berlin Wall around them. The simplest of ingredients, simply prepared, and the first good dinner on Irish soil.

# Brown Soda Bread

This recipe comes from my oldest friend Merci, whose husband John has mussel rafts

MAKES A 450G / 1LB LOAF

175g / 6oz coarse stoneground wholewheat flour

275g / 10oz organic wholewheat flour

1 heaped tsp bicarbonate of soda

1 tsp molasses sugar

25g / 1oz butter

500–600ml / 16–20fl oz buttermilk

Preheat the oven to 230°C / 450°F / Gas Mark 8. Mix all the dry ingredients together with your hands, lightly rubbing in the butter.

Make a well in the centre, and add about 500ml / 16fl oz of the buttermilk. Working with a knife, from the centre, gather the mixture to make a soft, wet dough. You may have to add more buttermilk to make the mixture 'sticky wet'.

Grease a 450g / 1lb round or oblong loaf tin, spoon in the dough, and bake for 30 minutes. Cover the top with greaseproof paper and bake for a further 10–15 minutes.

Turn out on to a wire rack, and cover with a tea towel. Leave to cool before attempting to cut it.

# Monkfish wrapped in Parma Ham

SERVES 6

*1kg / 2½lb monk tails, cut into*
*5cm / 2in chunks, about*
*3 per person*
*a sprig of rosemary, very finely*
*chopped*
*2 tbsp olive oil*
*a spritz of lemon*
*200g / 7oz finely sliced Parma ham*
*3 or 4 bay leaves*
*12 cherry tomatoes*
*salt and pepper*

Preheat the oven to 220°C/425°F/Gas Mark 7. Heat the olive oil gently in a small pan, and when warmed, add the rosemary. Cook for about 30 seconds, you want it to soften slightly but not to brown.

Remove the oil from the heat, squeeze on a bit of lemon juice, and brush over the monkfish chunks as you go, seasoning them, and wrapping them up in their Parma ham parcels. Tuck them tightly together in a gratin dish, stew the bay leaves and the tomatoes you've rolled in a bit of extra olive oil on top, and bake for 15–20 minutes. Insert a skewer, and if they're just unresistant they're cooked. Dish up, pour over the fishy juices. We ate ours with Pommes Anna (see page 140) and a dish of young leeks baked in red wine and olive oil.

# Pommes Anna

SERVES 3–4

*675g / 1 ½lb peeled, thinly sliced
potatoes*
*85–125g / 3–4oz unsalted butter,
melted*
*sea salt*
*black pepper*

I cook this deliciously simple dish in a cast-iron, heavy-bottomed, stubby-handled frying pan that goes in the oven. Traditionally it should be lidded, mine isn't, so I use greased greaseproof paper.

Preheat the oven to 200°C/400°F/Mark Gas 6.

Wash the starch out of the potatoes in a colander, pat dry in a cloth, and place them in overlapping circles on the well-buttered base of the pan. Brush butter over each layer as you go, and season. Cover with greaseproof paper or a lid and cook in the oven. Check with a skewer after 45 minutes, but they can take up to an hour.

# Sugar-Topped Morello Cherry Pie

Morellos are almost impossible to find in England, they obviously all end up bottled or jammed. Use the best-flavoured fresh cherries you can find as an alternative.

SERVES 6

SHORTCRUST PASTRY
*225g / 8oz organic white flour*
*125g / 4oz unsalted butter*

FOR THE FILLING:
*750g / 1¾lb morello cherries,*
*pre-stoned weight*
*3 tbsp sour cherry fruit syrup.*
*I bought a bottle of Austrian*
*D'Arbo syrup in the supermarket;*
*worth it to intensify the flavour*
*1 tbsp Kirsch*
*2 dsrtsp cornflour*
*vanilla sugar to taste*
*1 egg, separated*
*1 tbsp demerara sugar*

Make a basic shortcrust pastry in the usual way. Refrigerate for half an hour before rolling out a slightly bigger half, and lining your greased pie dish.

Macerate the stoned cherries in the syrup, Kirsch and a couple of tablespoons of vanilla sugar, turning occasionally, until they have released their juices. An hour or two will do. Check the juice for sweetness, and add a bit more if you need to, remember, the cherries are tart.

Preheat the oven to 200°C/400°F/Gas Mark 6. Brush the base of the pie with the egg white. Spoon a couple of tablespoons of the cherry liquor over the cornflour you have sieved into a small bowl, and stir until completely dissolved. Return it to the cherries, and pour the whole lot into the pie dish. Cover with a pastry lid, crimp the edges, and brush a glaze of beaten egg over the surface. Make a small incision in the middle to let the steam escape, and bake for about 35 minutes. We ate ours warm with clotted cream, the ripe fruit coated in the thickened purple syrup.

# WESTPORT COUNTRY MARKET

'THE MAN GET OUTS HAVE ARRIVED,' a lad announced when Brid MacAuley turned up at the shop with her mangetouts. Another customer returned to Brid's market stall the following week clearly unacquainted with the French term 'eat all,' accusing her of selling pealess pods. Despite Brid's exhortations, the lady remained unconvinced, 'I couldn't find a pea in any one of them.' The food revolution is recent to the west of Ireland, but Westport, my local town, is selling things it wouldn't have even dreamed of a decade ago.

On the half acre of land which she and her partner Christy Smith bought with their house 13 years ago, and a further rented half acre abutting it, Brid supplies organic vegetables and herbs to the Westport Country Market and to local shops, restaurants and supermarket. They were clueless when they started. 'People said "they'll be gone within a year." I was out clutching these great Royal Horticultural Society books, and Chris, being an engineer, was planting everything exactly 6 inches apart and half an inch down.' Precision engineering translated into rows of impeccably hand-dug raised beds, and the erection of five poly-tunnels, to do permanent battle with the recalcitrant elements of the west, an oft brutal climate of tearing gales and lashing rain.

The first three years were as brutal as the weather. 'We could see the demand was there, particularly for the herbs; no one else was doing it. In 1987 I got together with five or six other local women, and we thought up the idea of having a country market in Westport. Twelve years later we still have 15 of the original members.'

On Thursday mornings in the town hall, at the southerly end of the beautiful octagon, the ladies bring in their duck eggs, hens and hand-churned country butter; their home-baked, gently oozing rhubarb tarts, sturdy loaves of soda and yeast breads, sourdough, scones, cakes and sticky cinnamon buns; bright bouquets of primary-coloured flowers, jams, and Brid's organic vegetables.

'The sad thing is, we're the only serious organic growers in Mayo now, fewer and fewer are going into it; they go into sheep and cattle, but no one wants to work on the land anymore. It's disastrous trying to get workers, the locals don't want to do it, and the land is in decline. Animal farmers are deeply demoralized at the moment. I go round giving talks, and the first question people ask is "What grants did you get?" They don't believe you can make a living out of it.'

Brid keeps prices roughly in line with the local supermarket, saying, 'If a supermarket lettuce is 5p cheaper, I think of it like this: you often have to cut half of it away, there is no waste in an organic one; it is unsprayed and hasn't been on the road for days. They're cut the morning we sell them and are still fresh a week later if you keep them in the fridge. Generally the standard of fruit and vegetables here is poor. The way forward for the west of Ireland, where agriculture is in a state of chaos, would be for local communities to start up community vegetable gardens. It's happening in the States. Ten people get together to buy a couple of acres, employ someone to do the growing, share in the profits and get their own vegetables off the land. Look at the land lying idle here.'

In the lean, turn-of-the-year months, there is only spinach and leeks to sell. The pressure is on in the summer months, when Chris works from 6am to 10pm, six days a week. 'He is completely committed,' Brid says. 'It's not just a living, it's a way of life, and for Chris it's an ideological thing, caring for the environment. Me, I want to know can we afford to go on holiday this year.'

March down the serried ranks of perfectly spaced green lettuces with their gaudy purple frills, the Peter Rabbit rows of crisp green cos, the tumbling branches of courgettes with the great trumpets of gold flowers, the tunnels of exotica; roof-high cherry tomatoes dangling like so many earrings, dark-ridged cucumbers, pendulous on their thin stems, clumps of wavy-leaved rocket and aromatic thyme, fronds of mizuna, and you will see nature more successfully nurtured against the elements than you ever did. If they ever had the time, Brid and Chris should take a look at their handiwork and admire it.

# Iced Almond and Garlic Soup

This is a deliciously creamy-cold, absolutely white soup I made with organic garlic and country market white bread. It dates back over 1,000 years to when the Moors ruled much of Spain.

SERVES 4

*225g / 8oz white day-old bread, crusts cut off*
*2 cloves new season's garlic, peeled*
*salt*
*2–3 tbsp olive oil*
*2 tbsp sherry vinegar or white wine tarragon vinegar*
*125g / 4oz organic Spanish almonds; Rapunzel is a good brand*
*600ml / 1 pint fridge-cold water*
*a handful of seedless green grapes*

Process the almonds until ground. Wet the bread, then squeeze it out. Tear it into chunks and throw it in the blender with the chopped garlic, salt and olive oil. Purée, then add the vinegar and almonds, and slowly pour in the cold water with the blender running. Process until smooth and creamy. Refrigerate for several hours, then ladle into bowls and toss in a few grapes.

# Aromatic Chicken with Potato, Rocket and Thyme Stuffing

The run-around hens from the country market tend to be a bit tough, so I make an aromatic thyme butter and spread it under the bird's skin. The stuffing is made with delicious cubes of fried potatoes, breadcrumbs, olives and lemon rind, as well as thyme and rosemary.

SERVES 4

*1½ kg / 3lb chicken*
*1 tbsp fresh thyme, chopped*
*50g / 2oz unsalted butter*
*a squeeze of lemon*
*salt and pepper*
*1 onion, thinly sliced*

*FOR THE STUFFING:*
*1 onion, finely chopped*
*8–9 small cloves of*
*new garlic, peeled*
*2 medium potatoes,*
*cut in small dice*
*1 tbsp fresh thyme*
*½ tbsp rosemary*
*4 black and 8 green olives, more*
*black would be overwhelming*
*a handful of breadcrumbs*
*8 rocket leaves*
*the rind of a lemon*
*butter and olive oil*

Preheat the oven to 200°C/400°F/Gas Mark 6.

Make the aromatic butter by mashing the butter, chopped thyme and a squeeze of lemon well together, season it and gently spread it with your fingers under the skin of the breast and legs.

Heat about 25g/1oz of butter gently in a frying pan, add the chopped onion, finely diced potato and whole garlic cloves, and sauté until softened and translucent. Add the herbs and olives, stir to coat. Then add a tablespoon of olive oil, throw in the breadcrumbs, and continue cooking until they are crisply golden and coating the potatoes. Test the potatoes with a skewer, they should remain cubed and be almost cooked through. Finally, add the rocket, coarsely chopped, for a few seconds. Take off the heat, add the lemon rind, season, and stuff the hen!

Place it on its side on the sliced onion in a roasting tin, squeeze on a bit of lemon juice, season, and roast for 20 minutes. Repeat on its other side for a further 20 minutes, then turn it breast up for the final 20 minutes, basting it with the juices, and sprinkling it with sea salt. Leave to rest for 10–15 minutes, then carve. The pan juices will give you enough unctuously sticky brown gravy. I served mine with Brid's broccoli and green beans.

# Plum and Hazelnut Pudding Cake

This is a sort of triple-decker cake, with the plums poached inside it, and a deliciously crunchy, sugary spiced glaze.

MAKES A 22CM/9IN CAKE

85g/3oz softened butter
85g/3oz sugar
150g/5oz organic white flour
1 tsp baking powder
pinch of salt
2 organic eggs, beaten
2 tbsp milk
50g/2oz ground hazelnuts
a dozen good, not overripe red plums

FOR THE TOPPING:
50g/2oz butter
65g/2½oz demerara sugar
1½ tsp allspice
2 beaten eggs

Preheat oven to 180°C/350°F/Gas Mark 4

Butter a 22cm/9in springform cake tin, and line the bottom with greased baking parchment.

Beat the softened butter and sugar together well, until light and creamy. Sift the flour, baking powder and a pinch of salt into a bowl. Whisk the eggs and milk together in a bowl, and beat them alternately with the flour into the creamed butter. Spoon into the cake tin, and sprinkle with the ground hazelnuts. Halve and stone the plums, and arrange them cut side up in concentric circles.

For the topping, melt the butter, stir in the sugar and spice, and amalgamate. Cool slightly, then whisk in the beaten eggs. Pour this over the plums and bake in the oven for about an hour and ten minutes, but test with a skewer after an hour, it should come clean even in the middle. Serve warm with thick cream.

# THE SHERIDAN BROTHERS, CHEESEMONGERS

SWITCHBACKING THROUGH THE MOUNTAINS, on a drive that could only be measured in Irish miles, we head for Galway's Saturday market. A long alley of stalls, from old barrels covered in planks of wood, to sophisticated canopied constructions, snakes down the side of the Protestant church. If you had to define the difference between this, and, say, a French or English market, it would be in terms of its Europeanism, each national identity preserved in the foods it has grown, produced and baked. Dutch, German, French, English, Irish. There is Willem with his charcoal brazier of fatly delicious homemade sausages reeking of garlic, and his oily lengths of smoked eel; hand-made fresh goat cheeses rolled in rosemary and wheels of Dutch cheeses; there are tiny Punch and Judy style booths with bubbling vats of sludge-thick vegetable curry and samosas; a stall with black iron griddles and lacey tossed pancakes; a Provençale tableau of olives, basil, all things sun-dried, honey and lavender; a German stall of sesame-seeded loaves and plaited milk breads next to piles of organic vegetables and Rachel Parry's bread stall, an object lesson in how to turn a famine into a feast.

The next door stall belongs to Kevin and Seamus Sheridan, who are double-handedly bringing about a cheese renaissance in Ireland and England. When a deli-owning friend couldn't shift his cheese, Kevin brought the Colooney, Gubeen and Laverstown to market and, with the aid of a cheese knife to let the locals taste his wares, sold the lot. Kevin had trained as a sculptor, older brother Seamus as a chef. 'I didn't have a notion about cheese, we learned as we went along, building up the stall, visiting all the producers and getting to know their cheeses, and travelling to England.' Both brothers are passionate about washed-rind cheeses, and convinced that the Irish climate is ideally suited to their maturation. 'Ireland is one big cave, particularly in the west. The humidity, the salt, the rain, it's like the cheeses are living in caves, we don't need cellars like the French. Cheeses tend to fit into their environment, and Ireland is perfect for the washed rinds. Milleens, Durrus, Ardrahan and Gubbeen, they need a lot of humidity. A good mean temperature and salt to kill off the bloom and black moulds. We're setting up a creamery in Meath for maturing cheese. There is no infrastructure for it at the moment like the *affineurs* in France, so everything here is sold pretty immature. The small dairies don't have the space. Most small producers are women who started off making cheese just for the family with the excess milk from the kitchen pail so as not to waste it.'

This renaissance has been a long time coming, and Kevin has a theory about it. 'The monks were big producers in medieval times, making cheese, smoked foods, preserving food in the winter. When the monasteries went, so did the learning and the knowledge of how to do it. Ireland was full of poor communities where there was no summer abundance, so there was nothing to store, no preserving, just fish and spuds.

I see the whole supermarket thing as a blip in the history of food, think how short a time they've been going. I'm optimistic about food in Ireland, the worse it gets the better it gets. People don't appreciate something until they nearly can't get it; that's what brings about a renaissance, and that's what's happening now.'

If there is a dark Irish cloud on the horizon, it's over pasteurization. Kevin fears there might not be any unpasteurized cow's cheeses here within the year. The high incidence of TB in cows has meant a new food safety authority being set up to protect consumers. Each herd is tested every six months, but if there's just one reactor, all cheeses made in the last six months have to be destroyed, and there is no compensation. This is despite the fact that it actually takes six months for the udders to become infected, and that is when the milk becomes infected. Kevin has searched for scientific proof that TB can survive the cheese-making process, but can't find any. 'It's never been found in any cheese. The acidity in the cheese means no infection can even survive two months, but everyone is sitting on a time-bomb here, and the bigger the cheese-maker the harder they are going to fall, they have so much money tied up in stock. It's no use waiting and seeing, or saying "I reckon", we have to talk to the food scientists and get hard evidence.'

Here is Kevin's lore on some of the washed-rind cheeses. All, he believes, take on something of the character of their producers!

Milleens. 'Comes from southwest tip of the Beara peninsula, from Castletown Bear in West Cork. It is made by the Steele Normans. Wild would be the word I'd use, it's most like a French washed-rind cheese, with its vibrant orange rind. It has a big smell like Munster, and a really spicy, tangy flavour. It's wild and unpredictable just like the people who make it! It tastes best when the cows are out from April to October, not eating silage. There's a first growth in spring, and a second in the autumn.'

Gubeen. 'This one comes from Schull in West Cork, from Tom and Giana Ferguson. It's a pasteurized cheese with an unpasteurized rind, one of the best and most consistent, and really well made. There's a lot of work in the ripening, it's light and calm – as they are.'

Durrus. 'Comes from Geffa Bates at Bantry, another small producer. It's made in a copper vat. It's so delicate and complex, so long a flavour, it's a masterpiece. It's subtle like a good Reblochon, made with extremely high quality unpasteurized milk. It's a pale beigey pink with a silky texture, nearly as good in winter as in summer.'

Ardrahan. 'From Mary Burns in North Cork. She makes it how you'd make brown bread, hands on, she's a pure Cork woman. Quite tough. It is earthy, clayey, very deep and gutsy, and whatever the positive word for inconsistent is. It has a rusty brown-red rind.'

# Cos Lettuce with Cashel Blue and a Cream Dressing

Cashel Blue is a richly creamy blue Irish cheese, fudgy textured with no hint of bitterness. It is delicious crumbled into this salad of cos hearts.

1 tsp French mustard
1 tsp sugar
2 tsp tarragon vinegar
a scrap of crushed garlic
1 hard-boiled egg, white and yolk separated
200–250ml / 7–8fl oz double cream
2 dsrtsp chives, chopped
125–175g / 4–6oz Cashel Blue
2 heads of cos lettuce, outer leaves removed; keep them for soup

Stir the first four ingredients together in a bowl with the egg yolk, then stir in the cream. Thin with a bit of milk or water if it has thickened too much.

Pour cold over the washed lettuce, then scatter over the chopped egg white, chives and coarsely crumbled Cashel Blue.


# Cucumber Soup

A perfect, mild-mannered, delicate soup to serve before or with a selection of Irish cheeses for lunch or supper.

SERVES 6

1 medium onion finely chopped
50g / 2oz butter
2 organic cucumbers
2 scant tsp flour
1.7 litre / 3 pints good jellied chicken stock
2 egg yolks
2 tbsp cream
flat-leaf parsley, chopped

Peel the cucumbers and chop them into dice. Stew the onion gently in the butter in a lidded saucepan for a few minutes, then throw in the cucumber, stir, cover, and continue to stew for about 10 minutes until tender. Liquidize.

Beat the egg yolks with a couple of tablespoons of thick cream in a small bowl. Add a ladle of the soup and whisk it in, then return the mixture to the pan. Heat through gently but do not boil. Serve with a twist of parsley in each bowl.

# JOHN KILCOYNE, MUSSEL MAN

WHEN JOHN KILCOYNE WENT TO SECONDARY SCHOOL IN WESTPORT in the early '60s, from the little village of Kilsallagh ten miles away, the big farmers described country people such as himself as 'herring chokers'. 'Just as shellfish were seen as poor people's food,' John says. 'That attitude is going, but it's not gone. I believe about 80 per cent of Ireland's population lives within five miles of the sea, but I'm still exporting most of my mussels to France. Of the 150 tons a year I produce, only 10 tons is taken up by local restaurants, and it was hard enough to convince people of their better quality.

'I was always interested in fishing, and I would have been watching it as a possible way of life. Various state organizations involved in aquaculture funded some research on the Spanish system of rafts and ropes where mussels are suspended off the bottom, it was seen as good employment for the Gaeltacht (Irish speaking) areas. They did research here in Killary, and identified it as a perfect mussel hatchery and growing area, with a good mix of saline water and fresh water running off the mountains, depth, good tides with movement to wash away the effluent, and reasonably sheltered conditions. The essential is a good mix of salt and fresh water for the phytoplankton on which the mussels feed. A few of us decided to put out some rafts in our spare time, and within a couple of years we had our first good commercial crop.'

What I find extraordinary, is that mussel farming in Ireland didn't get off the sea bed sooner, so to speak. The Spanish have used rafts for 500 years, and the French Bouchot system in northern Brittany, of great wooden stakes driven into the sea bed, goes back even further, and was initiated by an Irishman who was shipwrecked there. So, a decade ago, John went full-time to sea, and 'Set out to make a fortune by mussels; fairly quickly disillusioned by that, but I stayed with it. It sounds like a terrible cliché, but you're working in such proximity with nature. The problems make it more fascinating, the weather, the physical work; you're dealing with a living organism and you have to treat it with respect. We're up against algal blooms, but they're natural occurrences, the challenge is not to beat them but to live with them.

'The great satisfaction is of working on the sea and with the sea to produce what is a top quality food. You're out in a northwesterly wind with steep waves banging the boat about, but that's not a minus. I wouldn't want to miss the moods, grey clouds, blue clouds, a gale blowing.'

Not being fully acquainted with the sex life of *Mytilus edulis*, the indigenous gentian-shelled bi-valve in question, John explains the fertilization process, 'They don't have sex in the conventional sense, anyone who knows what a mussel looks like would figure that one out. Spawning takes place around April, when the females release their eggs, and the males their sperm, into the water. Three weeks later the larvae emerge, and three weeks after that they become spat. I can tell when the spawning has happened, the mussel meat is very spent looking, and the gonad is transparent. We hang the collectors down, coiled near the surface, when they're ready to settle.'

In a few weeks, the spat, like black beads of glistening sand, attach themselves by their byssus threads, or beard. I had always wondered why mussels were bearded. They have tiny suction cups which secrete glue with which they attach themselves, and John informs me that one company has sunk millions into trying to reproduce this and make a superglue for underwater use.

'I'm constantly learning about these animals, I've given up forcing them to grow in the time and conditions and densities that I want them to grow in,' John says. 'That way you don't produce quality. I've stood back from my own superiority and observed how they do well for themselves.'

# Killary Bay Mussel Chowder

A milky, saffrony broth with soft, salty-sweet mussels and crispy bacon.

SERVES 6

3kg / 6½lb mussels
150ml / 5fl oz dry white wine
large pinch of saffron threads
50g / 2oz butter
2 medium potatoes
2 sticks celery and 2 leeks
50g / 2oz plain flour
900ml / 1½ pints milk
1 bay leaf
125g / 4oz smoked streaky bacon
flat-leaf parsley, chopped

Clean and de-beard the mussels. Heat the wine in a large saucepan, throw in the mussels and cook briefly until the shells open. Take them out of their shells, putting all the juice back into the pan. Add the saffron to the hot liquid.

Cut the potatoes into small cubes and finely chop the celery and leeks. Melt the butter in a saucepan, add the potatoes, celery and leeks, sprinkle with flour, turning the vegetables to coat, then stir in the mussel liquor and milk. Add the bay leaf, season and let simmer until the vegetables are just tender.

Fry the bacon until crisp, then drain and chop. Add the mussels and fried bacon to the mussel liquor mixture, scatter with a handful of chopped flat-leaf parsley, and serve in bowls.

# La Mouclade

A creamily curried dish, good on its own as a starter, or with rice as a main course.

SERVES 4

a good pinch of saffron
1.8kg / 4lb mussels, cleaned
25g / 1oz butter
125ml / 4fl oz dry white wine
1 small onion, finely chopped
2 cloves garlic, finely chopped
1 tsp good curry powder
1 tsp ground celery seed, celery salt
will do if you don't have it
2 tbsp Cognac
1 scant dsrtsp flour
250ml / 8fl oz double cream
flat-leaf parsley or coriander
salt and pepper

Put the saffron in a bowl with a tablespoon of hot water. Put the mussels and wine into a pan, cover, and cook until they open. Put them in a colander over a bowl, and catch all the juice in it, then keep the mussels warm.

Melt the butter in a saucepan, add the onion, garlic, flour and spices, and cook gently for 2–3 minutes. Add the cream, simmer again for a couple of minutes, season and pour the sauce over the mussels. Scatter with the parsley or coriander and serve with rice, bread or on their own.

# Mussels with a Red Pepper Sambal

A delicious cold dish of mussels to eat with drinks, ice cold Fino or white wine.

SERVES 4

450g / 1lb mussels, cleaned
125ml / 4fl oz dry white wine
½ red pepper, seeded
2–3 inches of cucumber
a spritz of lemon
a dusting of paprika
salt and pepper

Heat the wine in a pan and cook the mussels covered until the shells open. Remove the top shells, and put two mussels into each half shell, putting all the mussel liquor back into the pan. Reduce this down to about 4 tablespoons of juice, season, and add lemon juice to taste. Seed the red pepper and chop into minute doll-sized pieces. Skin and seed the cucumber and chop as the pepper. Scatter the pepper and cucumber over the mussels on their serving dish, and brush over the juice. Chill , then sprinkle a tiny pinch of paprika or chilli over them.

# THE MUSSEL STORY A YEAR ON

ALTHOUGH IRELAND IS A MARITIME NATION, it might as well be landlocked it is becoming so difficult to find good fresh fish. Crayfish, lobsters and crabs head for Spain or France, as do the scallops, turbot and mussels. We catch petrolly glazed mackerel chased inshore by the dolphins in summer, and the bony 'cole fish', which we know as pollack. Each year I anticipate a sack of plump mussels from John Kilcoyne's rafts in Killary Harbour, Ireland's only fjord, that is the huge watery divide between counties Mayo and Galway. This year I haven't tasted as much as a single succulent bivalve. The bay is closed; mussel farming is in crisis all round the Irish coast, and if the Department of the Marine or the EU don't rouse themselves into revised legislation soon, there will be no mussel fishermen in Ireland. My fear is that as we are talking about only 100 people, including rope farmers and bottom dredgers around the coast, the ministry for obfuscation and delay will do what they do best. After all, 100 votes in one constituency would hardly be important, but across the country constitute no political clout whatsoever.

The story is as follows: in 1996 a new toxin was discovered in Killary Harbour. Up until then, the species of algae that caused DSp – diarrhoeic shellfish poisoning – was a summer phenomenon, so the weekly testing was stopped at the end of September. 'The term toxin is a bit frightening to the public,' John Kilcoyne says. 'It is not due to massive pollution; it's a perfectly natural phenomenon. Filter-feeding shellfish feed on a range of microscopic plants which float in sea water. At times some of the phytoplankton increase in number, and at the increased level they can be toxic to human beings. It requires monitoring. I wouldn't produce shellfish without it.'

To guarantee public health, a 'bio assay test' was carried out on mice, and if they survived six hours, the mussels were deemed safe for human consumption. But in 1998, in response to a complaint from the French authorities on the basis of some people getting ill, which has never been proven to be directly from Irish mussels, the French demanded that all mussels imported from Ireland should be tested over 24 hours. The French and Spanish operate a seven-hour test; the English five hours and the Dutch six hours, but the Irish went further and imposed the 24-hour test even on their home market. The impact is decimating this fragile industry.

'Look, I wouldn't even mind a ten-hour test,' John continues, 'On the results we've had over the past 12 months we would have had the bay closed for only two weeks. As it is, it has been closed for eight months over the last year. No one is going to get poisoned, and no one is going to eat Irish mussels. Between '96 and '98 when we operated the six-hour test no one was poisoned and there were no closures. My business was largely with local restaurants. I'd a personal relationship with all of them. I'd a daily reaction to the mussels, and I'd have known if there was a problem within 24 hours. Our problem is a combination of French distrust of food production that isn't their own, and a terrible weakness of our own authorities, the Department of the Marine. The nature of the industry in France is that a lot of mussel producers also import and distribute. If they block imports, it makes their own product more valuable. What we want is a European standard that applies to everyone. The Department of the Marine should be one of the most important departments in the Irish Government. We've a huge coastline, it's a major natural asset, but they are understaffed and they're not fighting for us.'

John's recent trip to England with a van full of Killary mussels met with considerable success. Portland Shellfish and several other specialist markets who want particularly good-quality mussels wanted to do business with him. 'The irony is, if they'd done two tests back to back with the British regulations, we'd have passed. I had two years of the six-hour test and there was no problem, but I now see people getting ill with the 24-hour test because it isn't being policed properly. Some irresponsible people are falsifying the tests, they're the ones who need policing.'

On the border between Northern and Southern Ireland, the British side of Carlingford Lough and The Foyle are dredging away happily, while the southern Irish section of the bay is closed down.

If the EU were to put a sensible structure in place, John and his colleagues would be saved. 'We've written to MEPs to start lobbying. I think the British authorities respect their shellfish industry, and when it comes for them to have their say, they're not going to campaign for a 24-hour test, but one based on their knowledge and experience.' In the meanwhile, John can only continue the backbreaking work of thinning growing mussels on the ropes in the daunting weather that bruises and buffets this coast, wild storms rearing up cruelly out of the finest and clearest of days. This year he has harvested only 40 tons out of a possible 150. And if the Department of the Marine procrastinates any further, his and the livelihood of all Ireland's mussel fishermen will lie in ruins, and the country will see the end of what it should be known for across Europe, the juiciest, most yielding, salt-sweet flesh of their native mussels.

# Ginger Biscuits

Perfect for the aftershock of swimming in the Atlantic breakers, or for any warming tea time

225g / 8oz caster sugar
125g / 4oz butter
1 tbsp golden syrup
225g / 8oz plain flour
2 tsp cinnamon
1 level tsp ground ginger
1 tsp bicarbonate of soda
1 small egg

Cream the butter with the sugar until light and fluffy. Add the egg, then the syrup and beat together well.

Mix the dry ingredients with the sieved flour and amalgamate well with the egg mixture. Knead into a lump, then break off walnut-sized pieces, roll into a ball, and place on a greased baking tin. This quantity makes about 30 biscuits. Bake for about 45 minutes in a slow oven, or until golden brown. Remove and leave to cool a minute before transferring to a rack to cool further.

# Gooseberry and Elderflower Tart

A truly tart tart, with scented gooseberries bursting on the tongue. No soggy pastry if you sugar the bottom layer of pastry, add a spoon of potato flour, and preheat a baking sheet to cook it on.

SERVES 6

shortcrust pastry (see page 142)
500g / 1 and a bit lb gooseberries
125–175g / 4–6oz caster or soft brown sugar, depending on the sweetness of your tooth
a slug of elderflower cordial, Rock's make the best one
1 tbsp potato flour
25g / 1oz butter, cut small
milk
1 egg, beaten
demerara sugar

Preheat the oven and a baking sheet to 180°C / 350°F / Gas Mark 4. Divide the pastry into two halves, one slightly bigger than the other. Roll out the bigger piece and line a shallow, greased dish, leaving some overhang. Sprinkle some sugar over the surface, then throw in the gooseberries. Sprinkle over the potato flour, the rest of the sugar and the elderflower cordial, then dot with the butter. Roll out the remaining piece of pastry for the lid, place it over the top, then seal with a fork all round the edges. Cut a cross in the middle through which the steam can escape, brush with beaten egg, then scatter a bit of demerara sugar over the surface. Place on the hot baking sheet and cook for about 25 minutes. Turn the heat down a bit and continue to cook for another 20–25 minutes until golden and bubbling. Cool for at least 15 minutes, then serve with clotted or Jersey cream, or homemade custard.

# Baked Mackerel

I hesitate to offer so simple a recipe, but think of this in the way of a reminder. Now is the time of year when the mackerel are being chased inshore in shoals, and are oily, firm fleshed and a treat for the children if filleted after cooking – mine insist on mashed potatoes to soak up the juices. Buy mackerel only if they look shiny and rainbow coloured, then have them gutted but not beheaded. I find butter makes them less oily than olive oil, so I put a walnut-sized knob of it on each fish, spritz them with lemon, stuff a few parsley stalks into the cavities, then salt and black pepper them. An average mackerel needs 15 minutes cooked in this way in a roasting tin, at 190°C/375°F/Gas Mark 5. Baste once with the buttery juices. If you insist on saucing them, a couple of handfuls of sharp, lemony sorrel cooked gently and quickly in a bit of butter is perfect. Acidity is the key. If you are feeling brave, spread a bit of lime pickle over the skin 2–3 minutes before the end of cooking time, and whack the fish under the grill until it bubbles!

# Picnic Omelette

This is something to improvise with. Add a layer of spinach, whisk the eggs with cheese, add any herbs you fancy. I make mine in a 22cm/9in nonstick frying pan. Can be eaten hot or cold, but warm on a picnic is just perfect.

FOR 3–4

3 onions, peeled, thinly sliced, salted and gently cooked in olive oil until thoroughly softened
50g/2oz butter
6 large organic eggs
4 medium potatoes, steamed in their skins, cooled then peeled and sliced into 1cm/½in discs
2 tbsp basil, chopped
2 tbsp chives, chopped
salt and pepper

Make a base layer of onions and knobs of butter in the pan. Then put in your layer of potatoes, followed by the fresh herbs. Season.

Whisk the eggs well with a good scrunch of pepper – you could use 8 if you are 4 people, and pour them over the top. Set the pan over a low flame to cook.

When the eggs are completely set – mine took 15 minutes – season with salt, flip the omelette over onto a large dish and slide it back into the pan to brown the underside for a minute or two. Take off the heat and leave to rest until warm rather than hot. Tip your creation onto a sheet of foil lined with greaseproof paper if you are heading for the blue yonder, or slip onto a plate and serve.

# Cheese and Thyme Scones

I serve these with the Roast Cherry Tomato Soup on page 160. They form a delicious crusty lattice of russet-coloured baked cheese on top, and are suitably filling and strong flavoured enough to stand up to the broth. Start making them half an hour before the soup is ready.

MAKES 12 SCONES

225g / 8oz organic strong
white flour
1 tbsp baking powder
40g / 1 ½oz butter
pinch of sea salt
125g / 4oz good strong Cheddar,
Montgomery is the best
1 tsp English mustard powder
2 tsp fresh thyme leaves
pinch of cayenne pepper
150ml / 5fl oz of milk

Preheat the oven to 200°C / 400°F / Gas Mark 6.

Rub the butter into the sifted flour, salt and baking powder in a bowl. Add two-thirds of the coarsely grated cheese and the mustard, thyme and cayenne, and then gradually cut the milk in with a knife; you might not need it all but you want a soft dough. Roll out to 1.5cm / ¾ inch thickness, then cut with an upturned glass or pastry cutter.

Put the scones on a buttered baking tray, sprinkle with the remaining cheese, and bake for 12–15 minutes. Set on a wire rack for 5 minutes, then eat hot with lashings of good country butter.

# Easy Roast Cherry Tomato Soup

A perfect late summer lunch, deeply flavoured, yet made without butter, oil or cream, and strong tasting enough to survive a flask at sea.

SERVES 4–5

*1 kg / 2½ lb organic cherry tomatoes*
*3 fat garlic cloves, in their skins*
*1.2 litre / 2 pints intense jellied*
*chicken stock; mine was made by*
*poaching 2 fowl and then making*
*a further stock of the carcasses and*
*poaching liquor with vegetables*
*1 heaped tsp muscovado sugar*
*salt and pepper*

Roast the tomatoes in a roasting tin with the garlic for about an hour in a medium oven. The skins will have split, and the juices run.

Allow to cool until you can handle them, then skin them and the garlic, and put in the blender with 2–3 ladles of the hot stock. Whizz, then sieve, including the skins which you can press the flavour from.

Return to the pan with the rest of the stock, add the sugar and seasoning to taste, and serve. I resist the usual urge for basil, butter, cream or parsley. This is an intensely enough flavoured soup as it is, and utterly simple to make.

# AUTUMN

I AM CROUCHED DOWN SAS STYLE in a thicket of brambles and autumnal bracken with Italian chef Andrea Zunino, in search of the elusive porcini. Puck-like, we have traversed the Blackdown Hills, 'thorough bush, thorough briar', until I feel as though I have been dragged through several hedges backwards. There is that magical early morning forest stillness, broken only by the creak and whirr of two cock pheasants we put up from barely two yards away, and the tissue paper crackle of dead leaves as we scan the rooty banks of beech and oak and the copper-leaved layers beneath.

Andrea comes from Savona in Liguria, and has been running his family restaurant, Capriccio, in Taunton for 13 years with his wife Cathi. He goes home every spring, returning with red and white house wines from Piemonte, Parmesan, 'It should be matured for two years, in England it is often too old', and whole legs of Parma ham and salami from his favourite small, native producers, 'Done the artisan way is best.' Rucola, basil and lettuces he supplies the restaurant with from his allotment. It is everything a family restaurant should be, welcoming to the children, reasonably priced, and with home cooking from Andrea's region of the sort of honesty and unpretentiousness that never fails to please. If something isn't on the menu, it isn't a problem. In the autumn, a basket of fungi adorns the counter that separates the restaurant from the kitchen, a cornucopia of whatever Andrea has gathered. Every year I plead with him to take me out on a fungi forage, every year it never quite happens; the weather is too wet, the first frost comes early; the territorial imperative applies to porcini patches as fiercely as it does to property. 'They are the best mushrooms for taste and smell, the king of the mushrooms for Italians,' Andrea says. 'I come back to the same places every year since I first found them 15 years ago. Each time I cook them I bring the spores back to the place I found them, and scatter them. I'm sure that makes them return every year.'

We have found a dankly wet, mossy bank beside a rusty, muddied stream, and a half-buried heap of chanterelles rooted into it, fuzzed with moss, the heart-shaped tops exuding their characteristic scent of apricots, the flesh velvet-soft. It is like growing accustomed to the dark. Once we find one stash, we find another and another, the more fully grown with undersides ribbed and veined like cabbages. Then we find little puffs of hedgehog mushrooms; their spores hanging down like minuscule stalactites from their creamy fleshed roofs. But there is not a porcino to be seen, only the false ones with their reddened stems, which Andrea cuts into, abruptly turning the colour of the flesh a vicious metallic grey green. 'They turn silver spoons black. In Italy everyone knows which are the good ones and which are the bad.'

We have tramped the secret woods for nearly three hours without coming across a soul, or a single porcino. Suddenly Andrea sniffs and says, 'I'm sure we'll be lucky here.' Jutting almost arrogantly out of the earthy bank beside us is a single white-ribbed stem with a pale fawn cap. I wheedle it out of the earth, and sniff its intense, musky, damp-leaved fragrance. Inhale deeply. We have struck gold! 'We pass through this world too quickly, so we have to do things we enjoy,' Andrea says, 'The pleasure for me is much more in searching for them and finding them than in cooking and eating them.' I'm not so sure I agree, as we repair to the restaurant kitchen for a fungi feast every bit as pleasurable as the morning's treasure hunt

There are several important rules when preparing fungi. First and foremost be absolutely sure of what you have picked, so, if you can't go gathering with an

Italian, get a good guide, preferably with coloured pictures. Do not wash fungi – you will destroy the flavour if you do – with the exception of chanterelles that grow so buried that they are often sandy. Put them very briefly under running water, dry lightly, and cook immediately. Other fungi, like porcini, you can wipe with a damp cloth, or brush the dirt off with your pastry brush. Always cut even the tiniest mushroom before you put it in the pan, this will release the flavour which, with something like chanterelles, is extremely delicate. Do not cook them with other types of mushrooms, you will overwhelm them entirely. I think this is true of most mushrooms, even the intensely flavoured porcinis which would overpower anything else. The simpler the preparation and the quicker the cooking time the better. Mushrooms have wonderful affinity with eggs, and with fresh egg pasta. The following dishes are not ones that one can give specific quantities for. You might find one porcino; you might find a basketful.

# Pasta with Porcini

SERVES 2

*225g / 8oz preferably fresh egg*
*pasta, tagliatelli or papardelle,*
*dried will do*
*225g / 8oz porcini, cook more or*
*less if that is what you have found*
*olive oil*
*1 garlic clove and a bay leaf*
*1 small carton of whipping cream*
*knob of butter*
*flat-leaf parsley, finely chopped*
*salt and pepper*

Clean the porcini and slice them thinly. Heat a film of olive oil in the bottom of a frying pan, put in the garlic and bay leaf, and sauté until the garlic begins to brown. Remove it and the bay leaf, throw in the porcini, fry quickly, tossing and turning as you go, until they are just tender and have released their juices, a matter of a few minutes.

Season, pour in the cream, bubble it, and then throw in the pasta that you have cooked and drained and adorned with a knob of butter. Amalgamate briefly, add a dusting of finely chopped flat-leaf parsley, and serve.

Andrea freezes the porcini in pots before adding the cream stage. The flavour is not so intense, but it is worth doing this if you have a glut, to flavour winter soups and stews. He also dries them overnight, which you can do if you have a warming oven. Slice them first, then spread them on greaseproof paper on a baking sheet in a single layer and put in the oven. Rehydrate with a bit of warm water, and include the mushroomy water in a risotto, soup or stew.

# Chanterelles with Scrambled Eggs

Supermarkets are beginning to sell chanterelles, in case you can't get down to the woods. You can cook them as before with pasta, or on their own just fried like the porcini without adding the cream, or make this deliciously simple dish that I could eat at any meal time.

chanterelles
2 eggs per person
green olive oil
garlic
knob of unsalted butter
double cream
salt and black pepper

Prepare the chanterelles as above, slicing even the babiest to release the flavour. Throw them into a film of olive oil in which you have briefly fried a clove of garlic and a bay leaf, removing them when the garlic has begun to brown. Toss and cook quickly, then add a knob of good unsalted butter and two eggs per person, beaten with a splash of double cream, and gently worry the eggs with a wooden spoon until they are runnily set. Season and serve, on or without hot buttered toast.

# Raw Porcini Salad

porcini
green olive oil
lemon juice
black pepper
salt

If the porcini are firm fleshed and fresh, slice them as thinly as you can, and merely add a dressing of best green olive oil and lemon juice. And a scrunch of black pepper and salt. A wonderfully hedonistic starter.

# PROSPECT BOOKS

*'I think we ought to know about our culinary past, food and identity is terribly important, but no one takes food seriously in England.'*

SWEEPING GENERALIZATION THOUGH THIS MAY APPEAR, *agent provocateur* Tom Jaine is uniquely disposed to make it. His culinary credentials are impeccable. When Tom was 12, his stepmother married restaurateur George Perry-Smith. Christopher Driver described his Hole in the Wall in Bath as 'the single most influential restaurant of the post-war years.'

As a young boy, Tom would whip out of his boarding school after lunch, and into 'The Hole' for a second lunch. 'It was like being a Papist in the middle of a Methodist school.' Even then, restaurant life was considered a little racy. 'I really liked being part of the restaurant, it was so Bohemian. George had sandals and a beard and all that French stuff. I liked it, I liked the life.'

After reading Modern History at Balliol, Tom became an archivist. 'I would have liked to have been the new Simon Schama really, but archives don't allow that.' However, burrowing away as a backroom boy didn't last, and the scholarship, which in Tom's case is prodigious, was temporarily consigned to the back burner when George bought The Carved Angel at Dartmouth, and suggested that Tom ran it with Joyce Molyneaux. 'George had been 100 per cent father to me, I felt tremendous filial solidarity, so I thought oh well, whoopee!'

I ask Tom if The Carved Angel made a lot of money when it became successful. 'We never made a large profit. George will tell you me and money don't quite mix.' 'What happened?' 'I don't know.' 'You must know!' 'I don't know. George would say we didn't charge enough. He tried. We were quite mean and not hideously extravagant…' Tom's slightly wacky, professorial charm and wit tail off into a sort of boyish helplessness, 'I seem to be very good at business, but I'm just not.' He seizes the Old Holborn for another roll-up, and with huge hilarity recounts the selection process for the Good Food Guide, which he edited consummately between '89 and '94. 'I had to be passed by the appalling boss of the Consumers Association. He thought I was a limp-wristed git from start to finish. I nearly blew it at the interview.' After five years, Tom returned to Devon and became a baker. 'I was the world expert on bread, built my own bread oven, and wrote my bread book.'

Then, seven years ago, when Alan Davidson needed to offload Prospect Books to complete his great *Oxford Companion to Food*, Tom, who describes Alan as 'my other father figure,' bought it. 'Alan's twin prongs had been the ethnology and history of cooking. I've simply carried on where he left off. The distinction is, I'm probably keener on the history.' Prospect publishes between six and twelve books a year. 'We are not talking Grub St, we're talking micro publishing. I never expect to sell more than 1,000, and some books only sell 50. I edit, rewrite, typeset, design; the authors get no advances, only royalties. We just keep afloat.'

Last year's great success was *Traditional Foods of Britain*. Tom describes it as 'The most important book in any sphere published last year.' It is a book that clearly helps define our contemporary culinary identity, the issue closest to Tom's heart. 'We are quite specifically different from other European countries. Oh, we're brilliant magpies; we garner and garnish from our imperial past, but our identity is in crisis. I don't mean we should go out and eat historic dishes, but we should know what makes us different, not so that it makes us more different, but self-confident nations have that sense.' The 17th- and 18th-century facsimiles Tom publishes tell us precisely what made English food different; that we were using suet, which no other countries did; cooking puddings when others didn't, the idea of the pudding cloth is specifically English; that the French did not consider our cuisine beyond the pale in the early 19th century, they always considered us to be the best roasters. Read William Ellis's *The Country Housewife's Family Companion* of 1750 and you will see just how different the recipes are to, say, a French book of court cookery. 'It is the most wonderful book in the world. He's completely zany. It's one of the few 18th-century books that discusses the diet, farming, medicine and household of ordinary English people. Most books were about *haute cuisine*. It is almost a social studies book. The pig and grain cookery is thrilling, how to salt pork and prepare flitches of bacon, and the gruels, pottages, barley and wheat, we don't cook with grain these days, but the farmer or peasant did then.' Tom is hoping that Tomas Graves's delightful book *Bread and Oil* will underwrite the Ellis, which has sold only 39 copies, but cost him £5,000 to produce. Recent publications include Helen Saberi's brilliant *Afghan Food and Cookery*, which tells of the life, culture and hitherto undocumented cuisine of the Afghanis. Its chapter on cooking rice is inspirational.

The most exciting future publication will be the recipes of George Perry-Smith and Joyce Molyneaux which will arc the last 50 years, the period in which George began the process of redefining British food and taste.

No Arts Council grant has been forthcoming to the valiant and valuable Prospect Books. What does it say about our country, that we are not enabling someone whose driving passion, appreciation, and deep understanding of food scholarship is unparalleled, to flourish? If this slim volume of an enterprise should cease to exist, we will lose something priceless. Not elite and narrow, but fundamental, a utility, a slice of history that should exist for future generations.

# Chicken Liver Pilau

I used Helen Saberi's recipe for 'yellow rice cooked by the *dampokht* method' as the basis for my fragrantly spiced chicken liver pilau with a caramelized crust of onions.

SERVES 4

450g / 1 lb organic white long-grain rice
2 tsp sugar, I used light muscovado
600ml / 1 pint water or stock, I used almost another pint of stock at the stage I added the livers
2 tbsp olive oil
1–2 tsp char masala. I made mine by grinding 1 tsp each of cumin and green cardamom seeds, and adding 1 tsp each of ground cinnamon and cloves
salt

PILAU INGREDIENTS:
450g / 1 lb organic chicken livers
1 tsp saffron threads, ground and soaked in a bit of warm water
2 onions, peeled and finely sliced in half moons
225g / 8oz fresh or frozen peas, if fresh, cooked and drained
2 strips of lemon peel, without the pith
olive oil
salt and pepper

Preset the oven to 150°C / 300°F / Gas Mark 2. Rinse the rice very well in a sieve under cold water until it runs clear. Add fresh water and soak the rice for at least half an hour and preferably longer.

Place the sugar in a large flame-proof casserole and stir over a medium heat until the sugar dissolves and turns dark golden brown. Remove from the heat while you add the water or stock, the oil, spices and salt, then bring back to the boil. Drain the rice thoroughly, add it to the boiling liquid, and continue cooking over a low heat, with the lid on, until the liquid has evaporated and the rice is *al dente*, about 15 minutes. If you are just cooking plain rice, stir it once with a fork, carefully so as not to break the rice, cover with the lid and put in the oven for 20–30 minutes.

To make my chicken liver pilau, continue as follows: while the rice is cooking, de-vein the chicken livers but leave them whole, then sauté them briefly on each side. You are not cooking them at this stage, merely browning them, their insides should remain raw looking. Set aside on a plate, add a little more oil to the pan if you need to, and start cooking the onions with a bit of salt to draw out the juices. Continue to cook at a medium heat for the next 30 minutes or so while you finish off the pilau; you want the onions to brown and crisp delectably in the crusty juices, but not be charred and burnt. Meanwhile, add the saffron, peas and chicken livers to the pot of rice with the lemon rind. Gently bury the livers and peas under the rice with a fork, add up to 600ml / 1 pint of extra stock, cover and put in the oven for 20–30 minutes. Test the rice, and make sure the chicken livers are jewel pink. Serve in the pot, with the crispy brown onions on top.

# LINDSAY HOUSE

*FROM THE WATERS AND THE WILD*, the Yeats-inspired title of *The Richard Corrigan Cookbook*, is one of the handful of books I have been positively salivating for. There is nowhere I would rather eat, no chef I would more happily converse with, or spend a day in the kitchen with, than this talented Irishman. We have had heated debates about Irish politics, literature, food, and whether or not Richard is an Irish cook.

Behind the perfect Georgian façade of his restaurant, Lindsay House, where you ring a doorbell before being ushered into an unfashionably intimate, linen-laden dining room, is a welcome that could only be Irish. 'I want the hospitality to be warm, relaxing, effortless, for the place to have a sense of generosity about it,' Richard says. Down in the subterranean bowels of the kitchen, he has revitalized the arts of curing and brining. Barrels of ox and veal tongues rub shoulders with flitches of bacon, muslin-wrapped spiced beef, and boned, stuffed pigs' feet poking out above their blanket of jellied, saffron-hued fat. He is not a cook who would take the short cut to bought-in pancetta; his is the big-hearted, peasant-rooted cooking that his boyhood on a farm in County Meath inspired, the best ingredients transformed by real skills.

'My father hunted, shot and poached everything. We had no money, but no hunger. When we needed cash at Christmas we sold a calf. We had a huge orchard of plums, cherries and pears, we put our pears in the haystack to mature. Everything grew brilliantly in the bog, turnips, carrots, swedes. The buckets of milk sat in the dairy till the fat rose to the top, and we took the cream off for butter, we churned our own. Eels we line-caught in the River Boyne and kept in an old galvanized bath we shot holes in and lowered into the water. There'd always be a clutch of eels in it.'

After 'mitching' off school when he was 13, Richard started his culinary apprenticeship in earnest. It has been a long haul to Lindsay House, which he opened two years ago, gaining a Michelin star this year. So what, amid the deprivation and hardship of growing up in the rural Ireland of the '60s, has been most influential on his cooking? 'I think the way I was brought up has made me appreciate the seasons more than most people. On a farm you are always preparing for the next season. It's an endless cycle, and a hard way to live, but when in midwinter you are eating the lovely bottled fruits of summer it seems worth it.'

The book is dedicated to his mother Kate, alongside a poignant poem from Seamus Heaney's *Clearances*. Richard's mother died earlier this year, but what is clear is that she nurtured and instilled the 'great sense of values and tradition' that inform his cooking. Kate Corrigan remains Richard's greatest inspiration; she put down his early roots, he never left them behind. In that lies his greatest strength.

# Richard Corrigan's John Dory
# with Crab Juices

SERVES 4

*1 crab, about 750g / 1¾ lb*
*unsalted butter*
*1 tbsp each of shallot, celery,*
*mushroom and fennel, finely*
*chopped. I added leek*
*5 tomatoes, 4 of them chopped and*
*1 peeled, seeded and diced*
*1 tbsp brandy*
*about 300ml / 10fl oz water*
*sunflower or olive oil*
*about 1.3kg / 2¾ lb filleted weight*
*of John Dory*
*½ tsp chopped chives*
*½ tsp each of chopped tarragon*
*and dill*
*salt and pepper*

Remove the meat from the crab shell and set aside. Bash the shell into bits inside a large casserole.

Melt a knob of butter in a small saucepan and add the mirepoix of vegetables, the finely chopped shallot, celery, mushroom, fennel and leek, cooking gently for about 10 minutes. Add this to the crushed crab shell with the 4 tomatoes, stir for 2 minutes, then add the brandy and set alight. Pour over water just to cover, bring to the boil, and simmer for 20 minutes. Strain through a sieve into a clean pan, heat to boiling point, and reduce by a half. Whisk in another knob of butter.

Fry the fish fillets in a bit of oil for 3 minutes a side, then add the crab meat and juice and heat through for 2 minutes. Serve, adding the chopped tomato and herbs to each plate.

# Richard Corrigan's Almond Macaroons
## with Mascarpone Mousse and Strawberries

SERVES 8

FOR THE MACAROONS:
*100g / 3½oz ground almonds*
*1 heaped tsp cornflour*
*2 egg whites*
*squeeze of lemon juice*
*pinch of salt*
*200g / 7oz caster sugar*
*cocoa powder*

FOR THE CRÈME ANGLAISE:
*250ml / 8fl oz milk*
*250ml / 8fl oz double cream*
*vanilla pod*
*50g / 2oz caster sugar*
*5 egg yolks*

FOR THE MOUSSE:
*150g / 5oz cream cheese*
*150g / 5oz mascarpone*
*85ml / 3fl oz crème anglaise*
*40g / 1½oz caster sugar*
*450g / 1lb strawberries*
*icing sugar and lemon juice to serve*
*and a few pistachio nuts (optional)*

Preheat the oven to 190°C/375°F/Gas Mark 5. To make the macaroons, sift the ground almonds with the cornflour, then set aside. Whisk the egg whites, lemon and salt until frothy, add a third of the sugar, whisk until soft peak stage; add a third more sugar, whisk until glossy and thick; add the final third of sugar, whisk until stiff peaks form. Fold in the almonds. I spooned, Richard pipes the mixture on to a tray covered with baking parchment. Leave for 20 minutes to dry slightly, put in the oven and turn down the heat to 130°C/260°F/Gas Mark 1. Bake until off-white and slightly dry, about 15–20 minutes. Cool.

The crème anglaise is made by scalding the milk and double cream with the pod and seeds of a vanilla pod, then whisking it into the caster sugar that you have beaten with the egg yolks until pale over a pan of hot water. Discard the pod. Return the mixture to the pan and heat gently over hot water until thickened, about 10 minutes. Cool. This makes 500 ml/16fl oz, so I used the rest the next day with the banana tarts. Whisk 85ml/3fl oz of crème anglaise and the rest of the mousse ingredients together until smooth, then refrigerate until you need them.

Sandwich pairs of macaroons together with the mousse, then dust with sieved cocoa. Surround with chopped strawberries, and a purée you have made with half of the strawberries and icing sugar and lemon juice to taste. I didn't sieve mine, Richard does. Sprinkle a few chopped pistachio nuts over them, I omitted this. I think a raspberry purée would be delicious on the strawberries. All five children at dinner fell on this pudding with glee.

# Roast Chicken with a Sweetcorn and Ginger Stuffing.

It did make me slightly uneasy, stuffing a chicken with its daily diet of maize, and its own liver, but I promise you, this is one of the best stuffings ever; the ginger lifts it from ordinary to sublime. Do not add herbs, it would dull the pure flavours.

SERVES 6 WITH LEFTOVERS

*1 organic corn-fed chicken, mine weighed 3 and a bit kg / just under 7lb, and a sliced onion*
*2 corn cobs, cooked and the kernels stripped from the cob*
*1 onion, peeled and chopped*
*2 celery stalks, with the leaves, chopped*
*5cm / 2in fresh ginger, peeled and very finely chopped*
*the liver of the bird*
*seasoning*
*a handful of breadcrumbs*
*1 egg, beaten*
*olive oil and butter*

Preheat the oven to 200°C/400°F/Gas Mark 6. Heat a film of olive oil and a knob of butter in a frying pan and add the chopped onion and celery. Stir to coat, then add the ginger, and cook until palely softened. Throw in the liver, chopped into 7 or 8 pieces, and cook for a further couple of minutes, until still very pink. Remove from the heat and add the corn, seasoning, a scant handful of breadcrumbs and the beaten egg, and amalgamate. Spoon it into the fowl's bottom, pressing it down well. Secure with a cocktail stick.

Put your sliced onion on the bottom of the roasting tin, then lay the chicken on its side on top. Season and slather with a bit of olive oil. Cook for 30 minutes a side, then sit the chicken breast up, sprinkle over some coarse sea salt, and cook for a final 30 minutes. Remove and leave to rest for 15–20 minutes under foil.

Accompany with the usual roast potatoes, parsnips and other vegetables and gravy. I think bread sauce is not quite right with this, but I wouldn't dare not make it for the children.

# White Nectarine and Walnut Crumble or Crumble Tart

The walnuts on my tree are being squirreled swiftly away; I've resorted to buying organic ones. Try this with the golden plums that are on sale now if you can't find nectarines.

SERVES 6–8

6 or 7 nectarines
lemon juice
50g / 2oz vanilla sugar

FOR THE SHORTCRUST PASTRY
125g / 4oz organic flour
50g / 2oz butter

FOR THE CRUMBLE
85g / 3oz walnuts
85g / 3oz flour
85g / 3oz light muscovado sugar
50g / 2oz butter

Preheat the oven to 190°C / 375°F / Gas Mark 5.

Make a shortcrust pastry base with the organic flour and butter and line a deepish greased pie dish. Slice 6 or 7 nectarines, skin on, and put them in a bowl with some lemon juice and the vanilla sugar.

Make the crumble top by crushing the walnuts until bitty, but not sandy and greasy in a pestle and mortar. Whizz the flour with the light muscovado sugar and butter in the food processor until crumby. Add half the walnuts to the mixture. Put the fruit on the pastry, then a layer of crumble on top, and finish with a handful of walnuts. Don't use all the crumble mixture if it looks like making more than a thinnish topcoat, it would make the pudding too solid. Cook for 40 minutes, then serve with clotted cream. Don't make the pastry base if you are doing a plain crumble.

# Cream of Portobello Mushroom Soup

Good supermarkets have Portobello mushrooms in autumn; if you can't find them or field mushrooms, use organic chestnut mushrooms.

SERVES 4

450g / 1lb mushrooms
1 lemon
50–85g / 2–3oz unsalted butter
a pinch of ginger
1 tbsp onion, finely chopped
1 clove garlic, finely chopped
1 tbsp flour
900ml / 1½ pint chicken stock
125ml / 4fl oz double cream
salt and pepper

Chop the mushrooms finely and sprinkle them with lemon juice. Melt a large knob of the butter in a pan, and gently cook the onion and garlic until softened and pale gold. Add the mushrooms, sprinkle with a pinch of ginger, and cook until their juice has almost evaporated.

Melt another knob of butter in a pan, then stir in the flour until bubbling, and gradually add the hot stock — you can use veal stock instead of chicken. Whisk until smooth, and simmer for about 10 minutes. Add the mushroom mixture and continue to simmer for another 10 minutes. Season and stir in the cream. Liquidize if you want a smooth, velvety soup.


# Blueberry Clafoutis

A perfect autumnal pudding, with its purply juices bleeding into its custardy middle.

SERVES 6

450g / 1lb blueberries
25g / 1oz butter
85g / 3oz vanilla caster sugar
a splosh of Kirsch or vodka
2 whole eggs and 3 yolks, use 1 of the whites
a heaped tsp of potato flour
250ml / 8fl oz whipping cream
125ml / 4fl oz milk
a small handful of flaked almonds

Preheat the oven to 180°C / 350°F / Gas Mark 4.

Grease a deepish pudding dish. Melt the butter in a pan, and throw in the blueberries with a third of the sugar. Add the alcohol, and shake until the fruit begins to release its juice. Take off the heat. Beat the whole eggs and yolks with a further third of sugar, then whisk in the potato flour and stir in the milk and whipping cream. Whisk the egg white with the last third of sugar until glossy and thick, and fold it into the custard. Put the blueberries in the dish, pour over the custard and place inside a roasting tin half-filled with boiling water. Sprinkle over a scattering of almonds and bake for 25–30 minutes until faintly shuddery middled. Eat warm with crème fraîche.

# Quince Tart

This year my tree produced a record two dozen or so fuzzy-skinned quinces, but everything has come early and they are decaying so fast I can't leave them to scent a room, as I usually do, up until about Christmas. I love their scented graininess, and their rusty colour the moment they are peeled. This magic fruit, given to Aphrodite by Paris, is known as the fruit of love, marriage and fertility.

SERVES 8

*5 quinces, peeled, cored and cubed, if you only have 1 or 2, use apples too, which cook more quickly.*
*2 tbsp water*
*2 tbsp vanilla caster sugar*
*2 egg yolks and 3 egg whites*
*50g / 2oz butter*
*2 tbsp whisking crème crue*
*shortcrust pastry made with 125g / 4oz organic flour and 50g / 2oz unsalted butter*

Preheat the oven to 190°C / 375°F / Gas Mark 5.

Line a 22cm/9in tart tin with the shortcrust pastry. Gently stew the quinces in a covered pan in the water and sugar until tender. Liquidize in a food processor, test for sweetness, then add the egg yolks, butter and cream and whizz briefly. Scrape into a bowl.

Whisk the whites to stiff peaks, fold into the quince mixture lightly and quickly, plop into the pastry base, and cook for about 35 minutes, until well risen and airily set. Serve warm with cream.

# Baked Turbot in a Cream Sauce

SERVES 5

1.3kg / 2¾lb turbot
a few screws of black pepper
coarse sea salt
some knobs of butter
50g / 2oz unsalted butter
a small pinch of cayenne pepper
175ml / 6fl oz whisking crème crue
a handful of chopped parsley

Preheat oven to 200°C/400°F/Gas Mark 6. A glueily grey and tweedy-skinned fresh turbot is the most heavenly of fish, and should be cooked as simply as possible. I placed my fish on a large piece of foil on a baking sheet, scrunching the foil up around the edge of the fish like a protective nest. I then anointed the fish with a few screws of black pepper, some coarse sea salt and some knobs of butter, and put it on the middle shelf for 25 minutes. It was just unresistant right the way through when spiked with a knife point.

I poured the buttery, fishy juices into a small pan with a further 50g/2oz of unsalted butter, and heated it, having closed the fish up in its foil to keep hot. I then added a small pinch of cayenne and some seasoning to the melted butter, and the whisking crème crue, and stirred it until it bubbled hard. Throw in a handful of chopped parsley at the last minute, and then slice the fish and pour over the unctuous sauce.

I served a parsnip purée, pink fir apple potatoes and some gloriously day-glo ruby and rainbow chard for colour alongside the fish.

# KIT AND THE CASTLE

*'It's been like a divorce for me, it's been very difficult.*
*My restaurant is my passion and I care about it a lot.*
*A change of chef is something of a wrench.*
*When the moment of schism comes it is heartbreaking.'*

KIT CHAPMAN, PROPRIETOR OF THE ILLUSTRIOUS CASTLE HOTEL in Taunton, is speaking of the recent abdication of chef Phil Vickery, who both gained and lost a Michelin star during his eight-year tenure there. Jonathan Meades' lore has it that provincial towns are graveyards for good restaurants – truer still, I would hazard, if the restaurant concerned is hidden, like a burial chamber, within the tomb of a hotel. Somehow, over the last 20 something years, Kit has pulled off a treble, with Chris Oakes, Gary Rhodes and Phil Vickery all achieving Michelin single stardom, but as to whether Kit's culinary ambitions make sound economic sense, the answer is firmly in the negative: 'The big boys would close the restaurant immediately, without the beds it'd be bankrupt. And they'd be absolutely right, but how dull life would be.' I get the feeling that Kit would have to be carried out on a deep litter through his gracious, wisteria-clad portals before The Castle Hotel lost its toehold in the upper echelons of the gastronomic world.

His new chef, Richard Guest, is a delightfully witty, direct and dedicated Yorkshireman of 28. He is impressed but not intimidated by the Castle's lineage, 'I'd known about the Castle since I was about 17. Mr Chapman knows about food, has a point of view like Christophe did. I knew the sort of thing he'd go for when I was invited to cook – pressed tongue, the English side of things. He's an opinionated man, but he doesn't expect me to act on every opinion. He could be difficult if you wanted him to be, but I don't see it like that. He's interested, fair, and has eaten enough to know. I'll argue for the dishes that I want to keep. Mr Chapman has a helluva reputation, and I want to work for someone who loves and appreciates food. He's got manners, he comes down and thanks me when I've cooked for him. I'd hate to work for someone who didn't care.'

There has already been an unspoken altercation over a pyramid of crab jelly. I hear it from both sides, both equally relishing the telling. Richard says, 'I made this crab jelly, set in tomato water; it was almost liquid, so it's a dangerous dish. Mr Chapman hinted he didn't like it. I held on and on 'til the autumn came and it had to go. We never argued, but I'm damned stubborn, if I'd given in it would've looked like laying down and dying. IT WILL RETURN. I'm here all day and I've got to amuse myself somehow!'

'It was a wonderful creation, glorious to behold,' Kit tells me, 'But it ain't what we're about.

It was an architectural wonder of the world, but too poncey for us. Richard arrived on a Monday, and by the Wednesday he'd got a completely new menu in place. He wanted to shake the foundations of the kitchen, and he succeeded in doing so. It took chutzpah. He took an enormous risk. There came a moment when I took him aside and said there were certain ingredients I wanted a permanent moratorium on, lemon grass, chilli, coconut, salsas, anything pan oriental. He took it terribly well. After five weeks, things are beginning to evolve. He's been titillating metropolitan palates, this is a culture shock. What is interesting about him, is he's bringing his Francophile background and reapplying it in a very different context. The result is fascinating and fabulous. He literally swept the kitchen brigade off their feet.'

Kit has always had a clear idea of the sort of food he wants The Castle to be recognized for, and has been a constant champion of provincial English food. 'My own belief is that England has a noble tradition that is worth exploring. Food needs to have an affinity with its location, something that distinguishes it from everywhere else, food you wouldn't eat anywhere else in the world. The problem with London restaurants is that they're slaves to current food fads and fashions.'

The goals are as high as ever they were, Kit 'wants to be back on the front page of the *Good Food Guide* and I want the Michelin star back. We are NOT cooking to win stars, but I believe the cooking done here is worthy of one, I am totally convinced what Richard is doing is worth it, and it is a mark of credibility, of excellence. I believe in my kitchen. Regulars are saying it's the best food ever at The Castle.'

# Home-Cured Salmon
## with Marinated Vegetables and Spenwood

A mound of raw, sweetly fresh vegetables with the salt of the salmon and the cheese cut by the citrus dressing. Richard uses Spenwood, an English-style Pecorino cheese, but use the latter if the former eludes you. You need to prepare this dish at least eight hours before you want to eat it.

SERVES 4

*325g/12oz piece of salmon,*
*skinned and boned*
*1 cup sea salt*
*½ cup sugar*
*olive oil*
*zest of 1 orange and 1 lemon*

VEGETABLES AND MARINADE
*1 each of the following: small*
*carrot, small red onion, celery stick,*
*fennel bulb, red pepper,*
*butternut squash*
*juice of a lime*
*2 tbsp sherry vinegar*
*75ml/2½fl oz best olive oil*
*1 tbsp runny honey*
*zest of an orange*
*coriander seeds, freshly ground*
*sugar*

Pack the salmon in salt and sugar, cover and leave in the fridge for 4 hours. Wash off the salt and sugar. Pat dry and cover with olive oil and the zests. Leave covered in the fridge for at least 4 hours, then slice into thin strips.

Peel and wash the vegetables. Slice into thin strips with a peeler or mandolin. Season with salt, pepper, freshly ground coriander seeds and a pinch of sugar. Mix all the marinade ingredients together and then mix with the vegetables. Cover and leave to stand for an hour before using.

Mix the salmon strips with the marinated vegetables. Pile into a bowl with baby gem leaves and some shavings of Pecorino or Spenwood. If you feel like it, garnish with croutes of ciabatta sliced very thinly and toasted.

# Roast Partridge
## with Braised Celery, Cabbage and Liver Sauce

SERVES 4

*2 grey-leg partridges, with the
giblets*
*3 bay leaves*
*sprig each of thyme and rosemary*
*3 cloves garlic, peeled and roughly
chopped*
*4 shallots, peeled and roughly
chopped*
*50g / 2oz butter*
*225g / 8oz chicken livers*
*1 cup chicken stock*
*1 tsp butter for sauce*

FOR THE VEGETABLES:
*1 savoy cabbage cut into quarters,
stalk removed*
*6 sticks celery, strung and cut into
5cm / 2in pieces*
*300ml / ½ pint goose or duck fat or
dripping*
*300ml / ½ pint chicken stock*
*sprig each of thyme and rosemary*
*1 tsp chopped garlic*

Preheat the oven to 120°C / 240°F Gas Mark 2.

Melt the butter in a heavy pan, then add the herbs, shallots and garlic. Season the birds and add to the pan, cooking for 3 minutes a side; they should be golden brown. Transfer to the oven and leave to rest for 12–15 minutes, then take the breast and legs off the bone to serve. Bring the pan you've cooked the birds in back up to heat, and add the giblets and chopped chicken livers, frying them until golden brown. Deglaze the pan with chicken stock, scraping the bits as you go. Bring to a simmer, then strain everything through a sieve. Check the seasoning. Return to the pan and reduce by a third. Whisk in a teaspoon of butter.

Melt the fat in the stock, add the garlic, herbs and vegetables. Cover with a tight lid and simmer for 10 minutes. Remove from the heat and leave to cool in the liquid. Reheat in the same liquid, and remove the vegetables with a slotted spoon to lay on the plates. Put the partridge on top, and then the liver sauce. This is a triumphantly good, rich yet earthy dish.

# Marmalade Ice Cream

Richard says do not use top-quality Seville orange marmalade since it is too strong and will take over the dish. He uses Robertson's marmalade.

SERVES 8–10

*50g / 2oz Robertson's marmalade*
*1 tbsp Cointreau*
*30ml / 1fl oz stock syrup*

FOR THE ICE CREAM:
*600ml / 1 pint milk*
*300ml / ½ pint double cream*
*5 egg yolks*
*150g / 5oz vanilla caster sugar*
*75g / 3oz glucose*

You can buy the glucose at the chemist. It makes the ice cream easy to scoop. Mix together the marmalade, Cointreau and stock syrup.

Cream together the yolks and sugar. Bring the milk, cream and glucose to scalding point and pour over the yolk and sugar mixture, whisking as you pour. Churn in your ice cream machine. When it is almost frozen, fold in the marmalade mixture to create a ripple effect.

# CHOCOLATE HEAVEN

I AM WAITING UPSTAIRS FOR MICHEL ROUX, brilliant brace-of-stars chef at Le Gavroche, while he finishes the lunchtime service. Earlier in the year I had an epic dinner here – Odyssean, if that's possible – which ended, or rather didn't end until the indecent early hours. Michel appears, minus his hair. He has taken the Black and Decker to it the previous week, hair raising a four-figure sum for charity. We are both unashamed chocoholics, so the afternoon's mission, a chocolate tasting with premier chocolatier Gerard Colman of L'Atelier du Chocolat, is not exactly penance.

When we arrive, a huge trestle table is laid out as if for a convention of alchemists, perhaps the AGM of an exclusive brotherhood of the black arts. Each of us sits before a square tray studded precisely with black squares and circles. At the table's centre are three chocolate gâteaux decorated with beauteous minimalism. One has a surface broken by a shimmering liquid lake of spilled chocolate, another wrapped in a newspaper of chocolate pages written in gold. The self-control needed in the early stages is excruciating, as we shave and splinter each square to taste. But 20 chocolates made with best Valrhona and Callebaut, 35 per cent butterfat cream from Isigny Ste Mère, and Escure butter, is an intimidating prospect, even if you consider Cardinal Richelieu's brother Alphonse in early 17th-century France, who used chocolate 'to moderate the vapours of his spleen.' Not an excuse I'll be making in the near future. Though throughout its history, chocolate has been alternately praised and blamed for everything, from its supposed aphrodisiac qualities to its unexpected side effects. At the Court of Versailles in the 17th century, the Marquise de Coetlogon 'took so much chocolate during her pregnancy last year that she produced a baby as black as the devil. It died.'

I think I would rather subscribe to the aphrodisiac theory; we do at least know that the phenylethylamine contained in the black stuff is a naturally occurring chemical in the brain, responsible for the glow of euphoria we experience when we are in love.

So we sit in a miasma of pleasure – what a way to make a living. We move from the salted caramel – Michel and I force down the whole chocolate – to Gerard's tea-infused chocolates: Earl Grey, a slow wave of the tea and a rush of roses; verbena, an instant hit of its signature musty, leafy taste; orange blossom, what can I say? It tastes how it smells, and I don't mean like a bubble bath, sensational; jasmine, which we unanimously decide needs a stronger brew. We move on to banana and thyme, a beautifully balanced intense fruit and herb blast, and then to a taste that none of us can decipher. A sort of intoxicating vanilla-ey flavour underscored with new-mown hay. Gerard hands us a dish filled with a pile of dried black beans, the 'tonka' bean. We are all mystified. Alan Davidson's *Oxford Companion to Food* describes it as grown in Venezuela, Colombia, Guiana and Brazil, and containing a substance called coumarin. Thrillingly, the 'use of natural coumarin in food was banned in the USA in 1954.' I know no more. We move swiftly to the truffles, seductively 'enrobed' twice in dark chocolate, so the buttery light mousse of their innards neither leaks nor softens.

Cleverly, Gerard has overridden the guilt factor that seems to accompany the buying and eating of chocolate. When did you last buy yourself a box of chocolates? Do you know anyone who does? He's bagged up his sensational nougatine, slices of darkest chocolate penetrated with caramelized hazelnuts and almonds — I ate the whole bag at a sitting — his house truffles, and his utterly moreish chocolate-clad feuillantine wafers. Gerard makes chocolate for some of our top starred restaurants, though not all will do him the favour of admitting to it. Michel is happy to, he uses some of the chocolates he's selected specially, and sees Gerard as 'the leading light in the modern taste of chocolate.' On that, and the salted caramel, we both agree.

## Hot Chocolate Puddings

Another pudding to make the night before you need it. A moat of black chocolate seeps out when you cut into it, and its richness is best offset with thin pouring cream or good vanilla ice cream. You need six individual pudding moulds, I use ramekins

MAKES 6

5 eggs plus 5 extra yolks
125g / 4oz vanilla caster sugar
225g / 8oz unsalted butter
225g / 8oz best bitter chocolate
50g / 2oz plain flour, sifted

Beat the eggs, yolks and sugar together until pale. Melt the chocolate and butter in a bowl over simmering water. Remove from the heat and add to the egg mixture, beating as you go. Fold in the flour. Pour into the buttered moulds immediately. Cool, then refrigerate for a couple of hours.
Preheat the oven to 180°C / 350°F / Gas Mark 4. Bake for about 12 minutes, the tops will have risen and feel dry to the touch. Turn out with a bendy palate knife and serve. You can sprinkle a bit of cocoa powder and icing sugar over the top if you are feeling decorative.

# Devil's Food Cake

As sumptuous and excessive as the title suggests, this makes a wonderful pudding for 12. Most devil's food cakes are too dry, too sweet and not chocolatey enough. I've adapted this from *Baking with Passion* by Dan Lepard and Richard Whittington.

MAKES A 22CM/9 INCH CAKE

*150g / 5oz Valrhona or similar top quality dark chocolate*
*125g / 4oz vanilla caster sugar*
*125ml / 4fl oz milk*
*40g / 1½oz Green and Black's organic cocoa powder*
*3 eggs separated and 1 extra yolk*
*150g / 5oz soft unsalted butter*
*85g / 3oz light muscovado sugar*
*225g / 8oz plain flour*
*1 heaped tsp bicarbonate of soda*
*1 tsp salt*
*1 small pot soured cream*

ICING:

*200g / 7oz best bitter chocolate*
*50g / 2oz cocoa powder as above*
*100ml / 3½fl oz water*
*1 heaped tbsp golden syrup*
*50g / 2oz softened butter*
*225g / 8oz Billington's unrefined icing sugar, sifted*
*2 egg yolks*

Preheat oven to 180°C / 350°F / Gas Mark 4.

Butter two 22cm/9in springform cake tins, and line the bases with baking parchment. Put the chocolate, caster sugar, milk, cocoa powder and 2 egg yolks in a bowl set over simmering water. Stir until melted and custardy.

In your Kitchen Aid or mixer, beat the butter and muscovado sugar until light and fluffy. Beat in the remaining yolks, then the flour, salt and bicarb. Fold in the sour cream then the chocolate custard. Whisk the egg whites until stiff and fold them into the mixture.

Put half in each of the tins, and bake in the oven for 35–40 minutes. You want the skewer to come out almost clean. Cool briefly in the tins then turn out onto a rack.

*The Icing*

Melt the chocolate as above. Warm the cocoa powder, water and golden syrup until runny. Add the chocolate and stir to amalgamate. Remove from the heat and beat in the butter, icing sugar and egg yolks until smooth and creamy. Taste for sweetness. Cool until thick but spreadable.

Cut each sponge into two, then lash the icing on to each layer and sandwich together, keeping enough to spread all over the top and sides of the cake. Leave in a cool, but not cold place overnight.

# Roasted Figs with Cinnamon, Thyme and Honey

Anything as arterially challenging as the Devil's Food Cake on page 191 needs an antidote. Soft-skinned purple figs, around in the autumn, respond beautifully to the spicy notes of thyme and cinnamon, sweetened with honey and orange liqueur.

SERVES 6

*12 figs*
*3 heaped tbsp good runny honey*
*walnut-sized knob of butter*
*1 tbsp Grand Marnier or Cointreau*
*½ tsp cinnamon*
*1 tsp thyme leaves*

Preheat the oven to 190°C / 375 °F Gas Mark 5.
Heat the honey, butter, liqueur and cinnamon together until liquid. Make crosses almost to the bases of the figs, stand them upright in a roasting tin, splaying them out shamelessly as you go. Pour the liquid over each one. Roast for 15 minutes. Sprinkle a bit of thyme on each, return to the oven, switch it off, leaving the door ajar, and serve 5 or 10 minutes later.

# Sticky Gingerbread and Poached Pears

SERVES 8–10

*125g/4oz butter*

*50g/2oz molasses sugar*

*50g/2oz demerara sugar*

*2 eggs*

*two-thirds of a 450g/1lb jar*
*blackstrap molasses (Meridian*
*make a good one you can buy in*
*healthfood shops)*

*225g/8oz plain flour*

*1 tsp grated dried ginger root or*
*powder if you can't get it*

*5 knobs stem ginger and 2 tbsp of*
*the syrup*

*2 tbsp milk*

*scant ½ tsp bicarbonate of soda*

POACHED PEARS

*600ml/1 pint water*

*100g/3½oz vanilla caster sugar*

*a couple of slices each of orange*
*and lemon peel, all pith removed*

*a vanilla pod with its*
*scooped-out innards*

*1 tbsp orange flower water*

*6 firm but ripe pears, peeled, stalks*
*left on, sprinkled with lemon juice*
*to prevent discolouration*

Preheat oven to 160°C/325°F/Gas Mark 3. Grease and flour a 18cm/7in loaf tin.

Cream the butter and sugars thoroughly, then mix in the eggs one at a time, followed by the blackstrap molasses. Add the dry ginger root with the sifted flour, finely chopped stem ginger and syrup to the cake mixture. Warm the milk slightly and stir it into the bicarb until dissolved, then add to the mixture and fold in. Pour the mixture into the loaf tin, and bake for about 1½ hours. Check with a skewer. I favour a sticky, gooey cake, slightly sunken in the middle, so when you turn it out to cool on a rack, it looks like a depressed, blackened brick. When cool, wrap it up in greaseproof paper and foil; it keeps very well for a few days.

Make the sugar syrup by boiling the water and sugar with the peels, pods and vanilla grains. Boil furiously until you have a thick syrup, but don't let it brown. Add the orange flower water and the pears, then cook in a heavy-bottomed casserole at a gentle simmer until the pears are just tender when pierced with a skewer.

Leave to cool, and serve with the gingerbread and some crème fraîche. You can prepare the pears hours in advance.

# THE SHOOTING PARTY

'The British landed gentry invented rook pie for the peasants you know, you can't fool me,' Richard Corrigan declares as David Chambers, executive chef of the quintessentially English restaurant Rules regales us with tales of the squirrels and rooks he has sautéed on previous shoots. If Richard, Michelin-starred Irish chef of Lindsay House, had known at this stage that peacock was on the menu tonight, he might have toned down the class warrior act a bit. Sartorially speaking he's not dressed for it anyway, in his rather patrician Donegal tweed jacket, the colour of pea pods with freckles of saffron, and shocking golden lining, 'I asked for Protestant orange and they gave me Catholic.' We are in the back of a Land Rover on the Lartington Estate in the high Pennines, with similarly constellated Austrian chef of 1 Lombard Street, Herbert Berger. What more could a girl ask for than the great outdoors, and three fine chefs to cook her lunch? Our first catch of the day, the vicious-pincered *Pacifastacus leniusculus*, or signal crayfish. Delicacy they may be, but as gamekeeper Philip Morgan extracts them from the holding cage in the lake, they make the Resistance movement look tame.

We arrive at a log cabin looking out onto the turfy waters of the River Tee. We are greeted by John Mayhew, whose guests we are. Although he is the owner of Rules, and supplies a lot of the game from the estate and from the nearby grouse moors, he is passionate enough about food to enjoy the company of chefs even when he is off duty. Above us rears the bleakly treeless hillscape that is heathery homeland to the grouse; behind us, the raw-edged beauty of the Pennine Chain. John's log cabin is like stepping into fairyland. There are gas lamps, an old wind-up gramophone, and at one end, a leaping fire on which is perched a cast-iron device like library steps, so that you can cook at all temperatures from the intense heat of the top step, to the warming embers of the bottom. Donna, Philip's wife, is cooking the tiny garnets of beetroot, squeaky white head of cabbage and yellow courgettes we have chosen from the kitchen garden.

Richard shows me how to remove the crayfish entrails without being attacked, then we cook a pot of them under a canopy of dill fronds, on to which he pours a monsoon of champagne. Herbert sneaks off to doctor David's lamb, and eventually we sit down to lunch, finishing with delicious little treacle puddings Donna has cooked and warmed in billy cans.

At 6pm we head off to shoot duck. The pond is stocked with teal, mallard, wigeon and the 007 of dark-meated ducks, the golden eye. The birds take off, flying increasingly high and fast. As the light leaks out of the sky, John calls a halt, so that any injured birds the dogs haven't found can be picked up and swiftly, humanely despatched. Everything on the estate is run to give the game as wild and good a life as possible. Only a half dozen older bucks and does are culled in the winter. There are no clouds of birds like you see on some of the big shoots, where stray shot can pepper

and maim, and John will only allow people who eat game to shoot. 'I like the idea of good husbandry, that the birds are well looked after before they're eaten. That connection is the best one you can get as a way of life. The poults – baby pheasant and partridge – are brought in and kept under lamps for the first two weeks, then they're allowed out of their pop-holes to acclimatize before they're given their freedom.' Philip never shoots the birds he's reared, and is passionate about conservation. 'I'm putting in beetle banks to attract all types of wildlife, and to direct the game from one side of the estate to the other. As a result we've got loads of goldfinches.' 'For every 1,000 gamebirds we put down, we're lucky to shoot 180,' John continues. 'In effect we're giving back two-thirds of them bar the ones the foxes kill.'

It seems extraordinary that anyone operating to such high standards should need to be both persuasive and defensive, but that, I'm afraid, is the climate in which we live, bred and reared more on ignorance than on understanding of how acutely stewardship and conservation are taken by the serious countryman.

## Roast Wild Duck

Preheat the oven to 220°C/425°F/Gas Mark 7. Allow one duck per brace of people. I have always cooked wild duck very simply, roasting at a high temperature, resting, and using the juices as the main ingredient for any sauce. Apricots are a brilliant foil for the stuffing, particularly the little dried Hunza ones from Afghanistan. Apples and celery also work well, as do sharper berries like red and blackcurrants, or a sharp midwinter Seville orange in the sauce. You can use bitter marmalade instead. All the chefs agreed that, as Herbert put it, 'You can be very trendy and modern and exciting, but game is better cooked without too much fuss.'

For a rare bird, place the duck breast side up on a layer of sliced onion in a roasting tin. Add its liver mashed together with a lump of butter, some parsley, marjoram, salt, pepper and lemon juice. Roast for 25 minutes, then check with a skewer. The juices should run pink, but the bird should not feel resistant. Rest for a few minutes.

Richard Corrigan removes the duck legs from the carcass to make a *confit* with salt, sugar, thyme and Chinese 5 spice and star anise. He cooks the breast on the carcass by browning it in butter and corn oil in a pan for 1½ minutes a breast, then roasting for between 10–15 minutes in a hot oven. He serves it with Chinese leaves cooked in a pan with butter and ginger. He also suggests caramelizing some little bits of fresh pineapple in sugar and butter, and serving them with the breast, 'The gameyness of the duck against the pineapple is magical.' Herbert serves his with an apple and celeriac ragout infused with marjoram, David with a gingered Bramley chutney.

# Wild Apricot and Apple Stuffing

ENOUGH FOR 2 WILD DUCKS

*125g / 4oz Hunza apricots, soaked*
*overnight in apple juice, then*
*stoned*
*50g / 2oz breadcrumbs*
*butter*
*1 sharp eating apple such as Cox,*
*peeled, cored and diced*
*1 celery stalk, strung and*
*finely diced*
*1 tbsp chopped parsley*
*salt, pepper*

Sauté the celery gently in the butter until almost soft, then throw in the apple and continue to cook for a few minutes. Add the breadcrumbs, parsley and apricots, amalgamate, season and take off the heat. Stuff the birds' cavities before roasting.

# Port, Beetroot and Blackcurrant Sauce

Omit the beetroot if you want to keep things simpler, but they add a beautiful, garnet-hued earthiness to the dish.

SERVES 2

*1 miniature bottle of port*
*a ladle of duck or game stock*
*1 heaped tbsp redcurrant jelly*
*50g / 2oz black or redcurrants*
*50g / 2oz cooked, peeled and finely*
*diced beetroot*
*salt and pepper*

When the ducks are covered and resting, add the port to the duck juices in the pan, and bring to the boil. Add the stock, and bubble merrily for a few minutes to reduce a little. Add the jelly, blackcurrants and beetroot, bring back to the boil, then simmer for 5 minutes. Season.

# Guinea Fowl stewed with Treviso Chicory and Crème Fraîche

If you can't find the beautifully autumnal maroon chicory from Treviso, ordinary endives will do fine. Likewise, if you'd rather experiment with pheasant, do. This is an unctuously rich dish, the caramelly juices at once sweet and sharp; all it needs is some mashed potato.

SERVES 6

*3 jointed guinea fowl, leg and breast in one large piece*
*3 tbsp olive oil*
*50g / 2oz unsalted butter*
*7 or 8 heads of chicory*
*3 tsp molasses sugar*
*1 finely chopped onion*
*the juice of 1½ lemons*
*200ml / 7fl oz white wine*
*250ml / 8fl oz crème fraîche*
*salt, pepper*
*a handful of flat-leaf parsley, chopped*

Heat the oil and butter together in a heavy-bottomed casserole, then add the joints of guinea fowl, skin side down, and fry for a few minutes until golden and crispened. Turn over and repeat, then move to a plate with a slotted spoon. Halve the chicory vertically and put with the onion and sugar in the casserole, and cook until the chicory begins to caramelize, about 5 minutes. Add the lemon juice, return the guinea fowl to the casserole, and pour in the wine. Bring to the boil, then simmer gently for a few minutes. Pour in the crème fraîche, stir it in thoroughly, season, and put the lid on. Cook at a bare simmer for 35–40 minutes. Test that the meat juices run clear with a skewer. Pour the sauce into a saucepan, putting the lid back on the guinea fowl and chicory, and bubble the buttery, creamy juices until they're thickened and amalgamated. Pour over the casserole, add parsley and serve.

# JULIET HARBUTT, CHEESE GURU

LIKE A KIND OF ANTIPODEAN MISS JEAN BRODIE, Juliet Harbutt is addressing us, her charges, black spectacles perched perilously far down her nose, eyes heat-seeking out any anarchy in the ranks. 'If you don't like the class you're judging, TOUGH. And don't write down in your tasting notes "I wouldn't give it to my dog". That's no good for the producer. Stingy judges will be sent back to be more charitable.'

You know where you stand with this lady, who, laughingly refers to herself as 'Miss Ferocious, I'm a dictator. Well you heard me!' when we meet a week after her British Cheese Awards. I dare to hope that I have acquitted myself favourably as a 'new girl' invited to judge the Best Modern British Cow's Cheese under six months, and the Best English Cheese, though what we awarded the top gold medal to in the former category, neither I nor my judging partner could divine. Juliet works all year to create this unique event, which began somewhat more modestly seven years ago with 296 British cheeses. 'Most people can only name five British cheeses, in which they include Brie and Edam,' Juliet confides disparagingly.

'The reason we don't promote cheese in this country is because we don't see it as something to eat, we talk about cooking with it. This country is obsessed with cooking. Hard cheeses are good for cooking, but we should be promoting types and strengths, using the leftovers to cook with.' This year, Juliet shifted the British Cheese Awards to Stow-on-the-Wold and introduced a day for the public. Six thousand people came to sniff, taste, buy and talk cheese, and view the extraordinary collection of 688 cheeses from 146 cheese makers that we had judged. The Supreme Champion was the Irish Coolea. There were 70 judges, each expert teamed with a food writer or retailer. 'The experts can tell if a cheese is technically correct, you lot have the palate.' My first class, the under-six-month-cow's, consisted of 28 different cheeses; my expert, the quietly knowledgeable Simon Yorke from The Huge Cheese Company. Some cheeses left us gasping with horror – appearances and smell can be infinitely deceptive. The best looker was reminiscent of mouse droppings; the ugliest, in Simon's words, 'all grey and mouldy like grandad's garage,' can suddenly thrill the palate in a completely unexpected and brilliant way.

'Those who've done a good job get invited back,' Juliet tells me pointedly. She doesn't judge. 'I won't judge. I tend to know the cheeses, and if I don't, people think I do. Randolph (Hodgson, of Neal's Yard Creamery) and I do tend to tear our hair out and think 'how did they miss that one,' but it's not the Randolph and Juliet awards.' So why does she do it? 'I'm a nervous wreck for a month beforehand. But it's really important to the cheese industry, and I feel terribly proud of the cheese makers. I tend to think of them as mine. I'm so excited for them when they get a medal. We don't award 1st, 2nd and 3rd prizes, we give gold, silver and bronze medals, which are a symbol of excellence for the consumers. What is totally frustrating and mysterious to me, is how few cheese makers use the label after the event, only about 1 in 20. If you see a gold label on a bottle of wine in the supermarket, you think I'll try that. Maybe it's the British reserve, or apathy. It's why I, a New Zealander, have ended up running the British Cheese Awards presumably.'

## Onions Baked with Goat's Cheese and Thyme

Bearing in mind that all good cheese is worth eating raw, I bought a perfect Ragstone made by Charlie Westhead at Neal's Yard Creamery, and ate it with fresh figs before cooking with it. Just as delicious in this dish would be the Wexford goat's cheese Mine Gabhar.

SERVES 4

*12 small onions or 24 shallots*

*olive oil*

*200g / 7oz soft goat's cheese*

*1 tbsp chopped thyme or marjoram*

*2 cloves garlic, peeled*
*and finely chopped*

*cayenne, nutmeg, salt and pepper*

Preheat the oven to 180°C / 350°F / Gas Mark 4.

Blanch the onions in boiling salted water for 5 minutes to soften them. Drain and slice vertically in half. Oil a gratin dish and place the onions in it cut side up. Season with salt, pepper, nutmeg, a pinch of cayenne and add a bit more oil to moisten. Cut and crumble the goat's cheese over the onions, then sprinkle with the thyme and garlic, and bake for 40 minutes.

# Rumbledethumps

A dish said to originate on the Scottish borders, the 'rumbling' is the mashing, the 'thumping' is the beating down. Sending Juliet back to her notes, I discovered that Simon and I had awarded our top gold medal in the cow's under-six-month class, to a cheese called Old Stowey that is made on my doorstep in Somerset by an Indian called Amode Katirar. Call Monastery Cheeses on 01278 733566 for details of stockists. If you can't find it, a good, strong extra mature Cheddar like Montgomery, Green's or Keen's will work just as well.

SERVES 4–6

*450g / 1lb potatoes, boiled and
then skinned
1 large onion, peeled and sliced
450g / 1lb cabbage, cut into strips
50–85g / 2–3oz butter
125g / 4oz Old Stowey or strong
Cheddar
salt and pepper*

Cook the onion and cabbage in boiling salted water until tender, then refresh in a colander with cold water, and drain. Mouli or mash the potato with the butter, then mash in the cabbage and onion. Transfer the mixture to a gratin dish, cover with a layer of grated cheese, and brown under a hot grill.

# Taglierini with Baked Fennel,
## Cherry Tomatoes and Wealden Round

The same applies to this fabulously fruity unpasteurized soft cow's milk cheese as to the goat: eat it first, cook with it second. Another of Charlie Westhead's from Neal's Yard Creamery in Herefordshire. I bought the parsley and garlic, and the black pepper and garlic versions, both are organic.

SERVES 2

*2 fennel bulbs, well peeled and very finely sliced*
*2 dozen organic cherry tomatoes*
*2 cloves garlic, sliced*
*olive oil*
*butter*
*225g / 8oz taglierini or fine spaghetti*
*half of a black pepper and garlic 175g / 6oz Wealden Round, cut into pieces*

Preheat the oven to 200°C/400°F/Gas Mark 6. Put the fennel, cherry tomatoes and garlic into a small roasting tin, splosh on a few tablespoons of olive oil, and bake in the oven until the fennel is softened through and basking in the tomatoey juices. About 20 minutes.

Cook the pasta according to the instructions, drain, add a good knob of butter to the pan, then the soft cheese and taglierini, stirring on a gentle heat to coat. Add the vegetables in their juices, season and serve. You can add a good dollop extra of cheese to the top of each bowl to melt in as you eat it.

Wealden Round and Ragstone can be bought from Neal's Yard Dairy and all good cheese shops, or by mail order from The Fine Cheese Company (see pages 296–99).

I am pleased to say that Rick Stein and his producer, my old friend Dave Pritchard, have just won a Glenfiddich for their recent BBC series. I interviewed them while they were making it. The following recipes come from the accompanying book, *Rick Stein's Seafood Lover's Guide*.

# Omelette Arnold Bennett

I had forgotten this simple, rich comforter of a dish until reading the *Seafood Lovers' Guide*. Don't consign it to supper, Rick wants to see it reappearing on hotel breakfast menus.

SERVES 2

300ml / ½ pint milk
3 bay leaves
2 slices of onion
2 slices of lemon
6 black peppercorns
275g / 10oz undyed smoked haddock fillet
6 eggs
20g / ¾oz unsalted butter
2–3 tbsp double cream
2 tbsp freshly grated Parmesan
salt and freshly grated black pepper

Mix the milk with 300ml / ½ pint of water, pour into a large shallow pan and bring to the boil. Add the bay leaves, onion and lemon slices, peppercorns and smoked haddock and simmer for about 3–4 minutes, until the fish is just cooked. Lift the fish out on to a plate and leave until cool enough to handle, then break it into flakes, discarding any skin and bones. Preheat the grill to high.

Whisk the eggs together with some seasoning. Heat a non-stick omelette pan over a medium heat, then add the butter and swirl it around to coat the base and sides of the pan. Pour in the eggs, and, as they start to set, drag the back of a fork over the base of the pan lifting up little folds of egg to allow the uncooked egg to run underneath.

When the omelette is set underneath, but still very moist on top, sprinkle over the flaked haddock. Pour the cream on top, sprinkle with the Parmesan cheese and put the omelette under the hot grill until lightly golden brown. Slide it on to a warmed plate and serve with a crisp green salad.

# Devilled Mackerel with Mint and Tomato Salad

SERVES 4

4 x 325g/12oz mackerel
40g/1½oz butter
1 tsp caster sugar
1 tsp English mustard powder
1 tsp cayenne pepper
1 tsp paprika
1 tsp ground coriander
2 tbsp red wine vinegar
1 tsp freshly ground black pepper
2 tsp salt

FOR THE MINT AND
TOMATO SALAD:
225g/8oz small, vine-ripened
tomatoes
1 small onion, halved and very
thinly sliced
1 tbsp chopped mint
1 tbsp lemon juice

Preheat the grill to high. Slash the mackerel skin at 1cm/½in intervals on both sides, from the head down to the tail, taking care not to cut too deeply into the flesh.

Melt the butter in a shallow flameproof dish. Remove from the heat, stir in the sugar, mustard, spices, vinegar, pepper and salt and mix together well. Add the mackerel to the butter and turn them over once or twice until well coated in the mixture, spreading some into the cavity of each fish as well.

Transfer them to a lightly oiled baking sheet or the rack of the grill pan and grill for 4 minutes a side, until cooked through. Arrange the salad on 4 plates, sprinkling the layers with the lemon juice and some seasoning. Put the mackerel alongside and serve, with some fried sliced potatoes if you wish.

# OAKFIELD MUSHROOMS

IT IS NOT OFTEN ONE CAN DESCRIBE SOMETHING as totally atypical and unique. However, my trip to the twilit world of underground organic mushroom growing is just that. I have already telephoned the farmer, Oakfield Mushroom's Mark Komatsu, in advance, explaining that my love of mushrooms is in inverse proportion to my love of caves, and that the idea of suffering for my culinary art by traversing the dankly dripping depths 80 metres down and 500 metres into a hillside is the stuff of nightmares. Somehow I am persuaded that the reality is very different.

We meet on the outskirts of Bradford on Avon, and set off into a dimly lit tunnel where, after acclimatizing, claustrophobia, like myopia, recedes faster than the tide. The height and width of each quarried 'room' or 'street' – the 'streets' are even named, Trouble Street, Wine Street, Back Street – is more spacious by far than your average Celtic burial chamber, and there appears to be more danger of getting lost in this warren of domed, limy caverns with their alarmingly fissured ceilings, than of being crushed or trapped in the inner darkness. Suddenly a quite extraordinary sight emerges through the half-light. Ahead of us, the floor is covered in receding rows of huge compost bags, 2,500 of them, from which are erupting a frothy, cappucino-like topping of violet candy floss which, when touched – so off-putting as to be compulsive – has the texture of the lurid fairground spun-sugar-cloud-on-a-stick without the stick. It is softer, downier, more like rabbit fur. It is mushroom mycelium, or spawn, from which the mushrooms, in this case blewits, hence the lilac hue, are beginning to jut out in fully fledged form. There are patches bubbled like liquid sugar, which Mark tells me is the mycelium respiring. Creepy. Their distinctly marzipany odour wafts around the chamber. In this subterranean house of many mansions, there are similar-sized chambers of organic horse and chestnut mushrooms, and an experimental corner for oyster mushrooms. The perfect growing conditions prevail, a constant temperature of below 15 degrees Centigrade. This, the only extant mushroom quarry in England, has been used for mushroom growing since 1870.

We arrive in 'Back Street,' a cavernous recess that feels eerily apart from the overground world, but for the blaring of the resident ghetto blaster. A team of ladies is sitting perched on little metal wheeled trolleys, scooting between the mushroom bags and picking, with their little knives, amazingly fast and accurately. I ask why there are no men doing the job, and am told they just don't stick at it, they haven't got the patience or the manual dexterity. So there. These mushrooms, picked before lunch, will be in the supermarkets the next day. Almost worthy of that wonderful old British Rail Breakfast sobriquet 'morning-gathered mushrooms,' to which I always wanted to say, 'Which morning?'

Oakfield organic mushrooms are available from Waitrose, Safeway and Somerfield.

# Coriander Mushrooms

The inimitable Mrs David in her *Spices, Salt and Aromatics in the English Kitchen* observes that the flavourings in this dish are the same as those used for champignons à la Grecque, 'but the method is simpler, and the result even better.' Try it for yourself, it is one of those nigh-forgotten dishes that graces a cold table beautifully, makes a great starter, or, as Mrs David recommends, can be eaten hot with veal or chicken. If you miss the tomato element of the Grecque recipe, simply skin, seed and chop three large tomatoes and add them to the dish before you cover the pan.

SERVES 2–3

*175g / 6oz button or closed cap*
*mushrooms*
*lemon juice*
*olive oil*
*1 tsp crushed coriander seeds*
*2 bay leaves*
*salt, pepper*
*3 large tomatoes, optional*

Clean the mushrooms, and halve them if they are on the large side. Brush a little lemon juice over them. Heat a film of olive oil to cover the bottom of a heavy pan, and cook the coriander seeds for a few seconds over a low heat. Add the mushrooms and bay leaves. Season. After a minute, cover the pan and cook for another 3–5 minutes, but no longer.

Pour the mushrooms with their cooking juices into a serving dish and sprinkle them with fresh olive oil and lemon juice to taste. Serve chilled, or hot with veal or chicken.

# Eliza Acton's Mushrooms au Beurre

*1 pint of mushrooms*
*1½oz butter*
*cayenne pepper, mace*
*salt*

Eliza Acton's *Modern Cookery for Private Families* of 1845 includes this recipe which is simplicity itself, as elegantly so in her writing as in the dish, and to my mind it would be insulting to update her prose. Wipe the mushrooms clean with a damp cloth, then: 'For every pint of them thus prepared, put an ounce and a half of fresh butter into a thick iron saucepan, shake it over the fire until it JUST begins to brown, throw in the mushrooms, continue to shake the saucepan over a clear fire that they may not stick to it nor burn, and when they have simmered three or four minutes, strew over them a little salt, some cayenne, and pounded mace, stew them until they are perfectly tender, heap them in a dish, and serve them with their own sauce only, for breakfast, supper, or luncheon. They are very good when drained from the butter and served cold. The butter in which they are stewed is admirable for flavouring gravies, sauces, or potted meats.' And the bit I like best: 'Persons inhabiting parts of the country where mushrooms are abundant, may send them easily, when thus prepared… to their friends in cities, or in less productive counties. If poured into jars, with sufficient butter to cover them, they will travel any distance, and can be re-warmed for use.'

# A No-Fuss Puff-Pastry Vegetable Pie

It will have to be enough for now to tell you that this comes from Nigel Slater's new book *Appetite*, but if you think you can resist buying it after cooking and eating this pie, you must be what my children would term 'a seriously sad person.'

SERVES 4

*5 medium onions*
*butter or oil, enough to cover the*
*bottom of a medium-sized*
*shallow pan*
*325g / 11–12oz mushrooms*
*of any firm variety, or a mixture*
*chopped herbs, thyme, lemon thyme*
*or oregano, just enough to sit in the*
*palm of your hand*
*200g / 7oz crème fraîche*
*425g / scant 1lb puff pastry*
*(all butter )*
*a little beaten egg or*
*milk to glaze the pastry*

Preheat the oven to 200°C / 400°F / Gas Mark 6. Peel and roughly chop the onions and let them cook slowly with the butter or oil over a low heat for 20 minutes or so, until they are golden, soft and almost transparent. Tear or slice the mushrooms into large, bite-sized pieces and add them to the onions, adding a little more butter or oil if they soak it all up. Leave them to turn golden and tender, but stir them from time to time so they don't stick or burn. Season with the chopped herbs and stir in the crème fraîche, grinding in a little salt and pepper as you go. You want a mixture that is creamy rather than runny, so let it bubble for a minute or two to thicken. The pastry needs to be rolled into two rectangles about 35cm by 20cm / 14 x 8in (this is conveniently the same measurement as the ready-rolled frozen stuff). Lay one piece on a lightly floured baking sheet and spread the mushrooms and onions over, leaving a good finger thickness of bare rim around the edge. Brush a little beaten egg, milk or even water around the rim, lay the second rectangle of pastry over the top and squeeze the rims together to seal. It is worth being quite zealous about pinching the pastry, there shouldn't be any possibility of the filling escaping. Brush with more of the beaten egg or milk so that the pastry will take on a rich golden shine in the oven, then cut a couple of little holes in the top to let the steam out.

Bake the pie until it has puffed up like a cushion and is the colour of honey. You can expect this to take about 25 minutes. It is worth sneaking a look at the bottom to check if the pastry is crisp underneath (it should be fine because this is not an especially wet filling).

# SLOW FOOD

THE THREE OF US STAND ORPHAN-LIKE BY OUR BAGGAGE in the entrance to the Tre Galline, prepared, almost, to sing for our supper table. We have landed in Turin and sped straight here, to the city's oldest restaurant, but the 'Slow Food' festival has brought food producers, over 2,000 journalists, and thousands more to this beautiful northern Italian city, and there isn't a restaurant table in town. Our pleading finally pays off, and we are settled in the bar to await dinner with a bottle of the delicious local Nebbiolo Alba and a dish of local cheeses.

We have been billeted high above the city in a former convent, where a midnight curfew, narrow beds and bells are a reminder of the nuns whose presence still seems to breathe life down its quiet corridors. In the morning, fresh from our ablutions, we head for the Piazza San Carlo. It is barely past breakfast, though the feeling of being an extra in a Pasolini movie is enhanced by the groups of smart Italians who land, swift as starlings at the bar, down espressos, and take off again; and by the solitary Don-like figure musing over his banana silk tie and his Grappa in the corner. He polishes off a plate of dainty morsels on sticks, cigarette still in hand, inspects the tie, then, seemingly unhurried, orders another drink. Food and speed are arch-enemies in this country, and my mission, is to find out about Carlo Petrini's 'Slow Food' movement that has sprung out of the earth as convincingly as it abhors speed, and is rapidly taking root against the horrors of fast food here, across Europe to America and Australia.

In the hangar-sized Salone del Gusto, there are producers from 80 countries, but my interest is in the Presidi, or 'Ark' which 'Slow Food' is using as a symbol to promote and revive endangered products, and save them from extinction. Here is a country whose local councils and regional organizations are banding together to support their producers, willing saviours and preservers of the individual identity of each region's food.

'Slow Food' vice president Giacomo Mojola says 'To save the artisan producers we have to teach people to consume their products. This way we can improve local economies, keeping a close relationship between the product, its conservation, and the development of a district. To defend these small-scale artisans, we have to ensure they are paid a fair price; this is part of the 'Slow Food' message, if you are going to defend quality you have to spend money. A cheese made in a cottage in the mountain pastures can't cost the same as one made in a factory. We have to teach people to consume less and consume better. There are 100 products in the 'Ark.' *Violino di capra* – a goat 'ham' in the shape of a violin – had disappeared from the shops. 'Slow Food' got together local butchers, breeders and authorities in the mountains north of Lombardy, and set up a project to identify the best goat for the product. They helped guarantee methods of production, the ageing and salting of the goats' meat, even their feed.' The biodiversity 'Slow Food' preaches is augmented by an enviable determination to fight and outlaw over-rigorous food legislation. 'We support the regulations to protect people's health, but you can't cast doubt on methods that have existed for thousands of years and never done anyone any harm. Old methods of seasoning, ageing, maturing. Thanks to our fighting, there are exemptions in some regions from certain laws.'

My slow trail – the 'Slow Food' logo is the snail – down the Ark's aisles of meats, cheeses, vegetables, fruits, nuts, breads, confectionery, is an astonishing testament to the vigorous support this grass-roots movement has engendered. For a start, each stall is sponsored. There are perfect late Sicilian peaches, pesticide free and grown in parchment. Capacollo, a sensational salami from Martina Franca in Puglia, where the pigs, an especially long breed, are reared on acorns from the Macedonian oaks that were first planted there 15,000 years ago. The salamis are salted, peppered and immersed for two weeks in Bianco Martina, a dry white wine enriched and sweetened by boiling. Then, wrapped in caul, they are bound in white bandages and hung for three or four months before being smoked over oak bark, *Quercus troiana* from Troy. There is the dark-crusted *pane nero*, black bread, cooked in olive wood ovens in Sicily and made from wheat grown in the dry, warm Castelvetrano valley. Apricots grown in the volcanic soil around Vesuvio. Chocolate from Turin, first made here in the 17th century, and where the Swiss came to learn how to make it. A sticky, sweet Nettare d'Uva, made with Verdicchio grapes in the Marche east of Tuscany, which I am assured is 'good for depression and encourages euphoria,' and is best taken, medicinally of course, with a divine hunk of Lonza di Fico, a sort of pressed fig, walnut, almond, aniseed, rum and pastis log that is wrapped in dried fig leaves. There is Tuscan lardo, bacon from the pig's shoulder, kept in carrara marble boxes, or *conca*. The snowy fatted rectangles are rubbed with salt, pepper, garlic, rosemary, and heaped layer upon layer until the box is sealed under its morgue-cold slab of a lid for six months.

Peculiar though you may think it, I find the conversations and tastings with 'Slow Food' and the producers as saddening as they are truly inspirational. Ask yourself what we are doing to preserve our indigenous products and help our small, artisan producers, submerged as we are under the weight of post facto damage limitation in the wake of the horrifically ill-managed BSE and CJD crises, our obsession with food hygiene, and constant undermining of the dairy, the pork, and so many other areas of farming that our whole agricultural base and its infrastructure are on the point of collapse. Who even cares or knows whether we have regional foods, and is making sure that the young are guided towards enjoyable and healthy eating habits? Not a country where more of the population are looking for something cheap than looking for something good to eat. 'We have to teach people to consume less and to consume better' – it is Giacomo's words that stay with me as I leave the Salone del Gusto and consider the remarkably fast progress that 'Slow Food' has made in its short life.

# Shin of Beef in the Burgundy Style

Real slow food, perfect left to its own devices while you are left to yours. I made this with shin of organic beef on the bone, cut like a sort of grown-up ossi bucchi.

SERVES 6

*6 thick pieces of shin, on the bone*

MARINADE:

*1 bottle red wine*
*a glass of Cognac, or Grappa*
*1 large onion, sliced*
*a bunch of rosemary, thyme,*
*parsley and bay leaf*
*1 dozen peppercorns, salt*

FOR THE SAUCE:

*50g / 2oz butter*
*8 or 9 green streaky rashers*
*2 large onions, peeled and chopped*
*2 large carrots, diced*
*4 cloves garlic, peeled and chopped*
*flour*
*stock*
*bunch of herbs as above*
*1 tbsp sugar*
*salt, pepper*

TO FINISH:

*24 shallots*
*1 tbsp sugar*
*50g / 2oz butter*
*275g / 10oz button mushrooms*
*salt and pepper*
*flat-leaf parsley*

Put the meat in a large bowl with the marinade ingredients, and leave overnight or for at least 6 hours. Strain off the liquid and reserve, then heat the butter in a heavy-bottomed casserole. Snip the bacon into strips and brown gently. Dry the meat, then brown it on both sides briefly. Remove to a plate and brown the vegetables; you may need a bit more butter for this.

Sprinkle over a tablespoon of flour, coat the vegetables, then return the meat and add the marinade to the casserole. Bury the bunch of herbs, add the sugar, season and bring to the boil, then cover with a layer of greaseproof paper and a lid and cook at a gentle burble of a simmer for 2–3 hours.

About 45 minutes before you are going to serve it, put the shallots in a single layer in a frying pan, add the sugar and 25g / 1oz of the butter, and cook hard without a lid until the onions are well caramelized and coated in gloopy brown juice. Keep a watch, you don't want the sugar to burn but you want the shallots to have softened right through. Sauté the mushrooms briefly in another 25g / 1oz of butter, and keep them hot.

Remove the meat to a shallow, heatproof dish and keep warm while you bubble the sauce until thickened and reduced. Don't go too far, you don't want an over-concentrated flavour. Pour the sauce over the meat, surround with a heap of shallots and the mushrooms, scatter with parsley, and serve with plenty of buttery mashed potato.

# Steamed Lemon Curd Pudding

I made one with lemon curd, and another with lime curd and a couple of ounces less sugar. Which was best? I can't say, the ointment-thick lake of curd spilling around the tangy pudding was equally as divine, just different. Eschew cream, for once, the sauce is rich enough. I used Thursday Cottage curds, available in good supermarkets and delis.

SERVES 6

*175g/6oz caster sugar*
*125g/4oz butter*
*2 eggs*
*juice and rind of 2 lemons*
*125g/4oz flour*
*1 tsp baking powder*
*a bit of milk to slacken*
*1 x 310g/11oz jar Thursday*
*Cottage lemon curd*

Cream the sugar and butter together thoroughly, then beat in the eggs. Add the juice and rind of the lemons, then sprinkle over the sifted flour and baking powder. Add a bit of milk to slacken to a dropping consistency, but don't let the mixture become sloppy. Scrape the lemon curd from the jar into the bottom of your pudding basin, a snap-on lidded plastic one is fine if you don't want to cover and tie an old-fashioned pudding basin. Spoon the pudding mixture over the curd, cover, set on a trivet in a large pan, and pour boiling water to come half way up the sides of the basin. Simmer for about 1½ hours before turning out on to a large dish; remember there will be a lake of sauce.

# IN SEARCH OF THE WHITE TRUFFLE

How to describe a smell? If you have never smelt a white truffle, you cannot begin to imagine its heavy rancour; the alluring perfume that is at once a tidal wave of seduction, raw, earthy, sexy, come hither, yet almost – not quite – revolts, saying don't touch me, keep away, you don't want me, you can't have me. Analysis is supererogatory, but Mauro Carbone, truffle expert from the University of Turin, declares the white truffle's three main perfumes to be garlic, hay and honey.

I couldn't come to Turin at the height of the truffle season without heading into the Piemontese hills to hunt this elusive, underground nugget, or without visiting the Mercato del Tartufo, the famous truffle market in Alba. We begin with lunch at the magical Castello di Santa Vittoria, a 15th-century castle restaurant in the Roero hills that looks out across the coiling river Tanaro and the Langhe hills to the Alps, though today even the hills are shrouded in the famous *nebbiola*, a mist which hangs over them like a long skein of silk. There is a warm *fonduta*, or fondue, of supple, scented Fontina over which a snowstorm of white truffle is grated. Next, a simple dish of taglierini, lubricated with a bit of butter and cream, with more white truffles. Pasta, eggs, cream, rice are the perfect background for the truffle; it needs blandness and heat, which seems to flick a trip switch and liberate its intense perfume. Then we head for the hazelnut groves near the little village of Mango to meet Renato and his dog Diana. Diana bounds in ragged chevrons through the trees, and almost immediately starts scuffing up the sandy earth. Renato digs his metal-ended stick, a *bastone,* into the ground, then pulls a lethal-bladed *zappa* from the back of his trousers to help him delve around the hazel roots. The first truffles of the year, in early October, are usually found near the surface, but by December, they can be 30 to 40 centimetres underground. A female dog can be trained from six months, a male not until it's two; once trained, they are worth a staggering 500,000 lire. Renato gently eases the sandy earth away with his hands to reveal a perfect prune-sized black truffle, like a little lump of coal. 'So why don't you hunt with pigs Renato?' 'Because it's more difficult to get a pig into the car! Also, they're rougher, and they try to eat all the truffles.' Some dogs are muzzled, as there is a rather unsporting habit of laying down poisoned meat to kill your rival *trifulao's* dog. 'I take a different path every day,' Renato tells me. 'Sometimes I go out at 2am and search for eight hours without finding a truffle; the dogs work better at night, undisturbed by other noises.'

We repair to his house, the scales are found and jars of white truffles brought out for inspection. I choose a couple, and am bidden to keep them wrapped in kitchen paper in a jam jar, exchanging the wet paper for dry every day like a nappy, and returning them to the fridge where they will keep for over a week. I can, if I wish, place some eggs in the jar for a couple of days, they will absorb the truffle's perfume wondrously.

The following morning we stroll through Alba to the Mercato del Tartufo. To enter is to be overwhelmed. The perfume is all-pervasive. At the entrance, a glass case with four spectacularly large truffles, their strange, brain-like fissures and crenellations covered with a dusting of sandy earth, are watched over by a hawk-eyed guard. Each year, the finder of the largest truffle is rewarded with a gold truffle. I ask to meet the owner of the most princely specimen. Franco Robaldo flashes a gold-toothed, brown almond-eyed smile and begins. 'It was Tuesday night. It rained this week, so I knew it was better weather for truffles, the moisture, the humidity. Zara, my dog, always understands if it's a big or small truffle from the perfume; if it's big, she gets very excited and her tail wags very quickly. I always go to the same areas; I started with my uncle when I was a child, he still goes and he's 80. I write down the date and the time in each place, because if you close up the hole well, next year you will find more truffles, sometimes bigger, sometimes smaller. This is the biggest I've ever found, 660 grams. The emotion was incredible. When Zara found it I had to keep her away. I started digging with my fingers. It was becoming bigger and bigger like the emotions, and the fear, because if you break it it's worth less. When I'd uncovered it all the emotion was so great I couldn't breathe. It was like winning the lottery. I got home at 1.30 in the morning and brought it into the bedroom to show my wife. I kissed the dog for half an hour. My wife said, "You kiss the dog more than you kiss me".'

Franco's truffle should be worth nearly £900; perhaps his wife should be doing the kissing.

# White Truffle baked
## with Cream, Eggs and Jerusalem Artichoke

This was undoubtedly the outstanding dish of the trip, cooked by a young, talented chef, Silvio Berrino at the Ristorante Castello di Mango. I do not make a habit of giving recipes with ingredients that are difficult to find, I always try to suggest substitutes. This dish could, I suspect, be made with any intensely perfumed fungi like ceps, sliced wafer thin, but it will not have the magic of the white truffle. Try and buy one from any good Italian deli, you only need a tiny amount for this recipe. When I asked how Silvio had made it, I presumed it would be unreproducible, but, thrillingly, it worked perfectly, and I wasn't left with a heap of glass shattered by the heat of the oven.

SERVES 4

*2 anchovies, cut in half*
*12 dsrtsp of thick organic double*
*cream*
*4 Jerusalem artichokes,*
*4 organic eggs*
*white truffle*

You need a hot oven, 200°C/400°F/Gas Mark 6, and one white wine glass per person. In the bottom of each flute put half an anchovy. On top of it put a dessertspoon of thick organic double cream, Jersey if possible. Above that, spoon a dessertspoon of Jerusalem artichoke purée. (I steamed four artichokes in their skins until soft, popped them out of their skins, and put them through the coarse blade of my mouli.) Then break an organic egg into the glass. Add another layer of cream to cover the egg, you will be within a whisper of the top of the glass by now, and grate some white truffle over the surface. Miraculously the ingredients stay put in their layers. Put the glasses in a deep roasting tin, and pour boiling water up to the top of the stems. Bake in the middle of the oven. Check after 10 minutes, if the egg is no longer transparent, the dish is done. Mine took just short of 15 minutes. You don't want a really runny egg which will escape into the cream, but one where the yolk is a bit set around the edges. Each layer is a treasure trove of taste as you work your way to the bottom, the artichoke a perfect earthy foil to the truffle's delicacy, the salt sharp anchovy a brilliant contrast to the creamy richness.

# Tajarin di Casa alle Ortiche con Salsa di Nocciole

This simple yet perfect dish of homemade nettle noodles with Piemontese hazelnut sauce was a stunner of a dish from Carlo Zarri, who we dined with at the Villa San Carlo at Cortemilia. You can make it with plain fresh taglierini, but try to find the best fresh roasted hazelnuts you can. Piemonte is famous for its hazelnuts; I have never tasted such fresh, intense nuts as the ones I brought home from Alba.

SERVES 6

*700g / 1½lb taglierini noodles*

HAZELNUT SAUCE:
*a good-sized knob of butter*
*1 clove garlic, finely chopped*
*200g / 7oz hazelnuts*
*1 pinch of chilli pepper*
*100ml / 3fl oz extra-virgin olive oil*

Melt the butter in a large pot. Add the garlic, the olive oil, the hazelnuts that you have crushed but not ground (you want them nibbed rather than chunky) and the chilli pepper, and fry them together briefly.

Cook the pasta, drain and pour into the sauce. Stir well to coat, and serve. I served a sprouting broccoli salad with mine, which is a delicious accompaniment to any creamy or oily pasta dish.

# Sprouting Broccoli Salad

*broccoli, broken up into florets*
*best olive oil*
*lemon juice*
*sea salt*
*black pepper*
*red chilli, finely chopped*
*anchovies, chopped*

Steam the little florets, stalks and leaves, until *al dente*. Throw them into your serving dish, and toss when still hot in best olive oil, lemon juice, sea salt and black pepper to taste. Very finely chopped red chilli, fried for 30 seconds in the olive oil, is a good addition if you want to turn the heat up, and you can scatter a couple of finely chopped anchovies into the dish if you feel like it. Serve when it's still warm.

4

# WINTER

'I AM NO LONGER THE SLIGHTEST BIT INTERESTED IN FOOD, cooking or eating it,' George tells me, stooping over a pan of mornay sauce on the Aga, stirring vigorously and demanding of Heather, his wife, whether she's remembered to add the cream. 'Yes, and nutmeg and mustard,' she replies. 'There's not enough cheese in it,' he adds. 'I hate cooking, I like eating,' Heather says with a slightly mutinous twinkle. Soon a mantle of satiny sauce cloaks the cauliflower; tomorrow it will be sprinkled with more cheese and breadcrumbs for lunch with their accountant.

I am spending the night with George and Heather, after a somewhat protracted period of negotiation. George Perry-Smith does not give interviews. He never has. His capacity for self-publicity is not just non-existent, it is something he is genuinely, vehemently undesirous of. He is now 77, but I am sure nothing has changed on that front since he opened his famous restaurant The Hole in the Wall in Bath in 1950. I think I have been asking George, albeit in a rather circumambulatory way, for years, if he would agree to talk about his food, his life, the extraordinary mark that he and Elizabeth David have left, our culinary legacy. Every time I ask, George swiftly informs me of somebody else I should write about or know about, but not him.

This time, after an initial telephone call, during which he assures me he would have nothing of any value to say, he finally agrees. A couple of days before our meeting, I return to a message from George, clearly exercised beyond reasonable discomfort at the impending event, calling it off. Since the onset of heart disease three years ago, life has become extremely difficult, and George, 'always a worrier,' has been having sleepless nights at the thought of it. If I were to say that he has been the single biggest influence on my love of food and cooking, more so than even the great cookery writers, Elizabeth David, Jane Grigson, Claudia Roden – from George I learned by example, at the table – you will understand how I felt at losing the opportunity to pay tribute to him. Three weeks later I came home to a further message, 'This is George, I am eating humble pie.'

It is 18 years since I scoured the *Good Food Guide* for a hotel for my two-day honeymoon. There was only one place I knew I had to go to, a 'restaurant with rooms' called Riverside at Helford in Cornwall. The food read like everything you could wish for, local, home grown, abundant, unpretentious, original, classic. How many hotels can you think of where you could stay for a week or two and not get restaurant food fatigue? I rang and asked for a room for the following week. A voice at the other end burst into spontaneous laughter. There had been a cancellation; otherwise, it was clear people booked months in advance. I realized later it was Heather, who has been George's partner for longer than she would like to think.

The food, the ambience, the relaxed, unpushy informality and friendly, informed service were everything you could hope for this side of paradise. And if you got room three above the kitchen, you could awaken to the sounds and smells of George and the girls making fresh croissants, coffee and bowls of strawberries and oranges to eat on the terrace for breakfast. We returned twice a year, spring and autumn, from then on. The children came as babies, and have never eaten better high teas, chocolate and Tia Maria ice cream with hazelnut meringues being an early favourite. In the evening, Heather would listen out for them from the simple, linen-clad dining room as we ate brandade of smoked mackerel, lobster tart, fish soup with a rouille, and George's famous salmon baked in pastry with currants and ginger. When you ordered tarragon chicken, the whole bird would be brought to the table, with second helpings for the greedy. Vegetables came from the perilous ascent of kitchen garden behind, and on Sunday the famous cold table of pies, patés, terrines, rillettes, potted meats and salads would be laid out as it had been at 'The Hole.' The walnut treacle tart, decadently sticky, black and lemony, as seductive as the brandy-soaked macaroons in his chocolate St Emilion. I have judged every hotel, every restaurant since, if I think about it, according to Riverside standards.

When it closed 13 years ago, and we rented a little cottage at Helford from George and Heather, I plucked up courage and asked them to dinner. I won't pretend it didn't put the fear of God into me, it did. I poached wings of skate, and made a sauce with shallots and white wine, anchovies, butter and chervil, finished with a bit of lemon juice and cream. 'So when are you going to open your restaurant?' George asked in his quietly musical way. I think one probably only needs praise like that from someone of George's calibre once in one's life to feel, 'I'm on track, maybe I can cook,' but to know that the learning has always only just begun.

'How to seethe a joll of salmon,' in Andre Simon's *Encyclopaedia of Gastronomy* had inspired his most famous dish, salmon baked in pastry with currants and ginger. 'I still regard it as my trademark. The first time I did a whole fish wrapped in pastry, and sent these poor little girls like Heather out to cut it and serve it at table with not very good knives. I had to go back to the office and think could we adapt it for the restaurant, freshly cooked from the beginning? I didn't have much time for research, but we were brimming with confidence.' An eclectic stream of people beat a path to The Hole in the Wall to work for George, like Joyce Molyneaux, who later became a partner and cook at The Carved Angel at Dartmouth. 'I'd no idea she could cook, I didn't give people a job on the strength of their training, but on their attitude to food and people. Everyone always had something to contribute.' Staff worked in the kitchen and the dining room. 'It seemed quite obvious that cooks would cook better if they saw their food being served, and waiters would wait better if they understood the food they were serving.' The golden age lasted over 20 years, the menu beginning, 'Kissing don't last; cookery do' with its list of hot and cold 'beginnings' and its 'sometimes' and 'usually' list of main dishes, including bourride, cassoulet, Dover sole *à la dieppoise*, *queue de boeuf des vignerons*, ragout of shellfish.

By 1972, George had had enough. He decided to sell up, prompting the then editor of the *Good Food Guide*, Christopher Driver to write, 'You will have gathered I think that your news was greeted with a wail around the office as though Troy had fallen.' George has never been very keen on adulation, as you might have gathered. 'You could hear them at the door, "do you think we ought to bend down on our knees and kiss the threshold?" We were there to cook, not to become famous, just to cook.'

We have paused for dinner. The man who no longer cooks, and claims to live on Marks and Spencer's dinners, has roasted a chicken with a grass-green tarragon butter rubbed under its skin, and slivers of bright peppers bubbling in the buttery juices. We have moved from Cloudy Bay to a delicious 1971 Château du cru Beaucaillou, and Heather and I have been admonished for not putting all the peppers around the chicken. George is comparing us unfavourably to the gap year girls who he knocked into shape in a week in the Riverside kitchen. We are amused more than chastened.

Thirteen years ago they retired to their house high above the creek, which looks out onto the winding estuary, and the huge, gawky pine trees where raw-throated rooks caw at dawn. Looking across to Riverside in the early morning, I remember guests meeting and talking as though they were at a house party, and the bill, unique in my experience, seeming like an irrelevance, one always felt it was a privilege to be allowed to stay. So much of that feeling was due to Heather, who started at 'The Hole' in 1958, and finally married the boss nine years ago.

I've been allowed into George's study to read through his boxes of recipe cards. The dishes with which he reunited the English with their taste, inspired a love and understanding of things French, Spanish, Italian, and a pride in our own cuisine. 'So why didn't you write a book George?' 'I was too much of a snob to do it once everyone started writing them.' It is all there, a historical record of some of the best food cooked in England over the last half of the century, the documenting of the stirrings of a cosmopolitan food culture that is at once both true to its roots and to its indigenous ingredients. Christopher Driver called The Hole in the Wall 'The single most influential restaurant of the postwar years.' When I ring Simon Hopkinson on returning from George and Heather, and ask him, as a long-time admirer, what he feels, his first words are, 'He's an English god really. I think one of the things that gets him is not being remembered enough, never being talked about now except by a handful of people like you and me.' The corollary of not seeking fame, is, of course, the likelihood of not getting due recognition. Yet, ten years ago, Jane Grigson, referring to Elizabeth David and George, wrote of them as 'The two most important people behind such a revolution of interest in good food as we now enjoy in Britain.'

At the risk of incurring George's further displeasure, a genuine disincentive when contemplating this piece, I can only add to the likelihood of it, by saying that as far as I am concerned, he is still the master.

# Brandade of Smoked Mackerel
## with Dill Cream and Cucumber Sambal

This was a delicious starter that George used to serve at Riverside. If you are buying the puff pastry ready-made, do go for an all-butter one.

SERVES 6–8

225g/8oz puff pastry
225g/8oz skinned, boned fillet of
smoked mackerel
1 clove garlic, peeled
salt, pepper, lemon juice
50–85ml/2–3fl oz good olive oil
50–85ml/2–3fl oz milk
egg yolk for brushing patties

DILL CREAM
generous tbsp per person of lightly
whipped cream
lemon juice
pounded dill seed
salt and pepper

SAMBAL
cucumber, peeled and cut into
doll-sized dice
onion, finely chopped
celery, finely chopped,
red pepper, finely chopped
flat-leaf parsley
olive oil and lemon
salt and pepper

Pound the garlic in a mortar with just enough salt to melt it, add the smoked mackerel, and pound energetically until the resultant paste is smoother than you believed possible, checking for escaped bones as you go.

Prepare a *bain-marie* and in it warm the mackerel paste in a decent-sized pudding basin, and the milk and oil in two jugs; don't let them get too hot, just warm. Add the oil and the milk to the mackerel alternately, a little at a time, working each addition in thoroughly before adding more. The more you can work it in without making the mixture sloppy, as opposed to soft and light, the more interesting will be the contrast between crisp pastry and moist, light filling. Season to taste with pepper and lemon juice, and maybe a little salt. Chill. Roll out the pastry fairly thinly, and cut into rounds with a 7.5cm/3in cutter. Put a generous teaspoon of mackerel mixture on each, fold over and seal.

Keep the patties on a lightly floured tray in the fridge until the meal. Preheat the oven to 230°C/475°F/Gas Mark 8 and bake 3 per person, brushed with egg yolk, for about 12 minutes. Serve with a generous tablespoon per person of dill cream, made with lightly whipped cream, seasoned and sharpened with a squeeze of lemon, and some pounded dill seed to taste. For the sambal, peel the cucumber, and cut into tiny dice and mix with very finely chopped onion, celery, red pepper and parsley, dress with olive oil, lemon, salt and pepper, and put a generous tablespoon on each plate.

# Salmon Baked in Pastry
## with Currants and Ginger

George's signature dish, this is a classic despite its odd-sounding marriage of flavours, and is really not difficult to make. Everything can be prepared in advance for a quick assembly.

SERVES 6

*1 and a bit kg / 2½lb salmon, preferably wild, skinned, boned and in 2 thick fillets*
*rich shortcrust pastry, made with 450g / 1lb flour and 275g / 10oz unsalted butter*
*100g / 3½oz butter mashed with 3–4 diced globes of ginger in syrup and 25g / 1oz currants*
*egg yolk*

SAUCE MESSINE:
*tarragon, parsley, chervil, a handful of each, rather less of tarragon*
*½ onion*
*juice of a lemon*
*100g / 3½oz butter*
*2 tsp flour*
*2 tsp French mustard*
*2 egg yolks*
*600ml / 1 pint of single cream*

Preset oven to 220°C / 425°F / Gas Mark 7.

Season the fillets of salmon, then use half the butter, ginger and currant mixture to make a sandwich of the fillets, spreading the other half of butter on the top one. Wrap neatly in pastry (not a great clodge of pastry at the ends but a neat parcel), brush with egg yolk and bake for about 30 minutes. Serve with a Sauce Messine and a cucumber salad.

*Sauce Messine*
Put all the ingredients in a blender and whizz thoroughly until green. Cook very gently in a dish in a *bain-marie* stirring occasionally, until the sauce thickens.

# Chocolate St Emilion

'This has nothing to do with the Elizabeth David one. This is much lighter and nicer. I found a recipe for something called Hungarian Chocolate on the back of an England's Glory matchbox. It needed jazzing up, and I wondered how we could get this mixture into not a soufflé or a mousse, but so that it would stand up in a glass. Gradually we arrived at what we thought was perfection. It is named after the little macaroons that St Emilion is famous for.'

SERVES 8

225g / 8oz Menier chocolate
1 tbsp instant coffee
125ml / 4fl oz water
4 eggs
3-4 large macaroon
45ml / 1½fl oz brandy

Melt the chocolate in the water with the coffee. Separate the eggs, whisk the yolks, and add them to the chocolate at room temperature, mixing them in well. Crumble the macaroons roughly, sprinkle them with brandy, and mash with a fork. Whisk the egg whites stiffly and fold lightly, but thoroughly, into the chocolate mixture which should still be warm. Layer in glasses with the macaroon mixture.

# MICHAEL BROWN, EEL SMOKER

THE HEAVY BLACK METAL DOOR SWINGS OPEN to reveal them, hung in choir stall rows, hooked heads turned at a uniform 90 degrees to the right as though in deference to their choirmaster. Long, lean, snaky bodies the colour of gun metal stained with nicotine, their skins patterned in delicate overlaid chevrons, smoke circling upwards through their midst. As beautiful as the smoked eel is to the eye, it is to the palate; a combination of oily-rich smokiness and delicacy that is enhanced by the savoury saltiness of bacon, earthy beetroot, acidulous lemon and the nostril-aching heat of horseradish.

Down on the Somerset Levels, Michael Brown runs the country's premier eel smokery. He first came to the withy-strewn banks of the River Parrett, ancient, flooded flatlands with their network of drainage dykes and canals, in the mid '70s, to help a friend catch elvers. 'It was very romantic sitting out on the river by moonlight with my wife Utta, I thought "this is perfect, I can do this all summer, and write my travel pieces in the winter." The river was full of old blokes on bikes with buckets who'd come down to catch "a feed" of elvers, anyone was allowed to fish within tidal reach of the Parrett then. The elvers were sent to Germany for restocking. Eels have always been big there and in Holland, in fact both countries have bought elvers from the Severn since before World War 1 because more of them migrate to England from the Sargasso Sea.' A disastrous year in 1976 led Michael to start his eel business, he realized that man could not live by elver alone, 'I had to stretch finances across the year, so I started catching big eels in the summer months.

'The eels hurtle down the river into specially built racks which have risers like a ladder to take the force of the current out of the water, and filter the eels out like toothcombs. They arrive at the top of the ladder, and a keeper rakes them into his "keep" box. I deal with five or six tons a year. I smoke them very lightly so they stay succulent, I don't like an overpoweringly smoky taste. I allow the buttery, soft flavour to come out. I like them best plain, with lemon, black pepper, crusty bread and ice cold beer. They start migrating down river to the Sargasso in July, our biggest catch is early October. The problem is, their numbers are dwindling. The eel is fished at all stages of its life cycle. There is a closed season in France and Spain. Restocking is the way forward. We preach to our suppliers that they must put the elvers back.'

Gone are the days when scores of locals lined the water's edge on thundery evenings. A local farmer friend of mine, Nigel Male, remembers going 'clotting' with his uncle 40 years ago. The 'clot' was a skein of wool threaded with a needle through a handful of worms, and attached to a pole that they would lower into the river. Another pole was used to suspend a great bath on the river's surface, and when the eels had bitten, they were thrown into the bath.

At least here in the West Country something of the tradition survives intact, and Michael Brown has enhanced and made popular the reputation of this most delicious of sea 'snakes'.

# Crêpes Parmentier
## with Smoked Eel, Crispy Bacon and Horseradish

I remember a fantastic dish of eels stewed with crispy belly pork and garlic in the original Poons restaurant in Lisle Street in Soho. I think the affinity between the two is sublime. Here they are both smoked, so it's a head-on, full-strength flavour, with the creamiest of little starchy potato pancakes and a hit of horseradish. You can prepare the batter a few hours before you want it, and the horseradish, leaving your guests with the assembly job.

SERVES 6 AS A STARTER

2 fillets of smoked eel
8 rashers organic oak-smoked
streaky bacon

CRÊPES PARMENTIER
450g / 1lb floury organic potatoes,
peeled and cooked
50ml / 2fl oz milk
2 heaped tbsp potato or
ordinary flour
3 eggs and 4 whites
2 tbsp double cream
salt and pepper
butter

HORSERADISH CREAM
small carton of double or
soured cream
fresh horseradish root, grated
lemon
salt

Put the hot potatoes through the coarse disc of the mouli, or mash by hand. Put them in a bowl with the milk, flour, eggs, whites, cream and seasoning, and whisk together. Heat a tiny bit of clarified, unsalted butter in your pancake pan, and add tablespoons of the mixture, several if your pan is big enough, flipping them over with a palette knife when they begin to bubble and brown around the edge, a couple of minutes.

Keep warm on a plate in a warm oven while you make the rest. Allow a rasher of streaky bacon per person, and throw in a couple extra, and fry in their own fat until curled and crispened.

For the horseradish cream, I use either double cream or soured cream. If you can't get hold of fresh horseradish root, the only commercial brands I know that don't turn it into a noxious paste are the English Provender Company's Hot Horseradish, stocked by good supermarkets, and Source Foods Organic Horseradish Relish; ring 01495 371698 for stockists.

Depending on whether you want a runny or a stiffer result, do or do not whip the cream. Then stir in the horseradish a teaspoon at a time, tasting as you go. There is no going back! A spritz of lemon and a sprinkle of salt, and you have it.

Skin and fillet your eel by literally unpeeling it in one swift, satisfying move. Then chop your 2 fillets into 5cm / 2in chunks, and put one on each pancake, followed by the bacon and a dollop of horseradish cream.

# Hot Beetroot Purée

This makes the most dazzling and delicious starter with the plain, smoked eel fillets. It has a delectable sweet-sour sharpness and the earthiness of beetroots baked in their skins. A lot of organic box schemes are selling golden globes of beetroot now, so pick your colour, or do both, a sunset coloured sauce alongside the luminous, deep purply pink. I have adapted the purée from Michel Guérard's *Cuisine Gourmande*.

SERVES 6–8

3 medium-sized beetroots
3 tomatoes, skinned and seeded
1 tsp olive oil
150g / 5oz onions, peeled and thinly sliced
1 clove of garlic, peeled and crushed
6 dsrtsp good sherry vinegar, Valdespino, Lustau or Pedro Ximenez if you can find them
salt and pepper
1 tbsp double cream
150ml / 5fl oz hot chicken stock
flat-leaf parsley

Wash and trim your beetroots, leaving the root intact so the colour doesn't bleed. Bake them in individual foil parcels in a medium oven until cooked, pierce with a skewer after 45 minutes. Skin and slice them thinly as soon as they're not too hot to handle. Chop the tomatoes coarsely.

Heat the olive oil in a pan and fry the onions and garlic gently until softened but uncoloured. Pour over the vinegar, and add the tomato, beetroot slices and seasoning. Cook with a lid on very gently for an hour. Check on the moisture from time to time. Liquidize, or blitz in a food processor for a slightly coarser purée, with the cream and stock. Keep warm in a bowl over simmering water.

To serve, put a couple of 8–10cm / 3–4in slices of smoked eel on each plate, then add a generous ladle of sauce and a sprinkling of chopped parsley. You could offer slices of buttered rye bread if you wanted to turn it into a lunch dish. I served mine neat as a starter.

# GREAT WOOD CAMP

LIKE ALL GREAT IDEAS, THIS ONE OF MICHAEL'S was all the more impressive during the lengthy lucubrations over a good dinner than it appeared in the harsh light of day. Blame the Grappa, but I agreed to cook for his weekend camp for 30 children. The idea is to bring a group of disadvantaged inner-city kids to Great Wood Camp in the Quantocks, and give them a weekend of the great outdoors, with a huge range of activities, although, as I suggest to Michael afterwards, there are plenty of disadvantaged rural children who don't get the opportunity to do most of the things he has planned. The first problem is the budget. I have £3 per day per child to include cooked breakfast, packed lunch and supper. Loaves and fishes aside, there are certain standards below which I will not sink. I am not about to bargain for mechanically recovered sludge burgers, chips cooked in sump oil and mighty white. I ring Viv Jowett at Marks and Spencer headquarters hoping that she'll do a deal on their unsold bread and rolls. She asks rather a lot of questions, which, I answer unawares. Finally she says, 'Give me a list and Marks and Spencer will do the food. Use the spare cash for luxuries and the things we don't do.' Brilliant. Early morning at the M and S depot, and Viv appears with the trolleys. We stuff the car with a bakery, a meat shop, a fruit and veg shop and 10 dozen eggs, all it will take now is a shunt up the backside on the M4. Three hours later the field kitchen is in business, Michael's wife DD and I are dicing hills of onions, celery, carrots and garlic for the two lasagnes, *di magro* for the veggies and *al forno* for the carnivores. My Kitchen Aid is rebelling in the only way it knows how, by lobbing great lumps of pudding mixture out of the bowl at me like lemon grenades. Richard arrives. He is at a special school and has learning difficulties, but is a gentle and delightful boy fascinated by what's going on in the kitchen. 'Do chickens come out of those eggs?' he asks, then proceeds to tell me that he wants scrambled eggs for breakfast in the morning, which he will scatter with sugar and brown sauce. I hate to tell him it's a brown-sauce-free zone.

When the main group of children come, Michael addresses them by the roaring fire he has laid in the dining room. Nobody listens; they continue to chat and giggle. Most have stopped off for chips on the journey, so, with the exception of a few of the lads, I have over-catered by about 200 per cent. The lemon pudding will be great cold tomorrow. It is time for Michael's night walk, complete with a night line of string he has laid through the trees in Great Wood. Some are resistant. Don't like walking. Don't like the rain. Want to go off and have a fag. I search out Carl, Alex and Dan in their log cabin. Alex is horizontal and doesn't want to go. Carl says, 'Thank you for the nice food, I was the only one who ate everything.' It only takes one to make it worth it. I persuade Alex to venture out. The three boys fire questions at Michael from the off, about the army, the wild life, the owls, the woods. Eventually, when the rain comes sluicing down, I walk alongside Alex. His mother died of breast cancer two weeks ago. She played a major part in setting up 'Time Out Of Town,' the group that her friend Kim has brought the three boys down with. Alex is a credit to her, bright, keen, self-possessed, and unhappy with the knife culture that he says is a part of inner-city life. He wants to come and help in the kitchen. It won't be possible with the action-packed schedule, but I suggest to Michael that at the next camp we could include cookery.

At 7.30am a thin plume of smoke is rising over the camp. Michael is already on rasher, tomato and fried bread duty when I arrive. It's short-order chef time. An hour and five dozen eggs later, the hungrier children have eaten plates piled with fried and scrambled eggs and all the trimmings – twice – and DD has taken orders for 60 rolls for lunch. After a day orienteering, walking the hills, and visiting a working farm, the children return quieter, exhausted but in high spirits. They've vetoed the curry, so I've marinaded chicken breasts in olive oil, lemon juice, fresh thyme, tarragon and garlic, made a pot of spiced lentils for the veggies, cauliflower with and without béchamel, jacket potatoes, pans of slow-stewed onions cooked to a gloopy tangle in butter and olive oil, and a vat of plum crumble with brown sugar and flaked almonds. Everything goes, even the lentils!

On Sunday morning, after another breakfast and packed lunch marathon, I head for the abseiling, which is being run by Michael's army colleague Mark James, a successful climber of Mount Everest. The best sight of the weekend, is Richard being spurred on by Mark and the other lads as he finally plucks up the courage to abseil out of the top of the tower. He hadn't even wanted to attempt the small wall at the start. All that, and sugar on his scrambled eggs.

# Lasagne di Magro

This is a lovely dish, not worth leaving to the veggie population. It needs plenty of Parmesan to spruce up the vegetables. I made two versions, one with fennel the other with courgettes as the main vegetable. The mozzarella melts into a perfect, stringy goo over the dish.

SERVES 6

*3 medium courgettes or*
*4 fennel bulbs*
*2 medium carrots*
*125ml/4fl oz best olive oil*
*2 medium onions*
*225g/8oz shelled or frozen peas*
*salt and fresh black pepper*
*1¾ pints béchamel sauce, made*
*with nutmeg and a bay leaf*
*175g/6oz organic chestnut*
*mushrooms*
*1 box dried lasagne that needs no*
*pre-cooking*
*330g/11oz grated Parmesan*
*8 tomatoes, skinned and seeded*
*4 packets of buffalo mozzarella*

Preheat the oven to 200°C/400°F/Gas Mark 6.

Chop the courgettes and carrots into 2cm/¾ inch cubes. If you are using fennel, remove the outer tough layers, quarter the bulbs, then steam until almost tender. Heat the olive oil in a heavy-bottomed pan, add the peeled and finely sliced onions, and a bit of salt to release the juices. Fry gently until softened and translucent, then add the courgettes or fennel, the carrots and the peas. Season with salt and pepper. Cook until the carrots are *al dente*, but unbrowned, about 10 minutes.

Pour just enough béchamel sauce to cover the bottom of your greased baking dish, then add a layer of lasagne. Cover with a layer of the cooked vegetables, then a mantle of béchamel, followed by a handful of sliced raw mushrooms, one of Parmesan, and one of tomatoes. Repeat until you have used up all the ingredients.

Cover the top with slices of mozzarella, and bake for 25 minutes. Remove from the oven, and allow it to rest and cool for a few minutes before you serve it. As always, garlic bread and a plain green salad cannot be bettered.

# Lasagne al Forno

I had been minding my own business and making this classic dish in my own way for years before I came across Marcella Hazan's version. I am writing this in the hope that if you don't know it already, I might be able to convince you of its infinite superiority. A *ragu* is characterized by its mellow, gentle flavour, so don't blanch at the idea of adding milk to the meat first, it protects the meat from the acidic bite of the tomatoes you will add later. Remember to add salt to the meat as soon as you start cooking it, to leech the juice from the meat for the sauce, and do not think that lean mince is the answer. It ain't. You need a good marbling of fat for a sweeter *ragu*.

SERVES 8

*2–3 tbsp olive oil*

*a knob of butter*

*2 large onions, finely chopped*

*3 sticks celery, chopped*

*3 carrots, finely diced*

*3 or 4 cloves garlic, finely chopped*

*1 kg / 2½lb ground beef chuck, or similar, with plenty of fat*

*You can add ⅓ part ground pork to the beef if you wish*

*salt and fresh black pepper*

*2 bay leaves*

*250ml / 8fl oz milk*

*nutmeg*

*250ml / 8fl oz white wine*

*450g / 1lb tin of plum tomatoes*

*2 boxes dried lasagne, you will probably need 1⅓ boxes, of the sort that needs no precooking*

*freshly grated Parmesan*

*1.2 litre / 2 pints of béchamel, made with a bay leaf and nutmeg*

Preheat oven to 200°C/400°F/Gas Mark 6. Warm the oil and butter in a heavy cast-iron pot, add the onion, and sauté gently until softened and translucent. Add the celery, carrots and garlic, cook for another couple of minutes, stirring to coat well. Add the ground beef and a large pinch of salt, and grind over some pepper. Stir until the beef has lost its raw pink look. Add the bay leaves and milk, and simmer gently for about 10 minutes, until the meat has absorbed the milk. Add a suspicion of nutmeg, about ⅓ teaspoon. Add the wine, and let it simmer until it has evaporated, then add the cut-up tomatoes with their juice and stir thoroughly.

Cook at a lazy simmer, with just an intermittent bubble breaking through the surface, uncovered, for three hours or more. The fat will have separated from the sauce, but it will not be dry. Taste, and correct the seasoning.

Pour just enough béchamel to cover the base of your greased baking dish, then add a layer of lasagne, followed by a layer of the *ragu*, a layer of béchamel, and a good handful of Parmesan. Continue with two or three more layers, until your sauces are both used up, add a final sprinkling of Parmesan, and bake in the oven for about 30 minutes, The dish should be bubbling all over, and the knife should slip easily through the layers of lasagne. This *ragu* is great with spaghetti or tagliatelli, and makes a brilliant cottage pie.

# Guards' Pudding

Known as steamed strawberry pudding by my children. After cooking for 30 all weekend, it was as much as I could do to stick a leg of lamb in the oven, and make this delicious pudding with a pot of Shute Farm's strawberry jam, clotted with whole strawberries, when I got home.

SERVES 6

175g/6oz wholemeal breadcrumbs
25g/1oz self-raising flour
85g/3oz vanilla caster sugar
1 pot best strawberry jam, full of whole strawberries
3 eggs
125g/4oz melted butter
1 tsp bicarbonate of soda

Grease a 1.2 litre/2 pint pudding basin or plastic equivalent thoroughly. Mix the breadcrumbs together with the sifted flour and sugar in a large bowl. Melt the jam gently and pour it into the bowl with the whisked eggs and melted butter. Stir together. Dissolve the bicarb in a little bit of water, and stir it into the pudding. Pour into the pudding basin, and seal with pleated foil and string, or with the snap-on lid if you're using a plastic bowl. Place the pudding on a trivet, then pour boiling water to come halfway up the sides of the pudding basin. Cover with a lid and simmer for 2 hours.

Turn out, and serve with cream or if you want to be profligate, you can heat the contents of a second pot of jam to pour over the pudding with thick cream.

# Calves' Kidneys with Cabbage and Chorizo

The sweet, meaty mildness of calves' kidneys is one of life's great treats. I buy organic ones from Swaddles Green Farm; if you cannot get them, use lambs' instead, but it will be a different dish.

SERVES 4

*1 calf's kidney, fat and gristle removed, then you can separate the little nuggets and remove the outer membrane.*
*5cm / 2in chunk of good chorizo*
*½ savoy cabbage, shredded tinsel thin*
*seeded mustard*
*olive oil*
*salt and freshly ground pepper*

Cut the chorizo into matchstick strips, and soak it in a bowl in some good, fruity olive oil, 2–3 tablespoons. Blanch the cabbage in boiling water for a minute, hurl it into a colander, refresh under the cold tap, then drain it thoroughly.

Heat a film of olive oil in a pan and cook the kidney on a high heat for about 3 minutes, turning it to brown on all sides. Remove to a warming oven in a bowl, where it will exude some wonderful bloody juices.

Throw the chorizo and olive oil into a heavy-bottomed pan with the cabbage, and heat together thoroughly, adding a good tablespoon, or more to taste, of seeded mustard. Add the kidneys and their juices when all is hot and heavenly, and serve with acres of buttery mashed potatoes.

# Coq au Vin

I have a sense that this classic dish has fallen from grace, but it is just the kind of food I love, particularly at this time of year. My children agree. As with all classics, they should never be downgraded by the use of inferior ingredients, or by missing out things like the Cognac! Aim for a sauce that coats the fowl with a gluey, ruby-red richness and depth of flavour. Either use a whole jointed organic chicken, or, as I did, 6 good-sized legs

SERVES 6

85g/3oz unsalted butter
3 tbsp olive oil
125g/4oz diced organic green back bacon
18 shallots, but who's counting, peeled and left whole
18 organic mushrooms, halved
4 whole cloves of garlic
whole organic chicken, jointed or 6 good-sized legs
flour
a bouquet of fresh thyme, flat-leaf parsley and bay
4 tbsp Cognac
¾ bottle full-bodied red wine
1 tsp molasses sugar
salt and pepper
1 tbsp each of butter and flour
1 handful flat-leaf parsley

Preheat the oven to 180°C/350°F/Gas Mark 5.

Heat the butter and olive oil in a heavy-bottomed casserole, and throw in the bacon. Sauté briefly, then add the shallots, garlic and mushrooms and cook gently until the shallots are beginning to turn opaque and pale gold. Remove with a slatted spoon, and add the chicken pieces that you have shaken with some seasoned flour in a ziploc bag, then shaken the excess flour from. Brown first on one side then the other, for 5 minutes a side. Return the bacon and vegetables to the pot, add the bouquet, and season before covering with a lid and cooking until tender, about 25 minutes.

Set a saucepan on top of the stove on a moderate heat, warm the Cognac in a ladle, then pour it into the pan and set it alight. Let the alcohol burn off before adding the heated red wine and a teaspoon of molasses sugar, reduce by about a third, then thicken with some old-fashioned *beurre manie* made with a tablespoon each of butter and flour. Strain the sauce into the coq and keep hot until ready to serve. Scatter with the chopped parsley.

# Scallops with Parsnip Purée

The most important thing is the freshness and size of the scallops. My fishmonger, Phil Bowditch, in Taunton, has boats returning the same day the scallops are caught, so they are still alive in the shell. If they are beginning to smell, or look plumped up with water, avoid them. The scallop's sweet fleshiness marries beautifully with sweet legumes, Rowley Leigh cooks a particularly good combination of scallop with minted pea purée. I think roots work just as well with their starchy sweetness. I also love the clean, uncluttered simplicity of the two ingredients.

SERVES 2

*2 large scallops per person, for a
starter, cleaned and trimmed, the
white sliced in two,
the corals left whole
1 medium parsnip, peeled and cut
into chunks
a small knob of butter, and a tiny
bit of olive oil
salt and freshly ground pepper
little dusting of flat-leaf parsley*

Steam the parsnip until tender (keep the cooking water) and put through the smallest disc of your mouli (a processor would render it gluey) adding a tiny bit of cooking water to slacken it, and the butter, salt and pepper to taste. Keep warm. For the scallops, I use a ridged toasting machine, brushed with a tiny bit of olive oil before heating. You can use a griddle or frying pan, but need to turn the scallops at half time. When the surface is hot, quickly place the white discs of scallop on top. After about a minute, add the coral, close the lid, and wait about another minute. The moment the whites are translucent, they are cooked. Place a heap of parsnip on each plate, with the scallops on top, add the chopped parsley, season and serve.

# Minted Pea Purée

Much as I slavishly follow the seasons, and love fresh peas in summer, I love frozen peas, and not just the tiny green seed pearls of petits pois. I have just discovered Nutana's frozen organic peas, and they really taste of peas. You can buy them in the supermarket. Serve this instead of the parsnip with the recipe opposite, or with virtually any fish or meat dish.

SERVES 6

*1 onion, finely chopped*
*olive oil*
*a handful of mint*
*600ml / 1 pint good chicken stock*
*1kg / 2½lb frozen peas*
*sugar, salt and pepper to taste*

Sauté the onion gently in a bit of olive oil until softened and translucent. Add most of the mint, and cook briefly. Add the boiling chicken stock, bring it back to the boil, and pour on the peas, cooking them until they're done. Strain the liquid and reserve. Put the peas in the liquidizer and blend, adding a bit of the stock, but keeping the purée thick. Season with sugar, salt and pepper, and sprinkle over some really finely chopped mint leaves. Serve immediately, so it doesn't lose its green brilliance. Keep the remaining stock for soup.

# Lemon Cream Pots

A simple, citrus-sharp creamy pudding, which perfectly echoes the bistro era of the coq au vin.

SERVES 8

*125ml / 4fl oz lemon juice, about*
*3½ organic lemons' worth;*
*you can add a few drops of pure*
*lemon oil if you like, Boyajian do*
*one which is available in*
*supermarkets*
*85g / 3oz vanilla caster sugar*
*6 large egg yolks*
*375ml / 13fl oz organic*
*double cream*

Preheat oven to 160°C / 325°F / Gas Mark 3. Combine the lemon juice, lemon oil if using, and sugar in a bowl, and stir well to dissolve thoroughly. Test for sweetness. In a separate bowl whisk the egg yolks, then the cream into them. Whisk the lemon juice mixture into the cream one, then strain it into a jug through a sieve. Boil the kettle. Set 8 ramekins in a roasting tin, pour the creams into them, pour the scalding water into the tin halfway up the sides of the ramekins, and cover with a sheet of greaseproof to prevent a skin from forming. Bake in the middle of the oven until tremblingly set, about 30 minutes. They will carry on cooking once removed from the oven. Take the ramekins out of the water and cool on a rack before refrigerating for at least 2 hours or overnight.

# Winter Cabbage with Chestnuts, Bacon and Juniper

Perfect for little game birds at this time of year, I served mine alongside some briefly roasted partridges. This cabbage cooks as quickly as they do, unlike its red sibling. If you can't be bothered with fresh chestnuts, Merchant Gourmet do very good vacuum-packed whole chestnuts, which you can buy in the supermarket.

SERVES 6

*½ organic white cabbage*

*3 rashers organic smoked streaky bacon, snipped into strips*

*olive oil and butter*

*6 juniper berries, crushed in a pestle and mortar*

*18–20 chestnuts, cooked and peeled, or ½ packet Merchant Gourmet chestnuts*

*salt and freshly ground pepper*

Core the cabbage thoroughly, remove the tough stalky bits and shred finely. Blanch for a minute in plenty of boiling salted water, drain and refresh in cold water to arrest the cooking.

In a heavy-bottomed pot, gently fry the rashers in their own fat, then add a bit of olive oil and butter, the crushed juniper berries, and the cabbage. Stir well to coat the cabbage, season, put on the lid, and cook very gently for 15 minutes or so, but this is a very good-tempered dish; a few minutes either way won't hurt.

Add the halved chestnuts, stir them in and let them heat through, check the seasoning and serve.

# CLAUDIA RODEN

FLOATING BACKWARDS AND FORWARDS ACROSS THE CANDLE-LIT ROOM with shallow dishes and bowls heaped with exotically mosaiced mixtures of *mezze*, Claudia Roden is wearing a caftan and an incandescent smile. The occasion, to celebrate her new book *Tamarind and Saffron*, feels wholly un-English, although it is taking place in her north London home. That she should declare open house and cook on a scale not far removed from a lavish medieval banquet, is an unusual act of generosity in a world more attuned to the PR launch in the chicest new location. A couple of weeks later, I return, to talk over a late breakfast of gravadlax, herring and toasted brioche. Hospitality from another world. 'I don't want to embalm dishes, or change them for the sake of changing them, but I'm very into tradition; a dish belongs to a culture and civilization,' she begins.

It is 40 years since Claudia started writing her first cookery book, the classic *A Book of Middle Eastern Food*. She grew up in Egypt at a time when a lot of people didn't have their own oven, 'They might have a *mankal* – a charcoal burner – otherwise they sent their food to the public ovens all over Cairo, trays of stuffed vegetables, pies, roasts. The Africans and the Turks fried, in Syria, Lebanon and Egypt we baked. When I started writing my first cookery book in my early twenties, there wasn't a single cookery book in Egypt, everything was passed down from mothers or grandmothers. I started taking down recipes from the original, following them faithfully. Now after 40 years I can improve things a bit, follow my taste, but within the tradition. Tastes have changed, and over the years I have travelled, eating friends' food in Turkey, Morocco, Lebanon. Curiously none of the countries knew about each other's cuisine. They just thought the others cooked badly, so they weren't interested. Because Iraqis eat meat, they thought the Syrians were grass eaters like cows because they served so many vegetables and tabbouleh. The Turks in Istanbul thought they were so superior they didn't even want to know about regional food. Then there was the very grand Ottoman cuisine brought by the ruling classes to the Ottoman cities.'

Claudia's approach to food writing combines the academic discipline of the cultural historian, the anthropologist and the ethnographer, with the accuracy and attention to detail of a court transcriber. Her recording of the eating habits and dishes of a people, a place, setting them in their historical context, painstakingly and evocatively defining and distinguishing between culinary cultures, is something truly original, and, quite simply, no one does it better or more readably. So how did this lifetime's work come about? 'I came over to England as an art student. It is only when you leave a homeland and there is a fear of loss that you think you must do something. It is very often emigrés who write cookery books. I didn't know we ate Jewish food in Egypt until I left. Recapturing a place through food is beautiful, always the food is the good thing. First I wrote it for myself and my family who'd had to leave Egypt. My parents had to leave suddenly after Suez, it was a huge trauma for my father who was 59 and didn't speak any English. Home is here now, but I live in many different worlds. When you write about food in the way that I do you get very involved, say, with the Jews of Salonica, very passionate when you research into another world. The first book was a great labour of love. I thought I'm just doing it because it matters, it's important to do it, it will be of value to others. It took nine years to amass the recipes. I was fascinated by the Islamic world, generations of my family come from it. My first question was "What is a Syrian recipe?" I wanted to know why there were similar dishes in Morocco to those of Iran. I wanted a sense of unity out of all this variety, and I wanted to tell the story of something that mattered to me.'

Claudia's Middle Eastern classic has introduced at least two generations to the silken, smoky pleasures of *baba ghanoush* – aubergines with tahini – *ful medames* – the little earthy, Egyptian brown beans dressed in olive oil, lemon, garlic and parsley – as well as the revelation of the ancient Persian tradition of blending opposite with opposite, apricots with lamb, sweet with sour, strong with mild. '*Tamarind and Saffron* contains a lot of recipes from Middle Eastern Food, but rewritten with a strong awareness of how young people like to eat today. Simple good flavours, good combinations, something easy. I sympathize, but I still want them to cook. I've replaced the more labour-intensive dishes with things like lentils and rice with caramelized onions, and aubergines and cheese.'

Her smile has not, I believe, left her face during the whole of our three-hour conversation. It suffuses with its warmth, suggesting a serendipity of spirit. 'Really I am always happy. Do we have a happy gene? In Egypt there was not the Jewish thing of persecution, I have never been depressed.' Claudia has been presented with the Dutch Prince Claus Award for Culture, which has never been awarded to a food writer before. 'All the people who are doing something serious would like to be doing what we are doing,' she laughs. In Claudia's case it is a comment unworthy of her achievements. She is the most erudite of food writers, and her *Book of Jewish Food* stands alone this decade, I would venture, in terms of its scholarship, its accessibility and its originality.

# Chicken with Chickpeas

Claudia's mother used to make this dish with lemon and turmeric, which gives it a yellow tinge and a tangy flavour

SERVES 4

1 onion, finely chopped
2 tbsp sunflower oil
1 tsp turmeric
1 large organic chicken
225g / 8oz chickpeas soaked overnight
juice of one lemon, or more to taste
2–4 garlic cloves, crushed
black pepper or a pinch of cayenne
salt

Fry the onion in the oil in a large saucepan until golden, then stir in the turmeric. Put in the chicken and turn it until it is yellow all over. Add about 600ml / 1 pint of water, the drained chickpeas, lemon juice, garlic and pepper.

Bring to the boil and simmer, covered, for 1 hour or longer, turning the chicken occasionally and adding salt when the chickpeas have softened. Cook until the chicken is very tender, the chickpeas soft, yellow and lemony, and the liquid reduced,

# Baby Onions and Tamarind

You can find tamarind paste in Middle Eastern and Indian stores and many supermarkets these days. It gives the onions an intense sweet-and-sour taste.

SERVES 6

450g / 1lb shallots or pickling onions
2 tbsp olive oil
1 tbsp tamarind paste
1 tbsp sugar

Poach the onions in boiling water for about 5 minutes (this makes them easier to peel) and peel them when just cool enough to handle. In a pan just large enough to contain them in one layer, sauté the onions in the oil, shaking the pan and turning them to brown them lightly all over. Add the tamarind and the sugar and half cover with water. Stir well, and cook, covered, over a low heat for about 25 minutes or until very soft, adding water if necessary; lift the lid and reduce the sauce over a high heat at the end. Serve cold as a side dish, or as part of a *mezze*.

# Macerated Apricots and Nuts

This delicately fragrant sweet is an old Syrian speciality of Ramadan, the Muslim month of fast. It keeps very well for days, even weeks, covered with clingfilm in the refrigerator.

SERVES 6

450g / 1lb dried apricots (I use organic, unsulphured ones)
1¼ pint water
50g / 2oz blanched almonds
25g / 1oz pine nuts
25g / 1oz pistachios, coarsely chopped
1 tbsp rosewater
1 tbsp sugar, optional

Soak the apricots in the water overnight. Drain, reserving the soaking water.

Take a dozen of the apricots and blend to a light purée with the water in a food processor. Add to the rest of the apricots in a serving bowl and stir in the rest of the ingredients. Serve chilled.

# Chestnut Cake

Claudia Roden calls this her favourite chestnut cake in her lovely book *The Food of Italy*. You do not have to be purist and use fresh chestnuts, I use excellent whole vacuum-packed ones which good supermarkets sell.

125g / 4oz best bitter chocolate
100g / 3½oz blanched almonds or walnuts
450g / 1lb of chestnuts
5 eggs, separated
225g / 8oz caster sugar
125g / 4oz softened butter
grated rind of one lemon
2—3 tbsp Strega or Cognac

Preheat oven to 180°C / 350°F / Gas Mark 4. Butter and flour a 25cm / 10in cake tin. Grate the chocolate and finely chop the almonds or walnuts.

Blitz the chestnuts to a pulp in a food processor. Beat the egg yolks with the sugar. Add the butter, chestnut purée, nuts, grated lemon rind, chocolate and alcohol, and stir thoroughly. Beat the egg whites until stiff, then fold them in and pour into the cake tin. Bake for 50–60 minutes. Cool and remove from the tin. Serve cold.

# NORTHFIELD FARM

I AM IN PORK PIE COUNTRY. I have driven to this bastion of the raised pie crust, Melton Mowbray, to Northfield Farm, which specializes in rare breeds. A cold wind scythes across the open pasture as Ian McCourt and I walk out to see the pigs. The mothers, naturally gregarious, come to the gates to greet us, but there isn't a babe in sight, they are invisible, buried alive in their deep straw beds, little hummocks hermetically sealed against the winter chill. In the next shed are scores of Lilliputian Dexter cattle, a small, dumpy, ancient Irish breed whose undercarriages are as low-slung as a sleek sports car, short legged, sturdy with a sort of poodle-permed forelock. They are mostly black, with a smattering of recessive-gened interlopers which are deep dun or coppery red. Dexters have been Irish house cows for thousands of years, very milky for their size, but also good eaters, both sexes, for whom the Chinese proverb 'The closer to the ground the better the beef,' was clearly intended. 'Eat them or lose them,' is Ian's answer to the rarity factor. 'They are only rare because people stopped eating them. Dexters, like many rare breeds, take longer to finish, although present rules allow only 30 months before they have to be killed. It's got to change, they take longer to reach their optimum quality and value.'

It is just over two years since Ian, a syndicator of bond issues in the City, was sent home from work one afternoon. 'My secretary came into the office saying she'd got a list of six redundancies, but she could only find the names of five. I was the sixth. Coming back to Rutland on the train, I thought I don't want to go back to that life. It was a simple decision, although people said how brave it was; we'd got a lot of debt, we could either sell up or make a go of it.' Ian, brought up in London, had always loved farming and horses. His Irish grandfather had farmed at Houth, and Ian had bought a smallholding in the Fens with horses and a few Dexter cattle early in his City career. 'I read a 1905 farming book on agricultural breeds, and Dexter made the most sense, they're hardy, and very efficient processors of low-grade forage. When I killed the first one, there was a huge amount of meat; we gave it all away, everything from the brisket to the sirloin, and overnight I had a waiting list of buyers. Dexters are one of only three breeds, all Irish, never to have had BSE.' When the axe fell, Ian had never cut up an animal in his life. He went home to tell his wife Tessa, and the bank. 'I was delighted but devastated,' Tessa admits, basting a cushion-plump Aylesbury duck and a 'goose cut' shoulder of lamb for our lunch. 'When he told me, I was chasing escaped cattle. I was very, very cross: with life, with cattle, with the farm. It took me 24 hours, but then I said let's go for it. I was up at 5am feeding the animals, learning how to butcher and make sausages. I've always loved cooking, but I thought things like pork and leek, and beef, chilli, paprika and fennel sausages would never work up here, people wouldn't buy that sort of thing, but they do, they do, they do!'

Tessa has started cooking ready-made meals, dishes like Beef in Grainstore, Lamb Korma, Sweet and Sour Pork. 'A lot of children insist their parents buy our meals – Mrs McCourt's cottage pies are nicer than yours Mummy. Our strength is in simplicity. What's driven the business is a robust product, good marketing and a good story. What we're doing isn't particularly novel, but no one does it in such an integrated way.'

The McCourts have just bought one of the three licensed factories for making Melton Mowbray pork pies. It's another gamble. The aim is to set up 'The Rare Breed Meat Company' to make cooked foods, sausages and pies. 'I'm a total tart,' Tessa says, 'If they buy it and eat it I'll cook it, but quality is the most important thing.'

The former syndicator of bond issues and his formidable wife are about as likely to succeed as they are certain about their switch from city to rural traders. 'I don't think, genuinely, there's anything we'd rather do,' says Ian. 'We're passionate about it.'

# Pot-Roasted Brisket of Beef with Roast Root Vegetables

SERVES 5–6

*1 kg / 2½ lb brisket of beef*
*a selection of root vegetables, I used*
*1 large parsnip, 1 swede, and 3*
*carrots, onions and sticks of celery*
*olive oil*
*sea salt and pepper*
*bouquet of bay, parsley,*
*thyme and orange peel*
*about 1¼ pint of robust red wine,*

Brisket is a wonderful fat cut of beef to slow roast, with a run of lean stewing meat threaded through its middle.

Preheat the oven to 150°C / 300°F / Gas Mark 2. Assemble a selection of root vegetables. Cube the roots into 2.5cm / 1in squares, quarter the onions, or halve them if they are small, and cut the celery, carefully strung, into 2.5cm / 1in pieces. Brown the brisket on all sides in a bit of olive oil in a heavy-bottomed pot into which it should fit snugly. Throw in the vegetables with a bit more olive oil, brown, strew on some sea salt and pepper, tuck in a bouquet of bay, parsley, thyme and orange peel, then splosh on the red wine.

Cover with a sheet of greaseproof paper and roast for 2 hours, but another half hour won't hurt. If the red wine is reducing too much, pour on the same again. The vegetables should be tender when the dish is cooked, but if they are still a bit firm, keep the meat warm for 20 minutes while you finish cooking them separately. Serve this with lashings of buttery mashed potatoes. The children demanded thick-cut brisket sandwiches to take to school the next day.

# Shin of Beef with Mustard, Celeriac and Marsala

Dexter shin of beef is claret coloured and heavily marbled, so perfect for braising. I even used half shin and half steak for a steak and kidney pie, and there wasn't a shred of toughness in the densely textured, richly flavoured meat. The McCourts hang their beef for three to six weeks.

SERVES 4

1kg / 2½lb shin of beef
2 medium onions,
peeled and chopped
2–3 cloves garlic,
peeled and chopped
3 carrots, cut into chunks
a small celeriac,
cut into 2.5cm / 1in dice
2 sticks of celery and
leaves, chopped
¼ pint Marsala
750ml / 1¼ pint robust red wine,
or more, to just cover
2 dsrtsp seeded mustard
2 dsrtsp tomato purée
2–3 handfuls frozen
peas, optional
olive oil, salt, pepper, a bouquet
made as above

Preheat the oven to 150°C / 300°F / Gas Mark 2.

Cut the meat into generous 2.5cm / 1in cubes and shake them in seasoned flour. Brown the floured cubes of meat in olive oil in a heavy-bottomed pot, not too many at a time, on all sides, then set aside.

Put a bit more olive oil in the pot and gently sauté the onions and garlic for a few minutes until translucent. Add the carrots, celeriac and celery, cook gently on all sides for a few minutes, return the meat to the pot, and add the Marsala. Set light to it, let it crackle, burn off the alcohol, and let the flames die down before adding the bouquet, tucked well in, and the heated red wine. If it doesn't quite cover, add a bit of hot water.

Season, cover with greaseproof paper and a lid, and cook for about 2 hours. Take off the lid, stir in the mustard and tomato purée to enrich and thicken, and the peas if using. Return to the oven for 30 minutes.

# Moroccan Stuffed Tomatoes with Tomato Couscous

This was one of those inspired, moreish — and probably Moorish — dishes that come about when you want a new take on mince. I found large, organic Moroccan tomatoes in the supermarket, which looked too anaemic to respond to subtle flavouring.

FILLS 10 LARGE TOMATOES,
SERVES 4

10 large tomatoes
2 small onions, finely chopped
2 celery sticks, finely chopped
1 clove garlic, finely chopped
olive oil
450g/1lb organic minced beef
1 tsp each of allspice, cumin seeds and coriander
3 heaped tsp tomato purée
6–7 ladles chicken stock
50g/2oz pine nuts
375g/13oz organic couscous
salt and pepper

Preheat the oven to 180°C/350°F/Gas Mark 4.

Slice off the tomato lids, and take out the tomatoes' cores, seeds and juice with a serrated spoon. Reserve all the gunk in a bowl. Fry the onions, celery and garlic in a bit of olive oil. Then add the organic minced beef. Crush the spices in a mortar, sieve them if still husky and add to the pan. Add the tomato purée and some pepper, and cook until the meat is browned all over. Add 2–3 ladles of chicken stock, and simmer for half an hour. Top up with stock if it begins to dry out. Add the pine nuts you have toasted in a medium oven until golden brown, and cook a further 30 minutes. Season with salt and more pepper if needed.

Stuff the tomatoes with the mixture as full as you dare, sitting them in a roasting tin. Put their lids on, add 4 ladles of hot stock, and dribble over a bit of olive oil. Bake in the oven for 30–40 minutes, until the tomatoes are softened and sagging. Meanwhile, steam the couscous in a tea towel inside a steamer for 30 minutes. Fork it through gently, adding the tomato gunk that you have whizzed in the food processor and sieved. The couscous will turn a delicate pink and absorb all the liquid. Steam for a further 20 minutes, You could add some chopped fresh coriander at the end, I didn't have any. Spoon some couscous on to each plate, then add the tomatoes and some juice. Divine.

# GRAEME WALLACE, DEER FARMER

PAVAROTTI IS STANDING MOTIONLESS, head erect, his cool, patrician gaze levelled at the large bunch of females who he is clearly master of. 'He's a pussy cat in the summer, but in the winter he's wild," Graeme Wallace tells me from the safety of a 10-foot-high wire fence that separates us from the maestro's field. It is a truly extraordinary sight on a winter's afternoon: above, a watercolour sky, below, a loamy field in which a stag stands sentinel over an immobile herd of dun-coloured hinds, spindle legged, their winter coats tinged with roan and ginger, a single black blaze striping the spine of their elegant necks.

Graeme's herd of red deer high on the Blackdown Hills has eight stags, 80 breeding hinds, and 200 youngsters which are fattened up to eat at between 18 months and two years. They are semi-wild, but share the same sense of hierarchy as the completely wild herds. With a top speed of around 50 mph they can outpace a quad bike; in fact, Harry, one of the stags, chased one across the field during the hectic ardour of the rutting season. When they come to life and head towards us, it is neither a walk, a trot nor a canter, but a nervy, skittish prance, proud, fleet-footed, elegant.

It is 14 years since Graeme, exhausted by his move to the Blackdowns with 500 ewes, and the subsequent sleepless nights of the lambing season, decided to have a weekend off. He checked in to a deer farmers' conference in Wales. 'I don't know what possessed me, but everyone there was so friendly, so informative, so generous, I just thought yes, I'm going to give this a go. I was looking for something new. That autumn I found 12 acres and bought 30 deer, it was just a gut feeling. All these alternative enterprises promise you gold, they all call themselves "the realistic alternative," but I've seen trout farming and angora, they've been and gone. When I started, most people who were in deer were in it to sell breeding stock, that was high value in the mid '80s, but deer were still very much a hobby. I felt the key to the whole thing was selling the end product.' The final notch in the evolutionary belt came last summer, when Graeme took his wares to Cullompton Farmers' Market. 'Retailing was an absolute eye-opener, the feed-back, the contact with the consumer. It's what I love most, it was really a revelation, it made me think retail instead of wholesale, so my whole way of looking at the business has changed. Selling directly means 20 per cent more profit, but it also means I get people's appreciation. For 12 years I had none, just restaurants haggling over the price or the fact that we were late delivering. I've done a recipe leaflet because it's important that everyone has a good experience the first time they buy it, and a lot of the people I sell to have never cooked venison before. Our loin medallions are so tender they're the best things money can buy; if you didn't have teeth you could eat them! If the farmers' markets survive, that's how I want to go on selling. I'd been flogging myself to death, but suddenly I'm rejuvenated. I really enjoy selling, though I didn't think I'd ever say that.'

# Medallions of Venison with Red Wine and Juniper

If you like your venison to taste really gamey, keep it in the fridge for a couple of weeks in its vacuum pack before you cook it. Graeme hangs his animals for six days.

SERVES 2

4 medallions of venison
generous knob of butter
9 or 10 juniper berries
coarsely ground black pepper
salt
slug of wine and of port

This is the simplest and speediest of venison recipes. Heat a generous knob of butter in a heavy frying pan until golden and bubbling. Grind the juniper berries to as fine a powder as you can. Season the meat with coarsely ground pepper, then press in half the juniper to the side you are going to cook first, and put the medallions into the pan. After 3 minutes, sprinkle the rest of the juniper over them, grind a bit more pepper, and turn them over. They should take 2–3 minutes more if you like them rare. Season with salt and pepper before the end of the cooking time.

Remove, and let them rest in a warm oven while you scrape the pan juices and add a good slug of wine, and one of port if you have it, to the pan. Let this bubble and begin to reduce, then pour it over each portion. A robust root purée, either celeriac and potato or swede and carrot, and some spiced redcurrant jelly, and the dish is complete.

# Venison Liver with Gin, Port and Juniper

SERVES 3

600g / 1¼ lb venison liver
seasoned flour
butter
12 juniper berries, ground
2–3 tbsp gin
slug of port

I sliced the liver horizontally into the same thickness you would for calves' liver and tossed it in seasoned flour.

Add it to a frying pan of bubbling butter and sprinkle over the ubiquitous ground juniper berries, in this case a dozen, and cook it for just over a couple of minutes a side, until a knife blade goes in unresisted.

Keep it warm in a serving dish in a warm oven, deglaze the pan with a few tablespoons of gin, and when that thickens and is beginning to brown, add a good slug of port, and simmer it for a few minutes, before pouring it over the liver.

# Venison Steak and Kidney Pie

I had never tried venison kidney either; it made a wonderful gamey alternative to ordinary steak and kidney.

SERVES 4

*675g / 1½lb venison steak and kidney*

*seasoned flour to coat*

*3 small onions, chopped*

*3 large portobello mushrooms, or chestnut mushrooms if you can't get them*

*2–3 ladles good chicken or game stock, I used pheasant*

*1 glass each of Marsala and port, or substitute red wine if it suits you better*

*2 bay leaves*

*a heaped tsp of crushed juniper berries*

*butter*

SHORTCRUST PASTRY

*175g / 6oz flour*

*85g / 3oz butter*

*beaten egg*

Preheat oven to 150°C / 300°F / Gas Mark 2.

Sauté the floured meat in some butter until just browned on all sides. Remove to a plate, and add the onions and a bit more butter to the pan. Cook until softened and translucent. Cook the sliced mushrooms separately in a bit of butter, until they begin to exude their black juice. Return the meat to the pan, add the mushrooms, sprinkle over the juniper, add the booze, allow it to come to a bubble, then add 2–3 ladles of stock to just cover, season, and tuck in the bay leaves. Cover with greaseproof paper and a lid, and cook in the oven for an hour, no longer, venison is so unfatty it would start to toughen and dry out. Cool. You can do this a day or two before you want to eat it.

Make a shortcrust with 175g / 6oz flour and 85g / 3oz butter. Spoon the filling into the bottom of your pie dish and place a china bird or egg cup in the dish to funnel out the steam. Add a strip of pastry to the edge of the dish you have brushed with water, then place the rolled-out sheet of pastry over the top. Brush with a beaten egg wash, and cook in a hottish oven (190°C / 375°F / Gas Mark 5) for about 50 minutes. Serve with mashed potato and red cabbage.

At the same time, for the children, I also roasted a small haunch joint, weighing 1kg / 2½lb, which I placed on a sliced onion. I seasoned the venison and covered it with a thickly coated butter paper, and poured a couple of glasses of wine around. Dryness is the enemy of venison, keep basting. After 40 minutes cooking and 20 minutes rest in a warm oven, it was carved into thin, succulent ruby-red slices. Graeme had, of course, left the bone in. It will feed four people if sliced as above, which suits the grain of the meat best.

# Venison Liver Parfait

I had never seen a whole venison liver before. It is a deep, dark, garnet colour, almost black, and dense. It is curious how venison is complemented by things its own colour, cabbage, beetroot, juniper, port. This is a fantastic dish for a celebration, not difficult to make, but when you chill it, turn it out and cut it into rosy pink, lightly creamy slices it will delight even more than the chicken liver version.

SERVES 12

*about 600g / 1¼ lb venison liver*
*1 clove garlic, crushed*
*2 heaped tsp juniper berries,*
*well crushed*
*salt and freshly ground pepper*
*3 eggs*
*800ml / 28fl oz good double*
*cream, I used Loseley Jersey cream*
*3 large tbsp gin*

Preheat oven to 160°C / 325°F / Gas Mark 3.

Butter a 30 x 8 x 8 cm (12 x 3 x 3in) terrine with a lid, or a 900g / 2lb loaf tin. Chop the liver into chunks, and throw it into the food processor with the garlic, juniper, salt and pepper, and process until liquid and smooth. Add the eggs, and continue for a further minute, then add the cream and gin, and give it another few seconds. Check for seasoning, it needs quite a bit of salt and pepper, and you might want more juniper. Then sieve it into your terrine. Do not omit this stage, you want a velvet smooth texture. Cover with the lid, and stand the terrine in a *bain-marie* with hot water up to its middle in a roasting tin. Cook for an hour. Check that it is just firming to the touch, it will continue to cook when you remove it from its water bath and leave it to cool. It could need a further 10 minutes or so, but mine was beautifully pink after an hour. When cool, refrigerate for at least a couple of hours. To serve, dip the terrine into hot water, run a fine-bladed knife carefully around the edges, hold your breath and turn it upside down on to a serving dish. Then make a lot of wholemeal toast, and serve it with the best French unsalted butter you can find. I wrapped the remains of mine in clingfilm and kept it in the fridge for several days.

# L'ATELIER DU CHOCOLAT

GERARD COLEMAN, AN IRISHMAN FROM DUNDALK, and his partner Anne Françoise Weyns from Liege are hard at work. A large marble slab is covered in a window-pane-sized oblong of chocolate. To the right is a chocolate tank, where 30 litres of the shiniest, satiny dark stuff are sucked round by a pump, a fountain of chocolate disgorged into a huge metal tank, to be tempered by invisible paddles beneath its weighty gloss. These are the headquarters of L'Atelier du Chocolat, a chocolate 'workshop' that carries all the hallmarks of *haute couture*, each chocolate handmade with only the finest and purest ingredients.

It is about eight months since Gerard started the business. He had allowed himself a few months to experiment with flavours and textures first. His background as a pastry chef, working for Bruno Loubet, had led him to Belgium to study for 18 months. 'I was in Brussels making chocolates under Pierre Marcolini, who won the world cup in pastry and gâteau making in 1995. My aim is to produce the best-quality chocolates and eventually have a shop which also sells gâteaux, ice cream, cakes, and has chocolate window sculpture. I work mostly with ganache and infusions.'

For those of you ignorant on the subject of ganache, let me tell you a story. There was once an apprentice in 19th-century France, who was busy in the kitchen when he inadvertently spilled a bowl of hot cream into one of chocolate. The chef, in his anger, screamed '*Ganache*,' or 'Imbecile' at him, then set about rescuing what could have been an expensive accident, until he realized the ebony and ivory had been transformed by their marriage into something quite wonderful.

Gerard's ganache is made with the finest ingredients that money can import, 35 per cent butter fat cream from Isigny Ste Mère, Escure butter, Valrhona and Callebaut chocolate and unrefined sugar. 'In England there is so much mediocre chocolate. They import chocolate, and people think it's great just because it's Belgian or French. But even the good manufacturers have hundreds of grades of chocolate. I mostly use a 70 per cent, which is a very high grade chocolate, but it can be too bitter for some things, so I add a 60 per cent to balance it and make it sweeter. The average percentage in Cadbury's chocolate is about 15, so you can imagine what's left. I use Callebaut and Valrhona. Callebaut don't have their own plantations, they buy their beans in the market from different countries, then blend them together for a more generic taste. Valrhona have plantations in Venezuela, the Caribbean, Papua New Guinea and Trinidad. A lot of people say it is the best, it is the Bordeaux to Callebaut's table wine, but it depends what you are wanting it for. I use chocolate like a spice, I know how to balance it and blend it.'

On the chill black marble slab, where Gerard did all his tempering by hand until he'd saved £8,000 for the mighty tank, lie three 5-kilo bars of the best, one dark, one milk, one white. He shaves and teases little chips off each block to taste the raw quality. Then he places a small, black square on the slab, 'I've infused star anise and Costa Rica coffee into it.' The bitter-sharp acidity of the coffee is made mild by a milkier chocolate middle, which is then enrobed in the darkest chocolate. The spice underscores mysteriously, subtly, unexpectedly. We move on to 'salted caramel,' which Anne Françoise describes as 'So painful to make, I thought Gerard wouldn't want to do it. It's brilliant, but it was so difficult to get it right. The caramel has to be cooked at exactly the right temperature, we chucked 5 or 6 kilos away that was too liquid. It mustn't be too salt, too chewy, too liquid.' The result, with its brittle dark shell of chocolate, its softly fudgy interior that turns from sweet to salt on the tongue, is pure genius. And I normally hate caramel.

'We are making chocolates that are more French than Belgian, with a high cocoa content, mostly ganache; the Belgians make more pralines, and they're sweeter,' Gerard explains. He cuts into a *feuillantine*, made with crisp, Belgian pancakes that have been dried and shredded, then mixed with pralinée and speculoos – gingerbread spice. Again, what you taste at the beginning is not what you taste at the end. The surprise is the strength and length of flavour, from the fine, sandy crunch to the bitter chocolate and finally the warm winter spice, which my daughter Miranda compares to scented candles when she tries one later.

Even the chocolate truffles are unlike any I've eaten. 'A lot of people make them too dense, too hard. I make them with 70 per cent plain dark chocolate, then make a dark, moussey centre which is piped in, before dusting them with cocoa powder.' My bag doesn't make it down the M4. I arrive home with the tell-tale DNA print of cocoa – a dusty trace on my fingers. Gerard insists 'They should be eaten at room temperature like cheese or red wine. You don't get the full flavour cold.' He is experimenting with a raft of new flavours, caramelized pear, thyme and banana, sweet wine, melon and fennel, and different textures, 'Just as important, I won't just do new flavours for the sake of it.' Take my advice, these are the best chocolates you are ever likely to taste, each one a distillation of flavour, a miniature explosion of taste, a work of art; try them all.

# Chocolate Pots with Star Anise and Coffee

This was an experiment inspired by Gerard's use of the spice and coffee in his chocolate. It worked brilliantly in these richest of little chocolate pots, a crust of chocolate concealing a velvety smooth chocolate cream.

MAKES 5 LITTLE RAMEKINS

*175ml / 6fl oz good double cream*
*a heaped tsp fresh ground coffee*
*a heaped tsp whole star anise*
*85ml / 3fl oz Jersey milk*
*135g / 4½oz good, dark chocolate,*
*Valrhona or similar*
*2 egg yolks*
*1 heaped tbsp unrefined icing sugar*

Heat the cream with the coffee and star anise until just below boiling, then remove from the heat, cover and leave to infuse, which I did for an hour.

Preheat the oven to 140°C / 275°F / Gas Mark 1. Melt the chocolate very gently in the milk. Beat the egg yolks with the sugar, then add the chocolate milk mixture and the sieved coffee and star anise mixture, and beat together until blended. Pour into the ramekins and put them in a roasting tin with scalding water to reach halfway up the ramekins' sides. Bake for 45 minutes, remove from their *bain-marie*, let them cool, then put them in the fridge for a few hours before serving. If you are doubtful of this combination, you can omit the star anise and coffee, and just use the classic half a vanilla pod split, with the black grains extracted and used too.

# Rich Chocolate and Prune Mousse

Do not be alarmed by the unconventional method of making this richest and most delicious of mousses, whose darkly bitter density is cut by the prunes. After a night in the fridge, I transported it to a Sunday lunch party in Oxford, where it was pronounced a success by all present!

SERVES 8–10

*about 2 dozen organic prunes*
*pot of hot leaf-tea*
*150g / 5oz vanilla caster sugar*
*3 whole eggs, separated, and*
*3 extra yolks*
*1 tbsp Green and*
*Black's cocoa powder*
*200ml / 7fl oz double cream*
*85g / 3oz unsalted butter*
*225g / 8oz best bitter chocolate,*
*I used L'Atelier's 70 per cent*
*couverture chocolate*
*1 tbsp Armagnac or Cognac*

I poured hot leaf-tea, Whittard's Afternoon Blend, to cover the prunes, and left them in the bowl overnight. This way you don't need to cook the prunes, just remove them from the liquid and chop each one into thirds when you need them. Put 50g / 2oz of the sugar, all 6 egg yolks, the cocoa powder and the cream in the top of a double saucepan of simmering water. Keep whisking it over a gentle heat until it thickens enough to coat a wooden spoon. Take the top saucepan out of the bottom one, and, off the heat, add small pieces of the butter and chocolate and stir until fully melted. Add the alcohol and stir it in.

Whisk the 3 egg whites with the rest of the sugar. Do not add the sugar at the end, this method makes a thickly glossy meringue which you want to whisk to soft peak stage. Fold the meringue lightly into the chocolate mixture that you have decanted into a bowl and add the prunes. They will not sink to the bottom, the mixture is too dense. Pour into a large soufflé dish and refrigerate.

# Chocolate Brownies

MAKES 12–15

*125g/4oz softened unsalted butter*
*225g/8oz vanilla caster sugar*
*2 eggs and 1 yolk*
*200g/7oz best bitter chocolate*
*4 tbsp freshly made coffee*
*150g/5oz plain flour*
*1 tsp baking powder*
*a pinch of sea salt*
*a handful of broken walnuts,*
*optional*

Preheat the oven to 180°C/350°F/Gas Mark 4. Place a piece of foil in the bottom and up the sides of a roasting tin or earthenware dish. Mine is about 30 x 22cm/12 x 9in.

Gently melt the chocolate in a double boiler or in a bowl over, but not touching, hot water. Cream the butter until really light and fluffy, I do this in the Kitchen Aid. Add the eggs, one at a time, then the yolk, with the mixer running. Pour in the melted chocolate, then the coffee.

Remove the mixing bowl to a work surface and sift in the flour, baking powder and a pinch of salt. Fold it all in with the walnuts, pour it into the tin, and bake for 20–25 minutes. A skewer inserted into the mixture should come out a bit sticky. The interior should be a sort of fudgy goo, not a sponge. Leave to cool before you cut them into squares and turn them out.

# Spiced Fruit Loaf

A delicious spiced loaf speckled with organic vine fruits, a bit like a giant hot cross bun. My 10-year-old Charissa's tasting notes are as follows, 'Serve thickly coated with butter, and honey if you've got a sweet tooth.'

MAKES 2 SMALL LOAVES

*500g / 1 and a bit lb strong white organic flour, I used Shipton Mill's*
*a large pinch of salt*
*25g / 1oz fresh yeast, from health food stores or supermarkets with in-store bakeries*
*1 heaped tsp mixed spice*
*65g / 2½oz non-hydrogenated vegetable spread such as Biona or Suma*
*roughly 300ml / ½ pint water*
*65g / 2½oz organic raisins*
*50g / 2oz each organic currants and sultanas*

Sift the flour and salt into a large bowl and crumble in the fresh yeast. Add the mixed spice and the vegetable margarine in small pieces, and work it and the yeast in as you would for a crumble. Work in the water until you have a ball of stiffish dough. Leave it somewhere warm to prove for an hour and double in size, then knock it back with vim and vigour, adding the vine fruits.

Grease a baking sheet lightly with a bit of sunflower oil or the like, divide the dough into two, and put each round ball, like two large rolls, on the baking sheet. Allow to double in size again, about another hour. Preheat oven to 200°C / 400°F / Gas Mark 6 and bake for about 30 minutes. The loaves will be quite dense with a lightly coloured top. Cool on a wire rack.

# Cheese and Onion Bread

You can make this bread with all Cheddar if it's a good, strongly flavoured one like Montgomery or Keens, or use half blue cheese. The red onions give it a wonderful colour. The water in the onions slackens the dough considerably, so mix carefully.

MAKES 2 SMALL OR
1 HUBCAP-SIZED ROUND LOAF

*500g / 1 and a bit lb strong white organic flour*
*a good pinch of salt, this is a savoury loaf, but too much salt will kill the yeast*
*15g / ½oz fresh yeast*
*1 tbsp organic sunflower oil*
*1 medium onion, coarsely chopped*
*up to 300ml / ½ pint water*
*50g / 2oz mature organic Cheddar, or ½ Cheddar , ½ blue cheese*

Sieve the flour and salt into a bowl, and crumble the yeast in. Pour in the oil, mix it in a bit with your hand, throw in the onion, then start pouring in the water. Work the mixture into a stiff dough, then sit it in a warm place for an hour until it has doubled in size.

Knock it back vigorously, and either leave it whole or divide it into two. Form it into a flat round, and place it on an oiled baking sheet. Leave it for another hour to double in size, then sprinkle grated cheese over the top.

Preheat the oven to 220°C / 425°F / Gas Mark 7. Bake for about 25 minutes until starting to change colour and hollow sounding. Cool on a wire rack. Delicious eaten warm with unsalted butter, or try it with Marmite and watercress or goat's cheese.

# Buttery Lemon and Lime Cake

This cake was a happy accident. I found myself following the instructions for one recipe while using the ingredients for another, but it wasn't too late to change tack and invent something totally different that would be as good for a pudding as warm from the oven for tea.

SERVES 6–8

*200g / 7oz butter*
*325g / 12oz vanilla caster sugar*
*2 eggs*
*125g / 4oz self-raising flour*
*1 tsp baking powder*
*juice of 2 lemons (5 tbsp)*
*and the rind of one*
*juice of 1 ½ limes and*
*the rind of 1*
*a few drops each of Boyajian pure*
*lime oil and pure lemon oil,*
*optional, good supermarkets sell it*
*1 tbsp crème fraîche*

ICING:
*25g / 1oz unrefined icing sugar*
*2–3 tsp lemon juice*

Preheat oven to 180°C / 350°F / Gas Mark 4. Grease and flour a 22cm / 9in springform tin.

Cream the butter and sugar thoroughly, then add the eggs one by one. Sift in the flour and baking powder together, add the juices and fruit oils, then the crème fraîche, and fold in lightly. Pour into the tin and bake for 45–50 minutes, a skewer should come out clean. Stir the 2–3 teaspoons of lemon juice into the icing sugar for the icing, then spread it over the top. It should just cover it in a thin, sticky veil.

# LINA STORES

I FIRST STARTED SERIOUS FOOD SHOPPING IN SOHO when I was a student. I did the Friday night exodus from London in reverse, and on Saturday morning headed straight for Pâtisserie Valerie for a breakfast of hot brioche and apricot jam. Then on to the market and the shops, I would invariably have upwards of ten to cook for on a Saturday night in my one-room flat. There was still a faded French delicatessen on the corner of Wardour Street, Richards' the fishmongers in Brewer Street, and opposite, at Randall and Aubin, a breathtaking display of offal and game, as raw and tempting as anything else the neighbourhood had to offer. Standing out among the arteries of alleyways, hard by the latex and leather, was the illustrious Lina Stores. Nothing appears to have changed, the green-tiled façade revealing a pistachio interior, and floor to ceiling shelves of olive oils, tomatoes, anchovies and capers, squat sacks of rice, polenta, pulses and chestnuts nestling at knee height as you enter, wooden racks, hooks and baskets crammed and hanging with meats and fresh baked breads, casareccio, great elbows of ciabatta, oily foccaccia, and a mottled marble slab stacked with green and cream prinked-edged ravioli stuffed with spinach and ricotta, tortelloni stiff with veal and pork. There is a counter brimming with garnet-hued salami glistening with pearls of garlicky fat, prosciutto and culatello, the tenderest and sweetest of hams cut from the softest part of the leg. There are ivory doorstops of fresh and dried Pecorino, Gorgonzola, Taleggio and ricotta, with trays of olives and wonky wedges of straw-coloured Parmigiano which you can help yourself to. At the back, two tall fridges house Casabianca, the most meltingly creamy, lactic balls of buffalo mozzarella, jars stuffed with tiny parcels of fresh black truffles from Norcia in southern Italy, and tubs of homemade pasta sauces. Nothing is more than an arm's stretch away; it is my idea of a perfect shop, family run, courteous, noisy, buzzing yet unhurried, full although there is barely room for the customers. Pressed against the pastas, only a breath away from the scented fists of fresh basil, sage and rocket, with Tony passing titbits from the slicer, it is a home from home.

Gabriella Saccomani's mother and father took over the shop nearly 25 years ago. She and her husband Antonio – Tony – and Franco, a cousin, run it now, but her father Giovanni still comes in at 6am every morning. 'He is 72. He makes the sauces, Napoli and Bolognese, and he's famous for his rock cakes and apple pies,' Gabriella tells me. 'Mum is 71 and she still does the accounts and the VAT. The original Lina, who started the shop during the war, used to make the pasta by hand.'

'Last week I made beetroot and mascarpone tortelloni, and some with chèvre and rocket. I always do a pumpkin and ricotta one, but sometimes I put in feta cheese. The fancy people ask me to put parsley in it. I make 70–80 pounds of fresh pasta a day, more at weekends,' Tony says.

So will there be a third generation of this remarkable family at Lina Stores? The signs are not altogether promising. 'My son Gianni is studying Classics at Somerville College, Oxford, my daughter is doing her GCSEs.' Tony works from 6 in the morning until 8 at night six days a week, but there's no incentive beyond his family's highly developed work ethic. 'The rents have gone sky high,' Gabriella tells me. 'And no one can park. Last week the kitchen shop opposite closed down, five years ago it was Richards' the fishmongers. Everybody who works round here during the day knows everyone else. A lot of customers live round here, have babies, grow up, we know them over a lifetime. That's the lovely part of this business. We try to provide them with good-quality and top of the range foods they can't get anywhere else.' Tony adds, 'A gentleman was sent here from Harrods because he couldn't find a good balsamic vinegar. I've got a 30-, a 50- and a 100-year-old at £70 a bottle. I like to stock it, not for profit, but just in case anybody asks. I'd like to keep only the best, but you can't in a place like this. About 50 per cent of our customers have no problem with money, but for about 30 per cent of them money is short.' No one is going to slap a preservation order on Lina Stores, but for as long as the Saccomanis look after their customers and friends, I will keep coming back.

# Spaghetti Carbonara

You can use either fat chunks of pancetta for this, or tear up prosciutto or culatello. It is really just a glorious Roman version of eggs and bacon served with spaghetti. I use half Parmesan and half Pecorino, but do as your fridge dictates.

SERVES 6

500–750g / 18–24oz spaghetti
225g / 8oz pancetta, cut into small strips, or shredded prosciutto
2 or 3 cloves garlic
3 tbsp best olive oil
125ml / 4fl oz dry white wine
2 large eggs
50g / scant 2oz each of grated Parmesan and Pecorino
black pepper
flat-leaf parsley, finely chopped

Smash the garlic gloves with the flat of a knife blade. Warm the olive oil and garlic together in a small pan and remove the garlic when it has turned golden brown. Throw in the pancetta, and cook until browned and beginning to crisp. Pour in the wine, let it bubble for a couple of minutes, then turn the heat off.

Break the eggs into the bowl from which you'll serve the pasta, beat them, then throw the cheeses and the pepper in and beat again.

Add the cooked, drained spaghetti, I allow 85–125g / 3–4oz per person, and toss well to coat the pasta stickily. Reheat the pancetta quickly, pour it over the pasta, toss thoroughly with the parsley and some more black pepper and serve.

# Spinach Gnocchi with Butter, Sage and Pannarello

The quickest of suppers, but there is no need for excuses. Just sage and butter will do if you can't get Pannarello, or a few snippets of prosciutto thrown in with the sage. If you would rather have a more substantial sauce, Napoli is perfect, or any version of tomato sauce that suits you, with cream, with anchovies, with garlic and butter, with pancetta and chilli.

SERVES 4

*325–450g / 12–16oz*
*spinach gnocchi*
*butter*
*10–12 leaves sage*
*1 Pannarello*
*sea salt and black pepper*

Preheat oven to 180°C / 350°F / Gas Mark 4. Warm a large gratin dish in the oven, with a large knob of unsalted butter in it. Throw the gnocchi into a large pan of boiling water, turn the heat down to a blip, and wait for the gnocchi to swim to the surface.

Meanwhile, heat another knob of butter in a pan gently, and snip in some tiny bits of sage. Sage can overwhelm, so go easy. Fry briefly, until the herb releases its scent. Lift the gnocchi out of the pan with a slotted spoon, and put them into the buttery gratin dish, pour on the sage butter, scrunch over some black pepper and sea salt, and add cubes of Pannarello to melt in if that's the route you've taken. Return to the oven for it to melt for a few minutes.

# Winter Pasticcio

I used red onions, leeks and cherry tomatoes in this delicious dish of penne baked with roasted vegetables. Tony had a white globe of Pannarello, a cheese that melted like butter into the pasta and was sharp and strong in equal measure. You can use Fontina, and, as it doesn't turn quite so liquid, a couple of spoonfuls of mascarpone. Lubricance is what you're after.

SERVES 4

*4 medium red onions, peeled and quartered*
*4 fat leeks, the whites only, peeled and cut into 4cm / 1½in barrels*
*2 courgettes, cut into 2.5cm / 1in chunks*
*1 bulb fennel, ruthlessly stripped to its firm heart and quartered*
*2 x 200g / 7oz packets of organic cherry tomatoes*
*olive oil*
*2–3 sprigs of thyme*
*salt and pepper*
*325g / 12oz organic penne pasta*
*6 slices prosciutto or culatello*
*6 anchovies*
*a clove of garlic*
*a handful of basil leaves*
*175g / 6oz Pannarello or Fontina cheese cut into dice*
*2 tbsp mascarpone*

Preheat the oven to 190°C / 375°F / Gas Mark 5. Put the vegetables on a roasting tray and dribble on olive oil, rolling them around to cover. Scatter on the thyme, salt and pepper, and put in the oven until roasted and softened, about 30 minutes. Keep the leeks well bathed in oil so they don't brown. Cook the penne until *al dente* in plenty of fast-boiling salted water. Put the torn prosciutto, anchovies, garlic and basil in the food processor with 2–4 tablespoons of olive oil and blitz briefly. You want a coarse-textured gunge rather than a sludge! Turn the contents of the bowl into the drained pasta, add the vegetables, the Pannarello or Fontina and the mascarpone and amalgamate well; grind on some more black pepper. Turn into a greased gratin dish, and bake for 20 minutes. You can sprinkle it with flat-leaf parsley to serve and offer Parmesan if you wish, but it is delicious as is with a plainly dressed salad.

# A TRIP TO CORK

WHEN BORD BIA, THE IRISH FOOD BOARD, invited me over, I knew I was in for a gastronomic experience that would leave even Hannibal Lecter slavering for mercy, such is the carnassial tradition of this area famed for its 'fresh meat' – offal – its beef and its butter. Beef curing was a massive industry in Cork, particularly from the late 17th century until 1825, when it was exported to England, Europe, the USA, Newfoundland and the West Indies.

First, we head out of the city, abruptly entering into gently wooded country, until we reach the watery fingered peninsulas of East Cork and arrive at Belvelley, near Cobh. Frank Hederman emerges from his factory door to greet us, tall, blue-eyed with a shock of curly hair and an easy charm and wit. He opens the smokehouse door, a genie-like puff of smoke almost concealing the hanging bodies of the freshly hooked victims within, before he recoils, and, closing it rapidly, utters, 'I think we've seen enough, let's go and have lunch.' We head off to Ballymaloe, where the doyenne of Irish country house hospitality, Myrtle Allen, joins us for lunch.

Most memorable is an Irish green spinach soup spiked with an astringent whiff of rosemary, and Myrtle's famous caragheen pudding, a tremblingly white shudder of a dish that haunts the bowl like ectoplasm. Made with caragheen moss, a seaweed gathered on Ireland's Atlantic shores, it is infused with milk, egg and vanilla to give it the tremulous, satiny set favoured, one imagines, by languishing Edwardian invalids.

Frank Hederman was brought up by the sea. 'I found myself in this business by good fortune,' he assures me, though not so good, it would seem, in the early stages of experimentation. 'I built a smoking box like a large wardrobe, and fed it with wood from sawn up whiskey barrels. I'd sit and read the papers in my grandfather's armchair from cover to cover, and every so often there'd be a large bang. Spontaneous combustion from the alcohol.' Frank built his factory 'ahead of the posse,' on the advice of a Dutchman who has become something of a smoking-room mentor to him. 'Nothing really changes in the way the smoking is done, but the devil is in the detail. You have to learn how to treat the fish, how to pack them, fillet them, put them on spikes. The guiding light is to always try and make them taste better. We dry them for a lengthy period and then hang-smoke them, it creates a quite different texture to the stuff that's smoked lying flat on mesh where the oil has nowhere to go. We replace the oiliness with smoke.' So what separates Frank's fish from the rest of the shoal? 'It's the balance of flavours on your tongue, the sublime flavour of wood, salmon and the curing process. No one of these masks the other, it is gentle, light and it gives you a nice palate memory without masking the rest of your meal.'

We arrive late at the Ardrahan dairy. I had hoped to meet Eugene and Mary Burns, the makers of this fine cheese, which has just won two top prizes in the British Cheese Awards, but

Eugene has been rushed to hospital. Pauline, the third member of the business, shows us round the dairy, determined that we acquaint ourselves with the nature of this big-charactered cheese. Scrubbed up better than a surgeon, the cheeses are washed, turned and tended every two days, until a gentle ochre-coloured crust darkens the creamy, crumbly lactic interior. If you put your nose to one you can smell the pasture; its scent is at once grass, turning to hay, turning to silage. Pauline has been making the cheese for nine years and still hasn't tired of their infinite variety, 'If you look in the mirror you see the same old face. Go down to the dairy and it's alive, changing, you never get bored.'

Eugene has, tragically, since died, but the wonderful Mary is carrying on making their delicious Ardrahan cheeses.

# Ballymaloe Caragheen Moss Pudding

SERVES 6

6g caragheen moss
900ml / 1½ pints milk
3 level tbsp vanilla sugar
1 vanilla pod
1 egg

Soak the caragheen in cold water for 10 minutes, then remove and put it in a pan with the milk and the scraped-out vanilla pod. Bring to the boil, and simmer very gently for 15 minutes, semi-covered; watch that it doesn't boil over.

Pour through a sieve into a mixing bowl. The caragheen will now be swollen and exuding jelly. Rub all the jelly through the sieve and beat it into the milk with the sugar, egg yolk and grains of vanilla. Whisk the egg white stiffly in another bowl, and fold it in gently. Transfer to a serving bowl, and serve chilled.

Myrtle Allen put bowls of thick cream and soft dark sugar alongside the pudding. I served it chilled with a fruit compote.

# Spinach and Rosemary Soup

I've no idea how the Ballymaloe soup was made, but I've just made this for Saturday lunch and it is delicious.

SERVES 8

675g / 1½lb spinach, washed, tough stalks discarded

2 medium potatoes, peeled and cubed

1 medium onion, peeled and chopped

4 or 5 sprigs of rosemary

olive oil

butter

1.5 litre / 2½ pints of stock, I used pheasant stock

salt, pepper, lemon juice

Gently sauté the potato, onion and 3 sprigs of finely chopped rosemary in a little olive oil and butter in a heavy-bottomed casserole. Season. When the vegetables begin to soften and turn translucent, add the stock, bring to the boil, then simmer until the potatoes are just tender, about 10 minutes. Meanwhile, strip the rosemary from the other 2 sprigs, and put it in a mortar with a pinch of sea salt. Pound until the raw green herb is well crushed, introduce a spoonful of olive oil, and pound again until you have a beautiful verdant slick of oily green. Throw the washed spinach, with a bit of water still clinging to it, into another pan and stir briskly until the leaves begin to exude their own juice, a matter of a minute or two. Chop them down a bit before putting them into the pan with the stock and vegetables. Blitz in the food processor, return to the pan, heat until just at boiling point, squeeze on the juice of a scant half lemon, stir in the rosemary oil off the heat, check the seasoning and serve. The soup is a beautiful bottle green with the texture of plush velvet.

# Baked Plums with Dark Rum and Demerara Sugar

SERVES 6

*12 plums*
*2 tbsp demerara sugar*
*2 tbsp dark rum*
*2 tbsp water*
*2 or 3 clementines*
*½ lemon*

Preheat the oven to 180°C / 350°F / Gas Mark 4.

Put the plums, I used 'Laetitia,' in an earthenware dish, sprinkle with a couple of tablespoons of demerara sugar, the same of dark rum, and the same of water. Place a sheet of greaseproof paper over the top, and bake until just tender when pierced with the point of a skewer. About 20–25 minutes.

Test the juice. It will be too sweet. Squeeze the clementines and half a lemon, and stir the juice into the syrup. Adjust if you need to. The plums will have burst out of their jackets revealing their pretty pomegranate pink flesh. Cool them in the dish, then refrigerate.

# CORK MARKET

THE MOST REMARKABLE THING ABOUT CORK'S OLD ENGLISH MARKET – beyond its diversity, which is on a par with any French market you have idled through in envy, wondering in heaven's name why we have no equivalent – is its intrinsic regionalness. Preserving its ancient traditions seems to have emboldened Cork to espouse those of its nearer neighbours.

What delights about this market, which has been going since the late 18th century and is clearly in the throes of revitalization, is the unexpected juxtaposition. A knock-down-price, past-their-sell-by-date stall hard by The Alternative Bread Company's fabulous display of great coiled beehives of mushroom, garlic and parsley bread made in flowerpots; Greek-style Daktyla, their doughy discs like honeyed backbones scattered with sesame, coriander and parsley; poppy seed loaves; and the more traditional Irish bracks, sodas and treacle breads. On St Patrick's Day there will be 'golden drops' made with maize, porter bread laced with Guinness or Murphy's, and emerald-green pesto bread. Next door, a counter from another century, stacked with skirts and corned bodices, breasts of offal and crubeens – pigs' feet – the succulent by products of the mid-19th-century export trade, now all too easily forgotten as wealth distances itself from the cheap but tender sweet meats that were once the province of the poor. 'Corns' are the grains of salt with which so much was preserved, the 'bodices' are the ribs, traditionally boiled with 'turnips' – what we call swede – in a 'white stew.' Piles of pigs' heads are split ready for boiling, most sought after is the delicately fleshed muscle around the eye.

On Eddie Sheehan's marbled slab there are great sheets of salt ling, known, according to our guide, the eminent food historian Regina Sexton, as 'battleboard,' although the fish are not hardened into brittle starched sheets like Spanish *bacalao*. These more pliable strips are poached in milk, parsley and onion and served in a thick white sauce often flavoured with mustard. The 'buttered egg' stall is another reminder of a bygone era, the shells of the freshly laid, still warm eggs anointed with a coating of fresh butter, sealing the freshness in for up to a year. The quality of egg and butter are all, I only hope the rumour of margarine being used is ill-founded, that the people of Cork will ensure the tradition is properly preserved.

There is one remaining tripe and drisheen stall at the edge of the market. The national dish of Cork, blood pudding poached in milk and served with honeycomb tripe, has almost disappeared. Upstairs, at Kay Harte's delightful Farmgate Café, it is still on the menu. She has softened chunks of tripe in olive oil, then stewed them gently in milk, onions, thyme and a pinch of mustard. Thickened with cornflour, this palest of primrose dishes is finished with pieces of drisheen, the contrasting flavours at once mild, soft textured and complementary. You will have to go to Cork Market to try it, but I can promise you it is worth the trip.

# Chicken Liver Paté

Do not be alarmed by the unconventional method. I was given across-the-counter instructions, but I had to join up the dots. The pairing of the livers with the basil is a masterstroke, but remember it is really rich.

SERVES 8–10

*450g / 1lb organic chicken livers, left whole, but all green and thready bits removed*
*a splosh of Cognac*
*1 clove garlic, chopped*
*handful of fresh basil leaves*
*salt and pepper*
*125g / 4oz unsalted butter for the interior of the paté*
*50g / 2oz unsalted butter for the top*

Place the livers in a single layer in an earthenware dish, and scatter over the Cognac. It should not cover them, but they need to wallow in it for several hours. Turn them over so both sides absorb the alcohol.

The garlic, bunch of basil, torn and minus the stalks, and seasoning should be thrown into the brew just before poaching. Gently poach the livers in their brew on top of the oven, turning them over after a couple of minutes, and continue to stew until they are cooked on the outside, but rosy pink within. Do not overcook at this stage, or you will end up with a drab brown crumbly result.

Tip the contents of the dish straight into your blender with 125g/4oz of softened butter, and whizz until smooth. Check the seasoning, then scrape into a terrine and leave to cool. When cool, clarify the final 50g/2oz of butter by melting it, and removing all the curd-like sediment. Pour the buttercup-coloured clear liquid over the surface, place a couple of fresh basil leaves in the centre, and put it into the fridge until set. Serve with hot toast, but remember not to serve it fridge cold.

# Cod in Grain Mustard Sauce

SERVES 4

4 x 2.5cm/1in thick pieces of
really fresh cod, size according to
appetite, mine were about
325g/12oz each
coarse sea salt
pepper
fresh thyme
50g/2oz butter
50g/2oz flour
about ¾ pint milk
1½ dsrtsp grain mustard

Preheat the oven to 220°C/425°F/Gas Mark 7. Scatter a layer of sea salt over the bottom of a roasting tray, then the pulled leaves from a few sprigs of thyme. Sit the pieces of fish on top, skin side on the salt. Place in the middle of the hot oven. My pieces took 12 minutes, but test with a skewer that they are not resistant, but opaque. Their own liquid will have just started collecting on top.

Make a basic béchamel sauce in a small saucepan, by melting the butter gently, adding the flour, then pouring on the hot milk and stirring continuously for 10 minutes until thickened and smooth. Drop in the first spoon of mustard with some freshly ground pepper, stir briefly, and taste. Add the other half dessertspoon if you like the robustness, it is a very good foil for the fish.

Place the fish on a hot plate, the dissolved salt remains on the tray, and doesn't overwhelm the thyme-scented cod, then pour over some hot mustard sauce. I served mine with thinly sliced discs of swede cooked for an hour in a gratin dish with hot chicken stock to cover, and leek and potato cakes.

# Crème Caramel with Hazelnut Brittle

The milky, satiny soft Irish dishes made me go back to this forgotten classic, which, if you eschew the Caragheen Moss Pudding, is a delicious alternative. The brittle carries the burnt-sugar theme further and gives it another texture. I tried two versions, one in which I used extra burnt sugar from the base for the custard, resulting in a mahogany-coloured, stronger-flavoured middle, and the conventional method below

SERVES 4–6

*85g/3oz vanilla caster sugar*
*1 tbsp cold water*
*2 whole eggs and 2 yolks*
*2 tbsp vanilla sugar*
*1 vanilla pod, insides scraped out*
*600ml/1 pint milk*

HAZELNUT BRITTLE:
*85g/3oz vanilla caster sugar*
*100g/3½oz whole, skinned*
*hazelnuts*

Preheat the oven to 180°C/350°F/Gas Mark 4.

Gently melt the 85g/3oz caster sugar in a saucepan, until it is liquid and changes colour to a burnished mahogany. Just as it starts to bubble, throw on the cold water, and quickly pour the mixture into the base of a soufflé dish, rolling it slightly up the sides until it sets.

Break the eggs and yolks into a bowl, add the sugar and the innards from the vanilla pod, and whisk. Scald the milk in the sugar pan, and pour it over the egg mixture. Pour into the soufflé dish, then stand it in a roasting tin, hot water halfway up the sides of the dish, and cook in the centre of the oven for 35–40 minutes. It should have a tremblingly set shudder to it; it will go on cooking when it comes out of the oven. Cool it, then turn it out on to a large plate. A palate knife slipped around its edges is all you will need.

Scatter another 85g/3oz vanilla sugar in the base of a saucepan, and heat it to the same point as the caramel. Throw in the chopped hazelnuts, stir briefly, and deposit on a buttered baking tray. Leave to cool and set, then bash the brittle up a bit to serve alongside the crème caramel.

# CHRISTMAS

LAMB'S WOOL, FRUMENTY, WHIPCOLL AND POSSET are probably not what you'll be slurping from your wassailing bowl this Christmas, but I would hazard that their milky, spicy, creamy depths were charged to offer a bit of ballast, to line the Saxon gut in preparation for the feasting to come. Just in case you feel tempted, though, lamb's wool is a toddy of hot beer, wine, honey and spices with cream and a hot apple plunged into it; frumenty, a gruellish porridge of soaked wheat grain, boiled in sweetened milk and spices until creamy; whipcoll, Shetland Island's very own special brew, an egg noggy concoction of beaten yolks and sugar with cream stirred into it and flavoured with rum or brandy; and posset simply ale mixed with milk and nutmeg and supped with a communal spoon.

Without wishing to set you even further on a course of promiscuous consumption, I do feel that the secret of good drinking is eating. I hate drinking without eating; what civilized bar anywhere in Europe serves drink without little salt, savoury morsels to accompany it? Except England, where you're lucky to get a peanut or a pork scratching – and by the way, the real, homemade pork scratching, which I was first offered in a bar in Jerez with a glass of finest ice-cold Fino, is a mighty fine thing. At home there is no excuse. And the joy is, that the little sweetmeats you offer can take the place of a course, or be transmogrified into one later. Carême's dictum '*faites simple*' is the only proviso. A dish full of wonky wedges of the best Parmigiano Reggiano; fat cigars of capacollo, speck or prosciutto rolled around quartered figs; chestnuts that you can roast, glass in hand, until they burst open searing your hands as you peel them. Or try my latest, a teaspoon each of whole cumin and coriander seeds 'roasted' in a dry pan for a minute, then crushed in a mortar with coarse sea salt and pepper, and as much cayenne as you feel comfortable with, I use a third of a teaspoon. Stir in a couple of teaspoons of flour, dunk bites of de-veined and patted dry chicken livers, shaking off the excess spice mixture, and fry briefly in butter until crusted but oozy pink. Or make an advance party of stuffed vine leaves, little dark green Christmas parcels to eat hot, warm or cold.

To obviate the overkill of flesh, fat and dyspeptic combinations, dare I suggest that most seventies of things, the dip? I do not mean some hideously prinked bowl of cream cheese coloured pink with tomato ketchup and sundry unmentionable substances, rather a plate of *hummus bi tahini* striated with a slick of best green olive oil and a smidgen of smoked paprika or cayenne; a *baba ganoush*, the classic aubergine and tahini Middle Eastern mezze, over which you can strew Christmas jewels of pomegranate like confetti and serve with raw fennel, celery, mooli and carrots; a coarsely mashed guacamole of avocados threaded with finely chopped red chilli, fresh coriander and a sprinkle of lime juice – I served mine spread on button-sized homemade spiced meatballs; a purée of cannellini beans with crisply fried needles of rosemary or sage. Or some potted crab, its strata of white and brown meat and warming spices set in clarified butter, then poached gently in a *bain-marie*.

But let's get to the point. All this is peripheral. It never ceases to amaze me how even the most staggeringly competent of cooks tend to fall to pieces on Christmas Day, going into battle with the bird as if competing in some medieval jousting rite, instead of remembering that all they're doing is cooking a souped-up Sunday lunch. What induces this abject turkey terror, and to such a degree that alarms are set all over England, and birds tethered and consigned to the stove before even the dawn chorus has had the chance to make an enemy of sleep? And why is there a snooty school of anti-turkey terrorists, who mutter in superior tones that the turkey is a dry and tasteless bird? Only in the hands of an ignorant and unsympathetic cook I say, and only if the bird in question is an amorphous lump of intensively reared flesh, ill-fed, ill-plumped and ill-despatched. No organic Bronze, properly reared, roamed, killed and hung could fail to please, unless the guardian of the stove has cooked it to oblivion. So here are the golden rules for a tender, juicily fleshed bird, rules which I refuse to break because they are infallible.

First, stuff your turkey. I use the recipe on page 284, which has remained my favourite for too long to recall. Preheat your oven to 190°C/375°F/Gas Mark 5. Then weigh your stuffed bird, and calculate your cooking time: 33 minutes per kilo or 15 minutes to the pound applies up to a 6.5kg/14lb bird. So, a 6.5kg/14lb bird will take three and a half hours. Always calculate like this up to this weight, even if the bird is bigger. For each extra pound allow ten minutes per pound, so, for a 8.7kg/20lb bird, your total cooking time will be four and a half hours. Still not worth getting out of bed early for. I place the bird on its side, on a layer of peeled, sliced onions, and slap 175g/7oz of softened, well-seasoned butter on its skin. I then shroud the bird in foil, a double layer, clinching it tightly around the roasting tin, so the bird is sealed in. Just before half time, I turn the bird on to its other side, baste it with the buttery juices, seal it inside the foil, and continue to cook.

About 30–40 minutes before it should be ready, I remove the foil, turn the bird breast up, baste it, season the skin well with coarse sea salt and pepper, hit the 200°C/400°F/Gas Mark 6 button and allow it to crisp up. Rest the bird for 20 minutes in a warm place while you make your gravy. I simmer the giblets for 30 minutes with the vegetable water from par-boiling my potatoes and parsnips, adding the liver towards the end, then sieve this mixture into the roasting pan with the onion and meat juices, add a splosh of red wine and more meat juices from the carving board as frequently as they exude, and stir while they bubble away for a few minutes. Then I strain the lot into a jug, and hence into a *dégraisser*. The following recipes are of the gentle and undemanding sort that suit the turkey and pudding period particularly well.

# Potted Crab

I was about to make my usual version of this matchless, simple dish, when I found myself questioning the fact that classic potted crab is made only with the white meat. I flew in the face of convention, and produced this infinitely superior model for a dinner for my publisher Michael Dover. I think even Michelin-starred Richard Corrigan was impressed; he suggested that the reason for using only the white meat was due to the brown meat's turning so quickly. So make sure your crab is spanking fresh.

MAKES 12 RAMEKINS

*85g/3oz crab meat per person;*
*if you have a good fishmonger, he*
*will pick the crab for you, and*
*divide it into light and dark*
*about 400g/14oz best unsalted*
*butter*
*a blade or good pinch mace*
*a good pinch nutmeg*
*⅓ tsp cayenne*
*lemon juice*
*salt and pepper*

Preheat the oven to 150°C/300°F/Gas Mark 2.

Melt 225g/8oz butter gently, then pour it carefully into another pan, leaving behind the milky, curd-like solids. Add the spices, then turn the white meat into the spiced butter, amalgamate well, and taste. You should have a breath of spiced warmth, but not full-scale heat from the cayenne. Adjust accordingly, then add salt, pepper and a squeeze of lemon juice to taste.

Boil a kettle, and in the meanwhile fill each ramekin with a layer of the buttered white crabmeat, followed by a layer of brown meat. Finish with a layer of the white meat. You will just have enough room at the top of the ramekin for the final layer of clarified butter, which you add after poaching the crab. Place the ramekins in a roasting tin, pour boiling water to come halfway up their sides, and place in the oven for 25 minutes.

Remove, cool, then clarify the rest of the butter and pour over each ramekin like sealing wax. Place in the fridge. The ramekins should be removed 20 minutes or so before you make your brown toast so that they are cold, but not fridge cold. Then slip a slim knife blade all the way around the girth of each ramekin right to the bottom, turn them out on to the palm of your hand, and put each one, butter side up, on individual plates. The ones I served on Saturday night tasted as good as when I had made them the previous Wednesday night, but my fishmonger is very good.

# Stuffed Vine Leaves

MAKES 45–50

SERVE 8 PER PERSON FOR A
MAIN COURSE,
4 FOR A STARTER, FEWER WITH
DRINKS, DEPENDING ON
YOUR OTHER DISHES

*1 jar vine leaves in brine*
*100g / 3½oz organic basmati rice*
*250g / 9oz raw*
*minced lamb*
*2 tomatoes*
*1 small onion, peeled*
*and finely chopped*
*3 tbsp each of finely chopped mint,*
*flat-leaf parsley and celery leaves*
*50g / 2oz pine nuts*
*½ tsp cinnamon*
*½ tsp allspice*
*2 tbsp concentrated tomato purée*
*6 cloves garlic, cut into slivers*
*150ml / 5fl oz good olive oil and*
*the same quantity of water*
*juice of 1½ lemons*
*salt and freshly ground black*
*pepper*

First drain the vine leaves and put them in a bowl. Cover with boiling water and soak for 20 minutes. Repeat the process twice more, but with cold water, before a final drain. Cook and drain the basmati rice. Skin, seed and chop the tomatoes. In a large bowl, mix together the rice, lamb and tomatoes, onions, herbs, pine nuts, spices and tomato purée. Season.

Place a vine leaf on your work surface, vein side up, the stem end nearest to you. Put a heaped teaspoon of the lamb mixture in the centre of the leaf near the stem. Fold up over the filling, then fold both sides of the leaf towards the middle, and roll into a little cigar. Do the same with the remaining 49! Children are very adept at this sort of repetitive action.

Line a heavy-bottomed casserole with a single layer of unfilled vine leaves, slightly overlapping, to come about a third of the way up the sides. Pack in the stuffed vine leaves, one or two layers deep, placing occasional slivers of garlic between them. Add the olive oil, water and lemon juice, and weight down with an upturned plate.

Cook very gently on top of the stove for about 2 hours, until tender when pierced with a skewer. Check the liquid level after the first hour, you may need to add more water. You can leave them whole or cut in half to serve, hot, warm or cold.

# Chestnut Stuffing

Enough to stuff a turkey and make a separate roasting tin full, which you should cover with foil and cook for 1½–2 hours. I use Merchant Gourmet's plain, vacuum-packed chestnuts.

*3 tbsp olive oil*

*1 large onion, finely chopped*

*½ a head of celery, finely chopped*

*125g / 4oz walnuts, finely chopped*

*2 tart dessert apples, cored,*
*unpeeled and finely chopped*

*450g / 1lb tin chestnut purée*

*450g / 1lb organic sausagemeat*

*225g / 8oz wholemeal breadcrumbs*

*2 eggs, beaten*

*2 tbsp finely chopped*
*flat-leaf parsley*

*salt and pepper*

*450g / 1lb vacuum-packed*
*chestnuts*

Heat the oil gently in a frying pan, and fry together the onion, celery, walnuts and apple until golden and softened. Turn into a huge bowl and add all the remaining ingredients, mixing well; add the whole chestnuts last, chopped in quarters so that they don't break up during the mixing. Stuff the bird. Put the rest in a roasting tin and cook separately.

# Fish Pie with Rosti

My cousin Deborah, a very fine cook, with whom I always share recipe and restaurant gossip, dreamt up this delicious fish pie with a crisp top of cheesy rosti. The base layer of spinach, such a natural partner to smoked haddock, means the only other thing you'll need is a crisp salad of bitter leaves. The quails' eggs are well worth the trouble; you can buy free-range ones in good supermarkets now. Deborah bribes her children to peel them.

SERVES 6–8

675g / 1½lb cod
450g / 1lb natural smoked haddock
225g / 8oz tiger prawns, shelled weight
1 dozen quails' eggs
1 bay leaf
1 dsrtsp peppercorns
150ml / 5fl oz dry vermouth or white wine
300ml / 10fl oz milk
300ml / 10fl oz single cream
200ml / 7fl oz crème fraîche
900g / 2lb spinach
2 tbsp chopped flat-leaf parsley
85g / 3oz butter
2 tbsp plain flour
salt, pepper

THE TOPPING:
900g / 2lb potatoes, peeled
85g / 3oz butter
85g / 3oz good, mature Cheddar

Preheat the oven to 200°C / 400°F / Gas Mark 6.

Poach the piece of cod with the bay leaf and half the peppercorns in the vermouth and a little water for about 7 minutes, or until just cooked. Bring the milk to scalding point, pour it over the smoked haddock in a gratin dish, with the rest of the peppercorns, and let it rest for about 10 minutes. You may turn it over, the fish is smoked, so it is already cooked, but it needs to be tender so you can flake it. Drain all the fish, keeping both lots of fish liquor, flake, skin and de-bone it. Boil the quails' eggs for 3 minutes and shell. Gently steam the spinach in no more than the residue from the water you have washed it in, until it has wilted, 3–4 minutes, stirring so that it doesn't stick. Drain it thoroughly, and place a layer of it, with a good scrunch of black pepper at the base of an ovenproof dish.

Melt the butter, add the flour, and make a nutty golden roux, then whisk in the hot fish liquors. Stir in the crème fraîche, then the tiger prawns and parsley, season and remove from the heat. Place the cod and haddock on top of the spinach, pour over the sauce and prawns. Halve the quails' eggs, and push them into the mixture.

Grate the cheese, then coarsely grate the potatoes, a food processor will do it fine, and mix them together with the melted butter. Pile on top of the fish and bake for 45–60 minutes, until the top is seductively golden and crunchy.

# Irish Stew

A dish of consummate comfort and ease to leave cooking lazily after the Christmas overkill. If you can make it the day before, leave it to cool, skim off the fat and reheat, then do so. The potatoes need to be of the floury variety, so they thicken the juice. It is not essential to use lamb stock. I use water as often as not.

SERVES 8

*2–3 medium onions, peeled and thinly sliced*

*3–4 sticks of celery with their leaves*

*6 good-sized carrots, cut into thickish chunks*

*8 pieces of neck or scrag of lamb, on the bone*

*2–3 potatoes per person, peeled*

*125g / 4oz organic barley*

*salt, pepper*

Preheat the oven to 150°C/300°F/Gas Mark 2.

Place the onions in the bottom of a heavy casserole, then lay the celery and carrots on top of them, followed by the lamb pieces. Tuck in the potatoes, season, sprinkle over the barley, and just cover the ingredients with water, or lamb stock if you happen to have it.

Bring very slowly to the boil, cover with greaseproof paper and a lid, and either simmer at a mere blip on the top of the stove, or inside the oven for 2–2½ hours. You need nothing but a wide-brimmed soup bowl to serve it in.

# Fresh Grapefruit Jelly

Another devoutly-to-be-wished-for, after-the-fall sort of pudding. I can almost taste its astringent sharpness just thinking about it. If you can find pink grapefruit, it comes out a dreamy dusty pink.

SERVES 6

*juice of half a lemon*
*pared rind of a grapefruit*
*pared rind of an orange*
*85–125g/3–4oz caster sugar*
*300ml/½ pint water*
*6 or 7 leaves leaf gelatine, but*
*check the packet*
*600ml/1 pint freshly squeezed*
*grapefruit juice*

Put the lemon juice and rind and the orange rind into a saucepan with the sugar and 150ml/5fl oz of the water. Place over a low heat and leave to infuse for 10–15 minutes.

Soak the gelatine (read the instructions for how much to use first) for 10 minutes in the other 150ml/5fl oz of water. Add the soaked gelatine with its water to the saucepan, stir to melt, then strain and leave to cool.

Add the gelatine liquid to the freshly squeezed grapefruit juice, stir well, and pour into a mould or into individual long-stemmed glasses. Leave to cool completely, then refrigerate to set further. The jelly will keep well for several days.

# Steamed Blueberry Pudding

SERVES 6

*125g/4oz vanilla caster sugar*
*125g/4oz softened butter*
*2 eggs*
*125g/4oz flour*
*1 tsp baking powder*
*500g/1 and a bit lb blueberries*
*blackberry liqueur – I had a bottle*
*of Bramley and Gage's, but cassis or*
*even Ribena would do*
*golden icing sugar*
*cinnamon, optional*

Cream the sugar and butter thoroughly until light and fluffy, then add the eggs one at a time and mix thoroughly. Sift the flour and baking powder over the mixture, and stir in well. Put the blueberries in a pan with a good splosh of liqueur or Ribena, and shake a tablespoon or so of icing sugar over the berries to coat. Allow the fruit just to start bleeding its juices over the heat, before you remove the pan, it must not cook. A pinch of cinnamon goes well with blueberries, but is optional.

Pour the fruit over the creamed mixture, mixing it in well. You should have a slack mixture, on the slacker side of dropping consistency, which you scrape it into a buttered pudding basin. Secure with foil and string, or the lid if it's a plastic basin, and steam in a large pan with boiling water halfway up the sides of the basin, at a gentle pace for 2 hours. Turn out and marvel.

# Malted Milk Chocolate Pudding with Bailey's Custard

SERVES 6–8

125g / 4 oz butter
125g / 4 oz caster sugar
2 eggs
125g / 4oz flour
1 tsp baking powder
40–50g / 1½–2oz Prewett's malted milk drink
milk
100g / 3½oz bar Green and Black's organic milk chocolate

Bash the milk chocolate into small chunks. Cream the butter and sugar together until really light and fluffy, then add the eggs, one at a time. Sieve the flour and baking powder into the mixture and fold in, then add the malt powder and amalgamate. Add a splosh of milk at a time, until you achieve dropping consistency, i.e. the mixture will slide willingly off the spoon in a smooth heap, then stir in the chocolate, and scrape the mixture into a greased pudding basin.

Cover with foil, tie tightly with string, and steam in a large pan of just bubbling water to come halfway up the pudding basin for 2 hours. Turn out, and serve with this gloriously rich Bailey's custard.

# Bailey's Custard

If you lose your nerve over the custard, just make the delicious yellow substance without the liquor, there is NO substitute for the real thing.

SERVES 6–8

600ml / 1 pint full cream milk, Jersey is best
1 vanilla pod
6 egg yolks
85g / 3oz vanilla caster sugar
1–2 tbsp Bailey's Irish Cream liqueur

Scrape the seeds out of the vanilla pod and put both into the pan with the milk. Whisk over the heat, until the milk is at scalding point and the seeds dispersed, then take it off the heat, put a lid on it, and leave it to infuse for 20–30 minutes. Whisk the egg yolks and caster sugar together thoroughly, then strain the milk over them, add the Bailey's, taste, return to the pan, and keep whisking. Cook over a gentle heat, whisking constantly. The cream will look light and almost frothy, and begin to thicken imperceptibly after about 10 minutes. On no account try and speed things up by whacking up the heat, unless you want sweet scrambled eggs. Pour into a jug, or keep hot for up to 20 minutes over a double saucepan, and release copiously over the pudding.

# Brioche and Butter Pudding

The sweetly silken depths of this pudding with its sharp, almondy edge of best apricot jam, the whole apricots glazing the surface, is one of the greats — easy to make, even easier to eat too much of.

SERVES 6

300ml / 10fl oz Jersey or full-cream milk

300ml / 10fl oz double cream. Loseley's Jersey if possible

1 vanilla pod

3 eggs

125g / 4oz vanilla caster sugar

50g / 2oz unsalted butter

4 brioche, the best you can find, I use Baker and Spice's

a handful organic sultanas soaked until plump in hot water

½ jar best apricot conserve, I use Baker and Spice's Vallon de Genras, with the cracked kernel in the pot imparting its characteristic frangipane scent

Preheat the oven to 180°C / 350°F / Gas Mark 4.

Scald the milk with the cream and the scooped-out vanilla seeds and pod. Whisk the eggs and sugar together thoroughly, then add the milk and cream mixture and whisk a bit more. Melt the butter gently, then brush it over the brioches which you have sliced into four horizontally, putting them into your buttered pudding dish as you go, and sprinkling over the sultanas. Strain over the milk and egg mixture, place in a roasting tin, fill it with boiling water to come halfway up the sides of the pudding dish, and poach for about 30 minutes, or until just set and not over-browned. Remove from the oven, melt the jam with a teaspoon of water, then brush it generously over the eggy surface of the pudding. I think you'll find it doesn't need any cream.

# POST CHRISTMAS

LOOKING BACK ON THE CUSTOMARY EXCESSES OF THE FEASTING SEASON, several things stand out. A white-as-snow hillock of risotto made with tiny, sweet buttery leeks and pheasant stock scenting the rice. At its summit, a spoon of liquid Vacherin Mont d'Or dribbled over, tasting of all things earthy and flowery, a real antidote to the endless fowl and flesh. A simple lemony Madeira cake I made once we'd driven on to Mayo for the Millennium, crumbly, damp, a fistful of carbohydrates after a rousing march around the headland. The teaspoon dug deep into the tin of Oscietra caviar, which had travelled out strapped to an ice pack, my one inexcusable extravagance. Goose and apple sauce sandwiches for a 4.30pm lunch after another squally walk, accompanied by a compellingly vicious game of racing demon and the remains of a lemon pudding scraped straight from the dish.

The dregs of post-festive feeding always leave me starved of inspiration, unsure of what I want to eat and certain that I don't want to cook. The only thing that stands the faintest chance is fish. So I set off apathetically to my fishmonger Phil Bowditch in Taunton. He empties a box of palely beautiful spotty blonde rays on to the slab. 'There are more thorn back rays in the Irish Sea because of the stronger tidal flow, the thorns catch on to ledges on the sea bed so they can feed without being swept away, but these blonde ones from the English Channel are plumper. Twenty years ago you'd find vast big daddies. I remember a trawler at Lyme landing a 120-pound skate once, but now they average about 6 or 7 pounds.'

Phil has decided to fillet a wing for me, which, as he wryly points out, most fish counters wouldn't have the time or the skill to do. I normally poach the wings with their gluey, cartilaginous bones attached, but he insists that baking them in the oven like flat, ribbed blankets is as delicious a way to eat them. I am easily led. Phil is determined that I stick with local fish today, and that I help dispel the myth that crab is expensive just because it's a luxury food. The cock crabs that he sells all the year round, don't come out of the traditional pots, but from a beam trawler off Brixham. They are usually a bit sandy when they come up to the surface because they've been dragged along the bottom in a net about 20 miles off shore, but Phil scrubs them clean before boiling them.

Pressing the white meat that the combination of a crude rubber mallet and the more delicate forensics of a bent skewer have helped extrude, I am reacquainted with the satisfaction so easily afforded by successfully completing a simple culinary process. By the time the creamy, curdy solids of butter have been dredged, like the crab, from the murky depths of a sea of golden butter and clarified, and the knife-tip of cayenne, mace and nutmeg added, turning it tawny, it is all I can do to wait for the head of butter to set, before spreading it in a crumbly, melting mess on hot brown toast. Inspirational.

# Baked Skate

SERVES 3–4

*200g / 8oz of fish per person if filleted, 325g / 12oz or more if on the bone*

*butter*

*spritz of lemon*

*splosh of white wine*

*salt and pepper*

CAPER SAUCE

*85g / 3oz unsalted butter*

*2 tbsp capers*

*lemon juice*

*salt and pepper*

Preheat the oven to 200°C / 400°F / Gas Mark 6.

Butter a roasting tin thoroughly, and lay the skate down flat in the bottom of it in one piece. Squeeze on a spritz of lemon and sprinkle over a splosh of white wine. Season with salt and pepper and cook for 5 minutes, before testing the thickest bit with a knife. If it is resistant, return to the oven, another 5 minutes maximum should do. Transfer in serving portions on to a plate and keep warm, while you boil up the roasting tin juices and reduce them a little, beating in a few little extra knobs of butter as you go.

If your fishmonger doesn't fillet skate, poach the wings on the bone in water you have brought to the boil and acidulated with a tablespoon or two of wine vinegar. Drop the fish in, keeping the water at no more than a blip, and your fish should be cooked in about 6 minutes, again, test with a knife. Drain carefully, and keep hot.

I prefer a buttery, lemony caper sauce to the classic black butter one. Melt the butter in a pan and add the capers, rinsed or desalinated to the pan. Squeeze on lemon juice to taste, allow it to bubble for a few seconds, then scrunch on some black pepper, and add salt if the capers aren't too salty. Spoon over each piece of skate.

# Leek and Vacherin Mont d'Or Risotto

SERVES 4

*85g/3oz unsalted butter*
*4 slim leeks, cleaned, only the*
*tender whites chopped*
*into thin discs*
*325g/12oz carnaroli rice, good*
*supermarkets stock it these days, use*
*arborio if that's all they have*
*up to 900ml/1½ pint stock,*
*I used fresh pheasant stock, but*
*chicken or game stock are fine*
*1 small Vacherin Mont d'Or*
*salt and pepper*

Melt the butter in a heavy-bottomed frying pan, then sauté the leeks gently until wilted and softened. Add the rice, stirring to coat thoroughly in the butter, then start adding the hot stock a couple of ladles at a time, and keep stirring the rice until the stock is almost all absorbed. Add more stock, and continue stirring for about 20 minutes until the rice is just cooked, starchy, with a bite to it, but neither hard nor porridgey. You can cook this dish up to the final 10 minutes an hour or two earlier if it suits you, making sure there is a good pool of stock for it to absorb when you leave it.

Season with salt and fresh pepper, remembering that the cheese is quite salty. There should be enough liquid for the risotto to have a slightly soupy quality. Ladle into bowls, then drop a generous spoonful of the golden Vacherin over the summit of each serving.

# Potted Crab Two

SERVES 6

*325g/12oz white crab meat*
*175g/6oz unsalted butter*
*mace, nutmeg, cayenne pepper*

Melt the butter gently in a pan, then skim off the surface scum, and pour the butter into another pan, discarding the curd-like solids at the bottom. Add about half a teaspoon of cayenne and a little less each of mace and freshly grated nutmeg. Check, you want to feel the warmth of the seasoning without it overwhelming, and adjust accordingly.

Set aside about one-third of the butter, then stir the crab meat into the saucepan with the two-thirds. Spoon into individual ramekins, pressing the flesh down firmly. Pour the remaining butter equally over the top of each, so you have a thin layer of pure butter covering the crab. Cool, put in the fridge for an hour or two, or overnight.

Take the ramekins out and bring them up to room temperature before serving with hot brown toast.

# SUPPLIERS AND ORGANIZATIONS

**Ardrahan cheese**
Available from Neal's Yard Dairy,
17 Shorts Gardens, London WC2,
Tel: 020 7379 7646, and from
selected stockists, or ring 00 353
029 47156, fax: 00 353 029 78136.

**Aspalls** extra-dry, dry and
medium-sweet cider can be bought
from selected branches of
Sainsbury's and their apple juice and
vinegars from supermarkets and
healthfood shops.

**Asparagus**: Rob Mann sells his
asparagus at the Bristol Farmers'
Market on Wednesdays in May and
June, and from his farm daily,
Edcombe Farm at Rodney Stoke
near Cheddar, Somerset.

**L'Atelier du Chocolat:** The finest
chocolates, in my view, other than
Sally Clarke's eponymous truffles,
come from L'Atelier du Chocolat.
They have a range of 20 'delicately
enrobed ganaches' around five
themes, pure beans, herbs and
spices, nuts and seeds, fruits and
caramels. These are top-of-the-
market, handmade chocolates and
they come in beautiful, plain brown
corrugated boxes. They will also
make figurines or bars to order.
L'Atelier du Chocolat, Unit 25,
Elbourne Trading Estate, Crabtree
Manorway South, Belvedere, Kent
DA17 6NW.
Tel/fax: 020 8311 3337 for
stockists.

**Baker and Spice** 46 Walton St,
SW3 1RB. Tel: 020 7589 4734

**The Bay Tree Food Company**
at Lower Westcombe Farm,
Evercreech, Shepton Mallet,
Somerset BA4 6ER. Tel: 01749
831300. Fax: 01749 831233

**Phil Bowditch,** fishmonger at
7 Bath Place, Taunton, Somerset
TA1 4ER. Tel: 01823 253500.
To order fish, go to his website:
www.philbowditch.co.uk

**Bramley and Gage**'s gorgeously
sticky, fruity liqueurs are made with
the juice of the pressed fruit and
beautifully bottled. I love the raspberry and the Dittisham plum best,
but there are quince, blackcurrant,
blackberry, strawberry, and sloe and
damson gins. Mail order service and
catalogue: 2B Longmeadow, South
Brent, Devon TQ10 9YT.
Tel/Fax: 01364 73722.

**Brown and Forrest** sell a huge
range of smoked foods. Best of all is
their eel, one of which I was sent as
a present last year in a yard-long parcel, with brilliantly simple skinning
instructions. The faint-hearted can
order fillets, Craster kippers, hot-
smoked salmon or meats, or a
special Christmas hamper.
Brown and Forrest, The Smokery,
Bowdens Farm, Hambridge,
Somerset TA10 0BP. Tel: 01458
250875. Fax: 01458 253475.

**Caragheen** can be bought from
good health food shops, or direct
from Ballymaloe in 6g packets. Tel:
00 353 021 65253. Fax: 00 353 021
652021.

**Cheese:** for the best information
about cheese, check the website of
Juliet Harbutt, cheese lover and
chairman of the British Cheese
Awards: www.thecheeseweb.com

**English cheese retailers:**
CAMBRIDGE CHEESE
All Saints Passage, Cambridge
CB2 3LS. Tel: 01223 328672

CHANDOS DELI
6 Princess Victoria St, Clifton,
Bristol BS9 4VP. Tel: 0117 9243275

THE FINE CHEESE COMPANY
29/31 Walcot St, Bath BA1 5BN.
Mail order: 01225 448748.

HAMISH JOHNSTON
48 Abbeville Rd, London SW4 9NF.
Tel: 020 8673 5373
48 Northcote Rd London SW11
1TA. Tel: 020 7738 0741

JEROBOAM'S
96 Holland Park Avenue, London
W11 3AA. Tel: 020 7727 9359

PAXTON AND WHITFIELD
1 John St, Bath BA1 2JL.
Tel: 01225 466403
13 Wood St, Stratford on Avon,
Warwickshire CV37 6JF.
Tel: 01789 415544
93 Jermyn St, London SW1 6JE.
Tel: 020 7930 0259

THE TEDDINGTON CHEESE
42 Station Road, Teddington,
Middlesex TW11 9AA.
Tel: 020 8977 6868

**Chef Club Direct
and Heritage Fine Foods**
Tel: 01275 475252.
Fax: 01275 415167.
Email: info@clubchefdirect.co.uk
Website: www.clubchefdirect.co.uk

**Cider**: The Somerset Cider Brandy
Company Ltd and Burrow Hill
Cider, Pass Vale Farm, Burrow Hill,
Kingsbury Episcopi, Martock,
Somerset TA12 5BU Tel: 01460
240782. Fax: 01460 249220.
Email: apples@ciderbrandy.co.uk
You can also order from the website:
www.ciderbrandy.co.uk

**Clarence Court eggs:** Coach
House Farm, Cheltenham Road,
Broadway, Worcs, WR12 7BY. Tel:
01386 858007. Fax: 01386 858009.
E-mail: info@clarencecourt.co.uk
Clarence Court eggs are available at
the larger Tesco's and Sainsbury's and
most London Waitrose stores.

**Janet Clarke**: for her catalogue,
*300 Years of Food and Wine*, write to
Janet Clarke at 3 Woodside
Cottages, Freshford, Bath BA2 7WJ.
Tel: 01225 723186.
Fax: 01225 722063.
Email: janetclarke@ukgateway.net

**Cullompton Farmers' Market**
in Devon is held every second
Saturday of the month in the town's
car park, just off the M5 at Junction
28. Check your local Farmers'
Market details by telephoning The
Soil Association on 0117 9290661.

Of the varieties of Peter Whiteman's
potatoes I tested, Roseval, available
in some supermarkets, is a waxy,
glutinous pinky crimson; Salad Blue

a deep, dark purple until cooked,
then it makes a deliciously mealy-
textured Parma violet-coloured
mash, disconcerting but thrilling.
Golden Wonder is as rough skinned
as an unshaven cheek, and delicious
for baking; Linzer Delicatesse, a
thin, curvy Austrian spud with a
waxy, golden colour; the knobbly-
kneed Pink Fir Apple waxy and as
crisp as a water chestnut; and the
ultimate, Aura, a slightly yellow,
firm, sweet flavoured potato, as
waxy in its October largesse as in its
summer salad size. It takes my prize
for something we should re-intro-
duce and guard as royally as we do
our Jersey news in spring.

**Durrus** cheese, Jeffa Gill,
Coomkeen, Durrus, West Cork.
Tel: 00 353 027 61100.
Fax: 00 353 027 61017.
Also from good cheesemongers like
Neal's Yard Dairy, 17 Shorts
Gardens, London WC2.
Tel: 020 7379 7646.

**The Fine Cheese Company**,
29/31 Walcot St, Bath BA1 5BN.
Mail order: 01225 448748.
Website: www.finecheese.co.uk
They will make up boxes to order of
any combination of British, Irish,
French and Italian cheeses, special
cheese biscuits, jams, chutneys,
relishes, port and wine and are
agents for all Seggiano products
(see Seggiano).

**H. Forman and Son**, Britain's
oldest established salmon smokers,
sell wonderful wild smoked salmon.
They also trade in smoked marlin,
sturgeon and swordfish, and caviars
Beluga, Oscietra and Sevruga.

H. Forman and Son, 6 Queens Yard,
Whitepost Lane, London, E9 5EN
Tel: 020 8985 0378.
Fax: 020 8985 0180

**Fortnum and Mason**, 181
Piccadilly, London W1A 1ER. Tel:
020 7734 8040. For their food gift
brochure and details of their famous
hampers, ring 0845 300 1707.
Website:
www.fortnumandmason.com

**Frank Hederman** sells smoked
fish to Fortnum and Mason and is at
Borough Market monthly. Available
by mail order. Tel: 00 353 021
811089. Fax: 00 353 021 814323.

**Hill Station** ice cream is sold at
selected branches of Waitrose,
Sainsbury's and Tesco's. For further
stockists: Tel: 01249 816596.
Fax: 01249 816597.
Website: www.hillstation.co.uk

**Morecambe Bay Potted
Shrimps**: Furness Fish, Poultry and
Game Supplies, Stockbridge Lane,
Ulverston, Cumbria LA12 7BG. Tel:
01229 585037. Fax: 01229 582485.
Order delicious brown shrimps
caught by local fishermen off the
Cumbrian coast for over 100 years.

**Mustard**: Maille Boutique, 32 Rue
de la Liberté, Paris 6. Place de la
Madeleine.

**Northfield Farm Naturally
Reared Meats**, Cold Overton,
Rutland LE15 7ER.
Tel: 01664 474271.
Email:
enquiries@northfieldfarm.com
Website: www.northfieldfarm.com

**Prospect Books**. For a catalogue, write to Allaleigh House, Blackawton, Totnes, TQ9 7DL. Tel: 01803 712269. Fax: 01803 712311. Email: tom.jaine@prospectbooks.co.uk

**Restaurants:**

CAPRICCIO'S RESTAURANT, 41 Bridge Street, Taunton, Somerset TA1 1TP. Tel: 01823 335711

THE CASTLE HOTEL, Castle Green, Taunton, Somerset TA1 1NF. Tel:01823 272261

LINDSAY HOUSE, 21 Romilly Street, London W1V 5TG. Tel: 020 7439 0450

RULES RESTAURANT, 35 Maiden Lane, London WC2E 7LB. Tel: 020 7379 0258

THE STAR OF INDIA, 154 Old Brompton Road, London SW7 3RA. Tel: 020 7373 2901 Large parties and events catered for.

**Rocombe Farm** will despatch their dreamy, organic Jersey cream ice creams overnight. Drool over their brandy sodden Christmas pudding or 'very merry rum and raisin' ice cream, or trio of chocolates, Belgian, chocolate chip or Drambuie chocolate truffle. Or lighten up with a lemon or mango sorbet. Rocombe Farm Fresh Ice Cream Ltd, Middle Rocombe Farm, Stoke in Teignhead, Newton Abbot, Devon TQ12 4QL. Tel: 01626 872291. Fax: 01626 835777. Email: sales@rocombefarm.co.uk Website: www.rocombefarm.co.uk

**Seggiano:** all products are available by mail order from The Fine Cheese Company, Tel: 01225 448748, or on line at www.finecheese.co.uk . For other potential Seggiano stockists, more information, or a full list of stockists, tel: 020 7272 5588.

**Spiced Beef**: John O'Flynn and Sons, 36 Marlboro St, Cork, Eire.

**Swaddles Green Organic Farm**. My favourite meat producers have a luscious list, at the top end of which is a mighty Three Bird Roast, a turkey, stuffed with a goose, stuffed with a duck, all boned and stuffed with wild mushrooms and a mustard stuffing.
Or you can buy their geese, ducks and bronze turkeys, uncooked or cooked hams. The cooked come glazed with honey and orange, crushed juniper berries and sugar, or with a herb and mustard crust. They make duck and chicken galantines, stuffings, a Christmas pie with a lattice raised top of turkey and duck with figs and kumquats, and a selection of canapés, soups, ready-to-cook casseroles, puddings and cakes, plum pudding, mince pies, and brandy and lemon butter.
If you shun turkey, try their Christmas sirloin of beef with chicken liver pate and a mushroom duxelle.
Swaddles Green Farm, Hare Lane, Buckland St Mary, Chard, Somerset TA20 3JR. Tel: 01460 234387. Fax: 01460 234591. Email: orders@swaddles.co.uk Website: www.swaddles.co.uk

**Somerset Lamb Direct**, Bittescombe Manor, Upton, Wiveliscombe, Taunton, Somerset TA4 2DA. Tel: 01398 371387. Fax: 01398 371413.

**Suffolk Herbs** (to find out about growing your own organic herbs) E.W. King & Co, Monks Farm, Kelvedon, Colchester, Essex CO5 9PG Tel: 01376 570000. Fax: 01376 571189.

**Vegetables**: If you are interested in joining a box scheme, call the Soil Association on 0117 9290661. They also have an organic directory.

**Venison: Wallace's of Hemyock**, Hill Farm, Hemyock, Devon EX15 3UZ. Tel: 01823 680307. Fax: 01823 680017 Website: www.naturalmeat.co.uk Graeme attends the following farmers' markets, Bridport, Chard, Cullompton, Dorchester, Exeter, Glastonbury, Shaftesbury, Taunton, Tiverton, Wincanton and Yeovil.

**Willand Post Office, Devon**: Come off the M5 at Junction 27 and follow the signs to Willand.

**The Village Bakery**, Melmerby, Penrith, Cumbria CA10 1HE. Tel: 01768 881515. Fax: 01768 881848. Mail order delivery service. The organic Village Bakery at Melmerby will send the best raspberry jam or Seville orange marmalade and loaves of wonderful bread, including a naturally leavened Campagne and Hadrian, a spelt bread made with raisin pulp, and inspired by the Romans. Their chocolate almond cake made with Green and Black's dark chocolate is an alternative to their Christmas cakes. They make an award-winning Christmas pudding, with rum or brandy butter.

## Trade Associations, Growers and Trusts

ASPARAGUS GROWERS' ASSOCIATION
113 Eastgate, Louth, Lincolnshire
LN11 9QG

ASSOCIATION OF MASTER BAKERS
21 Baldock Street, Ware,
Hertfordshire SG12 9EH

ASSOCIATION OF SCOTTISH
SHELLFISH GROWERS
Polfearn, Taynuilt, Argyll, PA35 1JQ

BEE FARMERS' ASSOCIATION
Struan Apiaries, Burnside Lane,
Conon Bridge, Ross IV7 8EX

BRITISH DEER FARMERS' ASSOCIATION
(JOHN ELLIOT)
6 Pound Cottages, Streatly, Reading
RG8 9HJ

BRITISH GOOSE PRODUCERS'
ASSOCIATION
High Holborn House, 52-54 High
Holborn, London WC1V 6SX

BRITISH PIG ASSOCIATION
7 Rickmansworth Road, Watford,
Hertfordshire WD1 7HE

BROGDALE HORTICULTURAL TRUST
Brogdale Farm, Faversham, Kent
ME13 8XZ

ENGLISH APPLES AND PEARS LTD
Brogdale Farm, Brogdale,
Faversham, Kent ME13 8XZ

ENGLISH FARM CIDER CENTRE
Middle Farm, Firle, Lewes, Sussex
BN8 6LJ

ENGLISH QUALITY PLUM GROWERS'
ASSOCIATION
Cotswold Orchards, Broadway,
Worcestershire WR12 7JA

FARM SHOP AND PICK YOUR OWN
ASSOCIATION, HORTICULTURAL
DIVISION
The National Farmers Union,
22 Long Acre, London WC2E 9LY

FARMHOUSE CHEESEMAKERS LTD
23 Union St, Wells, Somerset
BA5 2PU

GAME CONSERVANCY TRUST
Fordingbridge, Hampshire, SP6 1EE

NATIONAL ASSOCIATION
OF CIDER MAKERS
6 Catherine Street, London
WC2B 5JJ

NATIONAL FEDERATION
OF GAME DEALERS
Hill Cottage, 26 Paddock Lane,
Mears Ashby, Northamptonshire
NN6 0EQ

NATIONAL SHEEP ASSOCIATION
Malvern, Worcestershire
WR13 5BR

NATIONAL SUMMER FRUITS
ASSOCIATION
The WFU Project line, Crundalls,
Gedges Hill, Matfield, Kent
TN12 7EA

RARE BREEDS SURVIVAL TRUST
The National Agricultural Centre,
Kenilworth, Warwickshire CV82LG

SAUSAGE APPRECIATION SOCIETY,
FOOD FROM BRITAIN
301-344 Market Towers, New
Covent Garden, London SW8 5NQ

SHELLFISH ASSOCIATION
OF GREAT BRITAIN
Fishmonger's Hall, London Bridge,
London EC4R 9EL

SOIL ASSOCIATION
86 Colston Street, Bristol BS1 5BB

SOUTHWEST OF ENGLAND CIDER
MAKERS' ASSOCIATION
Burrow Hill, Kingsbury Episcopi,
Martock, Somerset TA12 5BU

TEA COUNCIL INFORMATION SERVICE
Sir John Lyon House, 5 High Timber
Street, London EC4V 3NJ

TRADITIONAL LIVESTOCK
FOUNDATION
6 Green Park Road, Parklands,
Bromsgroves B60 2RD

TRADITIONAL POULTRY BREEDERS
Chadwick Farm, Chadwick Lane,
Knowle, Solihull, West Midlands
B93 0AS

WATERCRESS GROWERS' ASSOCIATION
22 Long Acre, London WC2E 9LY

# INDEX

# ACKNOWLEDGMENTS

This is turning into a highly elite, hand picked 'A' team, which has, I am pleased to say, barely changed over five years and three books. If the recipe works, and all that. The only problem from my point of view, in thanking this talented collective of individuals, is that there aren't enough superlatives in the OED.

Imagine, for a minute, this book without the photographs. Impossible; they are married to the text, but with an ease and grace and simplicity that is as immediate and accessible as it is a thing of beauty. David Loftus is, simply, the most talented food photographer I know. Were it possible to surpass the excellence of the pictures for our last book, *The Art of the Tart*, he would, and I believe he has. He sees to the heart of each shot more swiftly than anyone I've worked with, and his pictures have the purity of form and depth of image that others search long and hard for yet never seem quite to find.

We had only five days to photograph all the pictures for the book, with me doing the cooking, so a top drawer kitchen cabinet was a *sine qua non*. My teenage daughter Miranda, when handed the first recipe and told to get on with it, exclaimed, 'But I've never cooked it before!' My sympathetic reply: 'Nor will the readers have.' There are very few people one could place such trust in, but Miranda, a brilliant cook in the making, is already one of them. As is my cousin Deborah Richards, an unfazeable kitchen ally, who also did a turn of duty; she an experienced and outstanding cook as at ease in a crisis as with any new recipe thrown at her.

As for my editor, Susan Haynes, for some reason best known to ourselves she thrives on these schedule-busting food fests, usually taking on the role of troubleshooter as well, in her characteristically calm and mistress-of-the-proceedings way, and we dine out on the disasters afterwards. She is quite simply the best editor and friend you could wish for from gestation to publication, turning even the most arcane rituals of the process into fun. Also there from inception – if not pre-conception, since I always run my ideas by her first – is the divine George Capel. Keeper of the privy purse, sanity, chief map reader – after all, it is an agent's job to take charge of the course her writer steers – she is utterly unstinting in that increasingly rare virtue, enthusiasm.

At which point, enter the publisher, Michael Dover, who has championed all the books we have done together, and whose unprescriptive yet unfailingly wise counsel are all a writer could wish for. And his instigation of what I call the 'Dover Dinners', bringing writers, critics, publishers, and most nerve-rackingly for me as cook, Michelin-starred chefs to his table, are currently achieving legendary status. Some of the best recipes from this book have been served at the table of Michael and his lovely wife Ruth, and will, I hope, continue to be.

David Rowley is the inspirational art director who is actually prepared to put up with a writer who queries and questions everything about the look of the book, including the most important of shop windows, the cover. I would like to think that creative consensus is always achieved, but it is his talent that defines the look of this book. Alongside Nigel Soper's, our designer, whose sense of space and place and total sympathy for both text and image also achieve wondrous results. Jinny Johnson has had the long haul task of editing, interpreting, suggesting and collating the text and has, quite simply, been a joy to work with, as supportive as she has been professional. Beyond the call of duty, she even came to help on our final day's shoot and will certainly be asked back! Finally, my thanks to a very special editor, Rachel Simhon of the *Daily Telegraph* 'Weekend' and instrumental to this, as *Simply the Best* is based on the food, cooks and stories I have written about over my two years on the *Telegraph*.

Tamasin Day-Lewis Summer 2001

First published in the United Kingdom in 2001 by Cassell & Co.

This paperback edition first published in 2002 by Weidenfeld & Nicolson

Photographs by David Loftus
Additional photographs:
Pp 12–13: Telegraph/Guy Edwardes
Pp 90–91: Telegraph/Ron Thomas
Pp: 162–163 Images
Pp: 220–221 Bruce Coleman

A CIP catalogue record for this book is available from the British Library
ISBN 1 841 88202 X

Design director David Rowley
Editorial director Susan Haynes
Designed by Nigel Soper
Edited by Jinny Johnson
Proofread by Gwen Rigby
Index by Elizabeth Wiggans

Typeset in Perpetua
Printed and bound in Italy by Printer Trento S.r.l.

Weidenfeld & Nicolson
Wellington House
125 Strand
London WC2R 0BB